11+ Maths

For GL Assessment – ages 10-11

Passing the 11+ is no mean feat, but luckily this CGP book is the ultimate way to prepare for GL Maths. It's a one-way ticket to 11+ success!

With pages of study notes and step-by-step worked examples, it'll help you understand every topic. Then there are plenty of questions to put what you've learned into practice.

And if that's not enough, we've also included some mixed tests and two full practice papers with answers, so you're as ready as possible for the big day.

How to access your free Online Edition

This book includes a free Online Edition to read on your PC, Mac or tablet. You'll just need to go to **cgpbooks.co.uk/extras** and enter this code:

2926 5109 5275 4861

By the way, this code only works for one person. If somebody else has used this book before you, they might have already claimed the Online Edition.

Complete **Revision & Practice**

Everything you need to pass the test!

Contents

About the 11+

Section One — Number Knowledge

Section Two — Working with Numbers

Section Three — Number Problems

Section Four — Data Handling

Section Five — Shape and Space

Section Six — Units and Measures

Section Seven — Mixed Problems

Published by CGP

Editors:
Michael Bushell, Sarah George, Sean McParland, Caley Simpson

With thanks to Alison Griffin, Rachel Patterson and Glenn Rogers for the proofreading.

ISBN: 978 1 78908 600 3

Printed by Elanders Ltd, Newcastle upon Tyne.
Clipart from Corel®

Based on the classic CGP style created by Richard Parsons.

What's in the 11+

Make sure you've got your head around the basics of the 11+ before you begin.

The **11+** is an **Admissions Test**

1) The 11+ is a test used by some schools to help with their selection process.
2) You'll usually take it when you're in Year 6, at some point during the autumn term.
3) Schools use the results to decide who to accept. They might also use other things to help make up their mind, like information about where you live.

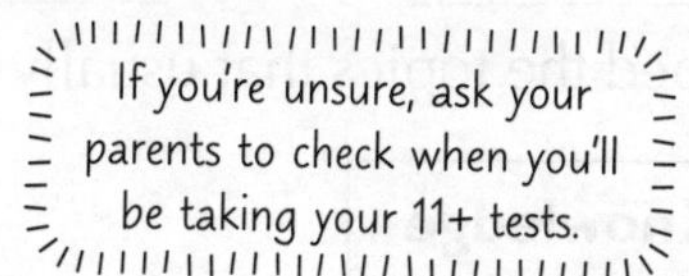

If you're unsure, ask your parents to check when you'll be taking your 11+ tests.

Some Schools test a **Mixture** of **Subjects**

1) Depending on the school, the 11+ can be a test on different subjects.
2) There are four main subjects that can be tested in the 11+, so you might sit papers on some or all of these:

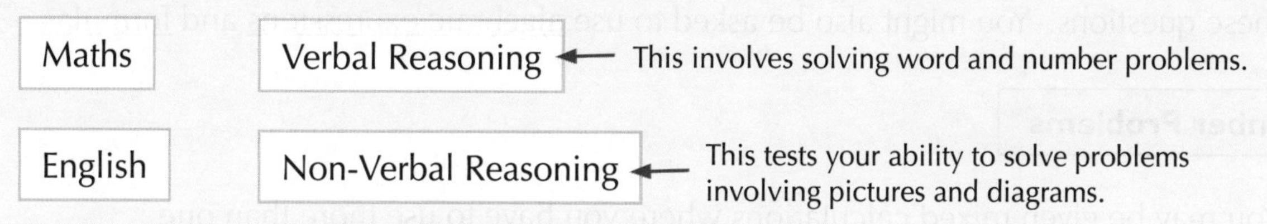

Maths
Verbal Reasoning
This involves solving word and number problems.
English
Non-Verbal Reasoning
This tests your ability to solve problems involving pictures and diagrams.

3) This book will help you with the Maths part of the test.

Get to **Know** what **Kind** of **Paper** you're taking

Your paper will either be multiple-choice or standard answer.

Look out for the tips at the end of each topic — they'll give you practical advice about the test, plus revision tips and extra hints to help you crack 11+ Maths.

Multiple-Choice

1) For each question, you'll be given some options for the answer.
2) On the separate answer sheet, you'll need to mark your answer with a clear pencil line in the box next to the option that you think is correct.

Standard Answer

1) You'll be expected to write down the correct answer for some questions, but you may have some options to choose from for others.
2) You'll usually mark or write your answer on the question paper.

Check which type of question paper you'll be taking, so you know what it looks like and where your answers go. Try to do some practice tests in the same format as the test you'll be taking, so you know what to expect on the day.

What's in the 11+ Maths Test

Get your brain ready for Maths by reading about the different topics in the test.

Maths involves Solving Number Problems

1) You should have covered most of the Maths topics that will be on the test at school. However, you may not have learnt about all of them yet, and the test might contain some types of question that are unfamiliar to you.
2) We've grouped the topics that usually come up into seven sections in this book.

You might not be tested on questions from every topic in the real test.

Number Knowledge

You'll need to be able to recognise different types of numbers. You'll need to look for number patterns and use place value and rounding to solve number problems.

Working with Numbers

You'll need to use addition, subtraction, multiplication or division to answer these questions. You might also be asked to use algebraic expressions and formulas.

Number Problems

You may be given mixed calculations where you have to use more than one operation (e.g. multiplication and addition). Or you could be given word problems where you need to use information in the question to find the answer.

Data Handling

Some questions use data in tables and graphs. You'll need to be able to find information in a table and know how to read different types of graphs. You also need to be able to find the mean of a data set.

Shape and Space

You may be tested on the names and properties of 2D and 3D shapes. Other questions may ask about symmetry, coordinates, volume, area and perimeter. You might also have to imagine shapes being rotated to solve shape problems.

Units and Measures

You may be tested on units and time. You'll need to be able to choose the correct unit for a measurement and to convert between different units (e.g. mm and cm).

Mixed Problems

There might also be questions that cover more than one topic. For example, you may be given a question where you have to read a graph and do some calculations.

How to Prepare for the 11+

Give yourself a head start with your Maths revision — be organised and plan ahead.

Divide your Preparation into Stages

1) You should find a way to prepare for the 11+ that suits you. This may depend on how much time you have before the test. Here's a good way to plan your Maths revision:

Use this book to revise strategies for answering different question types. Read through the study notes and follow the worked examples carefully — make sure you understand the method used at each step.

↓

Do plenty of practice questions, concentrating on the question types you find tricky.

↓

Sit some practice papers to prepare you for the real test. We've included two papers at the back of this book to get you started.

2) When you first start answering 11+ Maths questions, try to solve the questions without making any mistakes, rather than working quickly.
3) Once you feel confident about the questions, then you can build up your speed.
4) You can do this by asking an adult to time you as you answer a set of questions, or by seeing how many questions you can answer in a certain amount of time, e.g. 5 minutes. You can then try to beat your time or score.
5) As you get closer to the test day, work on getting a balance between speed and accuracy — that's what you're aiming for when you sit the real test.

There are Many Ways to Practise the Skills you Need

The best way to tackle 11+ Maths is to do lots of revision and practice. This isn't the only thing that will help though — there are other ways you can hone the skills you need for the test:

1) Practise your times tables with a friend by taking it in turns to test each other.
2) Divide up a cake, a pizza or a pie between a certain number of people. Work out what fraction each person is given.
3) Try drawing different shapes on a piece of paper. Use a small mirror to find lines of symmetry and work out what the shapes look like when they've been reflected.
4) Play games that involve counting like darts or Monopoly® to help you practise number calculations. You could also do activities like sudoku to help you to develop your problem solving skills, and play Battleships to practise using coordinates.

Place Value

Place value is about knowing the value of all the digits in a number.
You can use place value to compare numbers and work out which is biggest or smallest.

The **Value** of a **Digit** depends on its **Place** in a **Number**

Each Digit in a **Whole Number** has a different **Value**

1) This example shows you what each digit is worth in a 7-digit number — **1 256 297**.

Millions	Hundreds of thousands	Tens of thousands	Thousands	Hundreds	Tens	Ones
↓	↓	↓	↓	↓	↓	↓
1	**2**	**5**	**6**	**2**	**9**	**7**
1 million, or 1 000 000.	2 hundred thousand, or 200 000.	5 tens of thousands, or 50 000.	6 thousand, or 6000.	2 hundred, or 200.	9 tens, or 90.	7 ones, or 7.

2) Each digit has the same value as 10 lots of the digit to its right, e.g. 1 hundred is equal to 10 tens.

3) Whole numbers have a greater value when there are more digits, e.g. 1 256 297 has a greater value than 256 297 because it has a millions digit.

4) When comparing whole numbers that have the same number of digits, you need to look at the value of each digit. For example, 254 is greater than 249. They have the same number in the hundreds column, but 254 has a greater number in the tens column than 249.

Each Digit in a **Decimal Number** has a different **Value**

1) This example shows you what each digit is worth in a decimal number — **1.365**.

Ones	Decimal Point	Tenths	Hundredths	Thousandths
↓	↓	↓	↓	↓
1	**.**	**3**	**6**	**5**
1 one, or 1		3 tenths, or 0.3	6 hundredths, or 0.06	5 thousandths, or 0.005

2) Each digit has the same value as 10 lots of the digit to its right, e.g. 1 tenth is equal to 10 hundredths.

3) When comparing decimal numbers you need to look at each digit in turn. For example, 0.56 is greater than 0.53. They have the same number in the tenths column, but 0.56 has a greater number in the hundredths column than 0.53.

Place Value

11+ Example Questions

EXAMPLE: **What number is the arrow pointing to on this number line?**

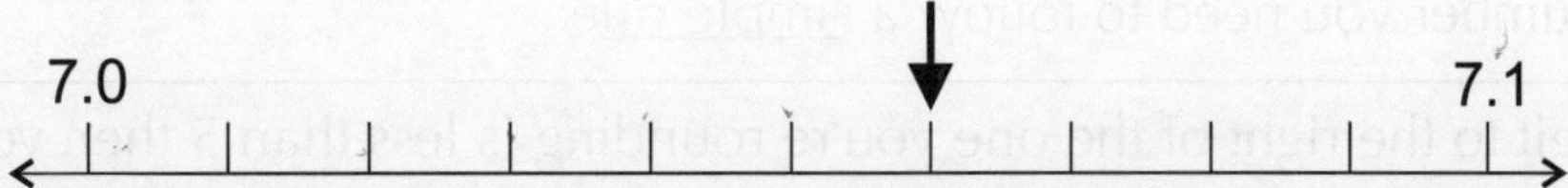

1) Look at the numbers given and how many points there are on the number line.

   The answer is between 7.0 and 7.1, and there are ten points on the number line. The difference between 7.0 and 7.1 is one tenth, or 0.1. 0.1 is made up of ten hundredths, so each of the ten points on the number line is equal to one hundredth, or 0.01.

2) Count along the points to where the arrow is located on the number line.

   The arrow is pointing to the 6th point to the right of 7.0 on the number line, which means that this point is equal to 6 hundredths or 0.06. So the value of this point is 7 units and 6 hundredths, or 7.06.

Luca, Steve, Flo, Sue and Tom all drove one lap around a go-kart track. They put their results in a table.

Name	Luca	Steve	Flo	Sue	Tom
Time (seconds)	49.7	49.65	49.92	49.84	50.1

Who drove the quickest?

1) To find out who drove the quickest you need to find the shortest time, which means that you're looking for the lowest value number.

   Look at the tens and the units of each driver's time. Tom's time is the slowest because 50 (which has 5 tens) is greater than 49 (which has 4 tens).

2) Luca, Steve, Flo and Sue all have the same number of tens and units in their time, 49. So you then need to look at the first decimal number of their times.

   They each have a different value for the first decimal place. Steve has a lower number of tenths than the others, 6, so his time is quickest.

Practice Questions

1) Which of these is the smallest number?

   A 8.47 **B** 8.543 **C** 8.465 **D** 8.449 **E** 8.43

2) Which of these pairs of numbers are equally distant from 7?

   A 6.97 and 7.3 **B** 6.89 and 7.11 **C** 6.8 and 7.02
   D 6.94 and 7.1 **E** 6.9 and 7.19

Check the place value of each digit...

When you're putting numbers in order, look at each digit of the numbers one by one. If they have the same digit in the same place value column, look at the next digit to the right instead.

Rounding Up and Down

You guessed it — you can round numbers up or down to give an estimated value.

The **Number 5** is **Important** when you're **Rounding Numbers**

1) To round any number you need to follow a simple rule:

- If the digit to the right of the one you're rounding is less than 5 then you round down.
- If the digit to the right of the one you're rounding is 5 or more then you round up.

For example, to round 17 872 to the nearest 100, you need to round the digit in the hundreds column.

When rounding down, the digit you're rounding stays the same.

17 872 — The digit in the hundreds column is 8.

Now look at the digit to its right, in the tens column, to see whether you need to round up or down.

17 872 — The digit in the tens column is 7, so you round up 17 872 to 17 900.

2) You can use this method for rounding decimals too. For example, to round 1.428 to one decimal place (or the nearest tenth), you need to round the digit in the tenths column.

Rounding to two decimal places means rounding to the nearest hundredth. Three decimal places means to the nearest thousandth.

1.428 — The digit in the tenths column is 4.

3) To work out whether to round this digit up or down you need to look at the digit to its right — in the hundredths column.

1.428 — The digit in the hundredths column is 2, so you round down 1.428 to 1.4.

11+ Example Questions

EXAMPLE: **What is 46.98 rounded to one decimal place?**

1) Work out which digit you need to round.

One decimal place is the first digit after the decimal point — 46.98.

2) Look at the digit to the right of the digit you need to round and work out whether you need to round up or round down.

The digit to the right of the digit you need to round is 8 — 46.98.

8 is more than 5 so you need to round up. Rounding up 9 tenths will give you 10 tenths, which is equal to 1 unit. This will increase the digit in the units column from 6 to 7 and leave 0 tenths. So 46.98 rounded to one decimal place is 47.0, or 47.

Rounding Up and Down

Which of these is 1500?

A 1508 to the nearest 10 **B 1448 to the nearest 100**
C 1562 to the nearest 100 **D 1498 to the nearest 10**
E 1504 to the nearest 1000

1) Look at each option one by one.

   A 1508: 0 is being rounded, 8 is more than 5 — 1508 rounds up to 1510 not 1500.

   B 1448: 4 is being rounded, 4 is less than 5 — 1448 rounds down to 1400 not 1500.

   C 1562: 5 is being rounded, 6 is more than 5 — 1562 rounds up to 1600 not 1500.

   D 1498: 9 is being rounded, 8 is more than 5 — 1498 rounds up to 1500.

   So the answer is D.

2) If you have time you can check your answer by looking at the last option.

   E 1504: 1 is being rounded, 5 is 5 or more —
   1504 rounds up to 2000 not 1500.

Round 43.389 kg to the nearest 10 grams.

A 50 kg **B 43.4 kg**
C 43 kg **D 40 kg**
E 43.39 kg

1) You need to find 43.389 kg to the nearest 10 grams —
   it'll be easier to round this figure if you convert it into grams.

   One kilogram is the same as 1000 grams, so
   multiply 43.389 by 1000. 43.389 kg is 43 389 g.

2) Work out which digit is in the tens column and look at the digit to its right (in the ones column) to see whether you need to round up or down.

   43 389: 8 is being rounded, 9 is more than 5 so 43 389 rounds up to 43 390.

   To convert this back into kilograms you just need to divide 43 390 by 1000.
   The answer is 43.39 kg.

Practice Question

1) Round 174 782 to the nearest ten thousand.

   A 174 800 **B** 180 000 **C** 170 800 **D** 170 000 **E** 175 000

You can use rounding to estimate answers...

For example, to check your answer to 4988 + 507, round the numbers to 5000 and 500.
5000 + 500 = 5500, so make sure your answer to 4988 + 507 is pretty close to 5500.

Number Knowledge

It's really useful to know a few facts about different types of numbers.

Whole Numbers are either Odd or Even

1) An even number is any whole number that can be exactly divided by two to give another whole number. For example, 6 is an even number because 6 ÷ 2 = 3.
2) An odd number is any whole number that can't be divided by two to give another whole number. For example, 5 is an odd number because 5 ÷ 2 = 2.5.

Negative Numbers are Numbers Below 0

1) You can use number lines to work out the value of negative numbers.

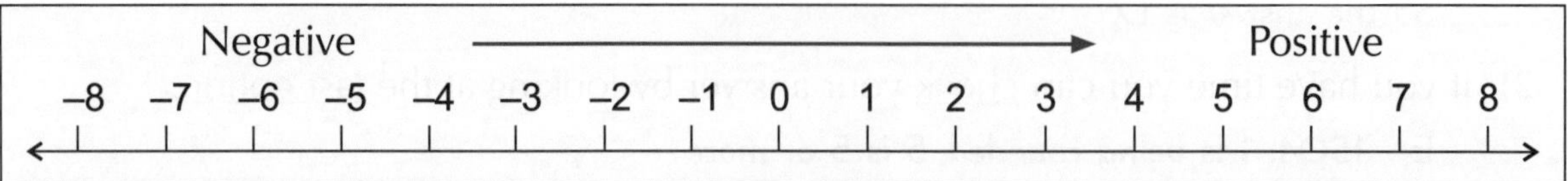

2) The numbers on the number line increase from left to right. So –1 is greater than –6.
3) Number lines can be used to help you with calculations that involve negative numbers. For example to work out 2 – 9, just count back 9 places from 2 along the number line:

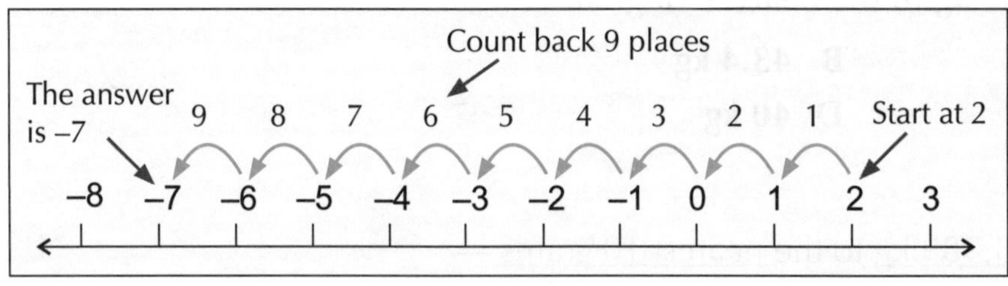

You can use **Symbols** to show whether one number is **Bigger** or **Smaller** than **Another**

There are two symbols you can use:

< means 'is less than'. For example, –3 is less than 2 or **–3 < 2**.
> means 'is greater than'. For example, 7 is greater than 5 or **7 > 5**.

Factors of a number are Whole Numbers that divide Exactly into it

1) The factors of a number are all the whole numbers that divide that number exactly (so there's no remainder). For example the factors of 9 are 1, 3 and 9: 9 ÷ 1 = 9, 9 ÷ 3 = 3 and 9 ÷ 9 = 1.
2) If a question asks for the common factors of some numbers, you need to find the factors that the numbers all share. Here's how to find the common factors of 12 and 36:

Find the factors of each number, then work out which factors are shared.

The factors of 12 are: 1, 2, 3, 4, 6 and 12.
The factors of 36 are: 1, 2, 3, 4, 6, 9, 12, 18 and 36.

1, 2, 3, 4, 6 and 12 are all common factors of 12 and 36.

Number Knowledge

A Multiple is the Result of Multiplying one Whole Number by another

1) The multiples of a number are just the times table for that number, e.g. multiples of 4 are 4, 8, 12, 16, etc.
2) If a question asks for a common multiple of some numbers, you need to find a multiple that the numbers all share. Here's how to find a common multiple of 3, 4 and 6:

> Find the first few multiples of each number and check if any of them are the same. If not, work out a few more multiples, then try again.
> The first six multiples of 3 are: 3, 6, 9, 12, 15 and 18.
> The first six multiples of 4 are: 4, 8, 12, 16, 20 and 24.
> The first six multiples of 6 are: 6, 12, 18, 24, 30, 36.
> 12 is a common multiple of 3, 4 and 6.

Prime Numbers only have Two Factors

1) A prime number is a number with exactly two factors — the number itself and one. For example, 23 is a prime number — the only factors of 23 are 1 and 23.
2) 1 is NOT a prime number — it doesn't have exactly two factors.
3) Apart from 2 and 5, all prime numbers end in 1, 3, 7 or 9 (but not all numbers ending in 1, 3, 7 or 9 are prime numbers).
4) The only even prime number is 2.

> The first ten prime numbers are: 2, 3, 5, 7, 11, 13, 17, 19, 23 and 29.

A Whole Number Multiplied by Itself gives a Square Number

1) For example, if you multiply 4 by itself (4 × 4) you get 16 — a square number.
2) The first 12 square numbers are:

1	4	9	16	25	36	49	64	81	100	121	144
(1 × 1)	(2 × 2)	(3 × 3)	(4 × 4)	(5 × 5)	(6 × 6)	(7 × 7)	(8 × 8)	(9 × 9)	(10 × 10)	(11 × 11)	(12 × 12)

3) You can show a number is squared using a small 2, e.g. five squared (5 × 5) can be written as 5^2.

A Whole Number Multiplied by Itself Twice gives a Cube Number

1) For example, if you multiply 2 by itself twice (2 × 2 × 2) you get 8 (2 × 2 = 4, 4 × 2 = 8).
2) The first 5 cube numbers are:

1	8	27	64	125
(1 × 1 × 1)	(2 × 2 × 2)	(3 × 3 × 3)	(4 × 4 × 4)	(5 × 5 × 5)

3) Cube numbers can be written using a small 3, e.g. 8 = two cubed = 2^3.

Number Knowledge

Roman Numerals are **Letters** which represent **Numbers**

1) There are letters for 1, 5, 10, 50, 100, 500 and 1000
— all other numbers are written as combinations of these numbers.

1	5	10	50	100	500	1000
↓	↓	↓	↓	↓	↓	↓
I	V	X	L	C	D	M

2) For most numbers, you find the biggest numbers you can that add up to make the number you want. Then you write the matching letters from largest to smallest. For example, 2 = 1 + 1, which is II, 6 = 5 + 1, which is VI and 13 = 10 + 1 + 1 + 1, which is XIII.
3) 4s and 9s are a bit trickier. For these, you write them as subtractions.
The number you take away goes before the number you take it away from,
e.g. 4 is 5 – 1 so it's IV, and 400 is 500 – 100 so it's CD.
4) For example, 198 = 100 + 90 + 5 + 3. 100 = C, 90 = XC, 5 = V and 3 = III, so 198 is CXCVIII.
5) You can write dates using Roman numerals. It's useful to remember that 2000 is MM and 1900 is MCM. For example, 1997 is MCMXCVII:

M	CM	XC	VII
/	|	|	\
1000	900	90	7

11+ Example Questions

Emily has bought some sweets. She gives them all away to her friends. Each friend got an equal number of sweets and they were all given more than one sweet. How many sweets could she have bought?

A 19 B 23 C 24 D 29 E 31

The question doesn't say how many friends Emily has — but she has more than one because it says she has "friends" and not "a friend".

1) You might recognise that all of the amounts, except 24, are prime numbers (prime numbers have no factors other than one and the number itself).

   If the number of sweets is a prime number, e.g. 23, then they can only be equally distributed between one friend or a group of 23 friends. The question shows that there is more than one friend and they all get more than one sweet. So none of these are right.

2) The answer to the question is C because 24 is the only number that has any factors other than 1 and itself. For example, if Emily had 24 sweets she could give 8 friends 3 sweets each, or 4 friends could have 6 sweets each, etc.

3) If you're not sure if a number is prime then you can try to find the number's factors.

   For example, you could work out if 19 has any factors other than 1 or 19.
   Divide 19 by possible factors to see if you get a whole number.
   This will take time so it'd be useful to memorise some prime numbers.

EXAMPLE:

What number is represented by the Roman numeral MDXXIV?

M is 1000, D is 500, XX is 10 + 10 = 20, IV is 5 – 1 = 4,
so added together they make 1000 + 500 + 20 + 4 = 1524.

Number Knowledge

Two of the numbers are missing from this sorting diagram. Which of the following could be the missing numbers?

	Multiple of 3	Not a multiple of 3
Square	36 144 ?	4 64 16
Not square	?	2

A 6 and 3 **B 3 and 25**
C 81 and 9 **D 81 and 3**
E 81 and 19

1) Both of the missing numbers are multiples of 3, one is a square number and one isn't. Start off by finding which of the answer options have two multiples of 3.

   3, 6, 9 and 81 are all multiples of 3, 19 and 25 are not — options A, C and D all have two multiples of 3.

2) Now work out which one of these options has only one square number.

   A 6 and 3 are not square numbers.

   C 81 and 9 are both square numbers (3 × 3 = 9, 9 × 9 = 81).

   D 81 is a square number, but 3 is not — D is the answer.

Which of these numbers will go into the shaded section of the Venn diagram?

A 8 **B 9** **C 27** **D 64** **E 85**

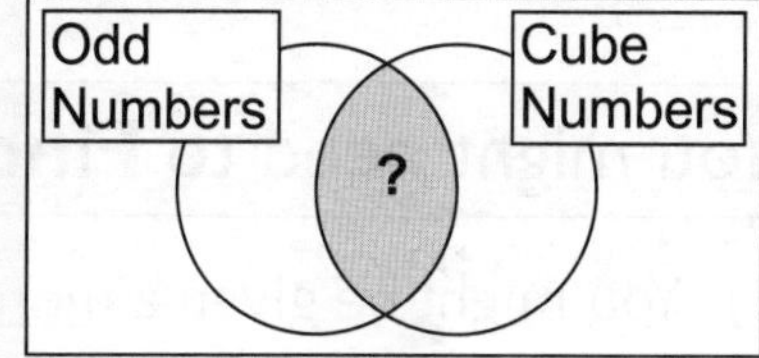

1) Data put into a Venn diagram must match its labels. Odd numbers must go in the left-hand circle of this Venn diagram, and cube numbers can only go in the right-hand circle. Where the Venn diagram overlaps the data must match both labels — so numbers in this section must be odd and cube. Data that doesn't match any of the labels must go in the box outside the circles.

2) Numbers that are both odd and cube must go in the shaded section. Start off by working out which of the options are cube numbers.

   8, 27 and 64 are all cube numbers: 8 = 2 × 2 × 2, 27 = 3 × 3 × 3, 64 = 4 × 4 × 4.

3) Then work out which of 8, 27 and 64 is an odd number.

   8 and 64 are even because they're divisible by 2.

   27 is odd because it isn't divisible by 2 — C is the answer.

Practice Questions

1) Which of these statements is true?

   A All factors of 24 are multiples of 2.
   B 13 and 52 have no common factors.
   C A prime number can be a multiple of 3.
   D A prime number can also be a square number.
   E All numbers ending in a 3 are multiples of 3.

2) Which of these numbers is not a factor of 72?

   A 4 **B** 6 **C** 7 **D** 8 **E** 9

Learn the primes at least up to 30...

It can take a while to work out if a number is prime, so it's worth being familiar with some of them. Remember, most primes end with 1, 3, 5 or 7, but not all numbers that end with those digits are prime.

Number Sequences

You need to follow the rule of a sequence to get from one number to the next.

Some **Number Sequences** follow a **Pattern** you **Already Know**

1) You might spot a pattern in a number sequence because you recognise the numbers.

   2, 3, 5, 7... — are all prime numbers going up in order.
   25, 20, 15, 10... — are all multiples of 5 going down in order.
   1, 4, 9, 16... — are all square numbers going up in order.

2) Once you know the pattern you can work out what the next number in the sequence will be.

   1, 3, 5, 7... are all odd numbers going up in order.
   So the next number in the sequence will be 9.

3) You can also work out later numbers in the sequence. For example, to find the seventh number in this sequence of odd numbers, follow the same pattern until the seventh number.

   1, 3, 5, 7, 9, 11, 13 — the seventh number in this sequence is 13.

You might need to **Find** the **Rule** for a **Number Sequence**

1) You might be given a more difficult number sequence, e.g. 4, 5, 7, 10, 14.
2) You'll need to work out the rule that the number sequence follows. One way to do this is to look at the difference between each number in the sequence.

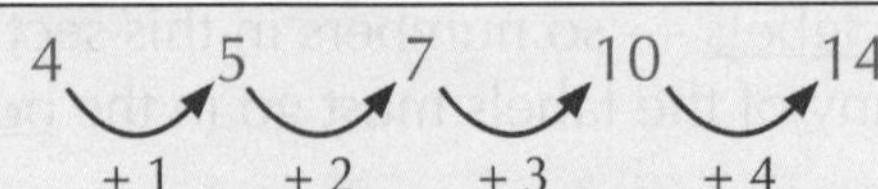

   The amount you need to add to get the next number in the sequence goes up by 1 each time. The next number in the sequence will be 14 + 5 = 19.

3) Make sure you look at all the values in the sequence when you're working out the rule. For example, the start of this sequence looks like it follows the same rule as the one above — but if you look at all the values, you can see the rule is actually to add together the previous two numbers in the sequence:

   2, 3, 5, 8, 13 → 2 + 3 = 5, 3 + 5 = 8, 5 + 8 = 13.

11+ Example Questions

Scott started from the number 14 and counted back in steps of 6.
Which of these numbers did he count?

A 4 **B 1** **C 0** **D –2** **E –4**

1) Write out the number sequence for this question and see which number is included in it. Writing out the sequence will help you avoid any mistakes.

   Make sure you apply the correct rule — subtract 6 each time.

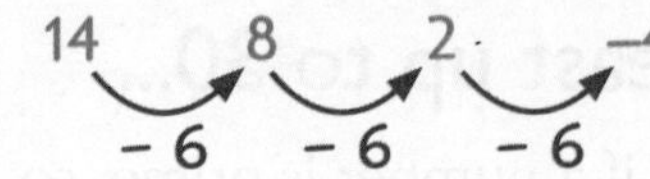

2) Out of the options you're given, only –4 appears in the sequence. So the answer is E.

Number Sequences

Look at the sequence 212, 205, 198, ☐, 184 ...
What is the missing number in this sequence?

1) First work out the rule for the sequence.

2) The numbers in the sequence go down in steps of 7.
   So the missing number is 198 – 7 = 191

Use the rule again to check your answer. 191 – 7 = 184, which is the next term.

There are 9 small triangles in this shape. The shape is three triangles high. How many small triangles would there be in a shape that's five triangles high?

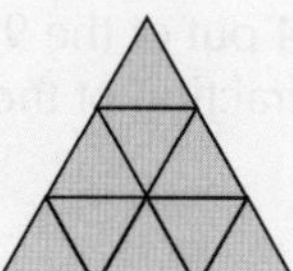

1) You need to find what the sequence is.

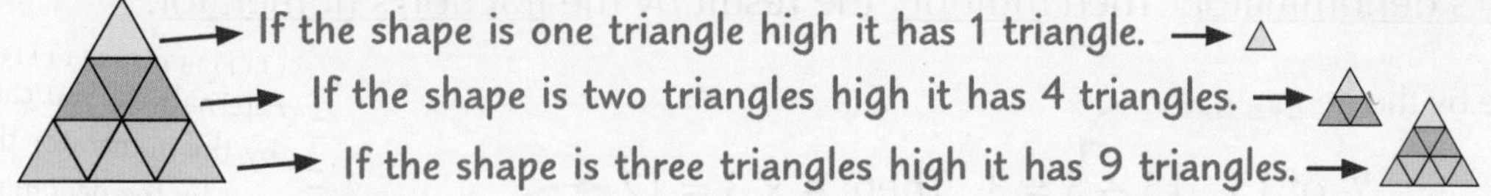

If the shape is one triangle high it has 1 triangle.
If the shape is two triangles high it has 4 triangles.
If the shape is three triangles high it has 9 triangles.

2) So the sequence for the number of triangles is 1, 4, 9. To find the 5th number in this sequence you need to work out if there's a pattern.

3) The difference between each number in the sequence increases by 2 each time — each row added has two more small triangles than the last one. Now work out what the 5th number in the sequence will be.
   The difference increases by two each time, so apply this rule until you reach the 5th number.

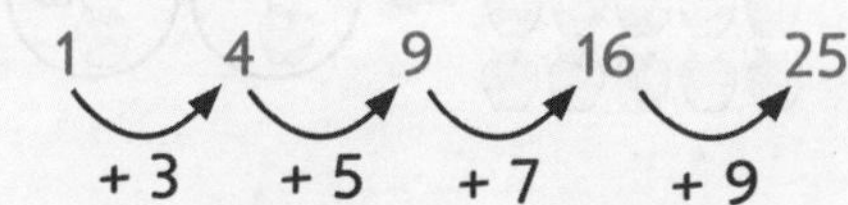

4) If the shape was five triangles high it would have 25 small triangles in it.

This is actually a sequence of the square numbers.

Practice Question

1) Jake is building a wall. He lays 4 bricks in the first hour, 5 in the second and 6 in the third. Each hour he continues to add one more brick than he laid in the previous hour. How many bricks will he have laid after 6 hours?

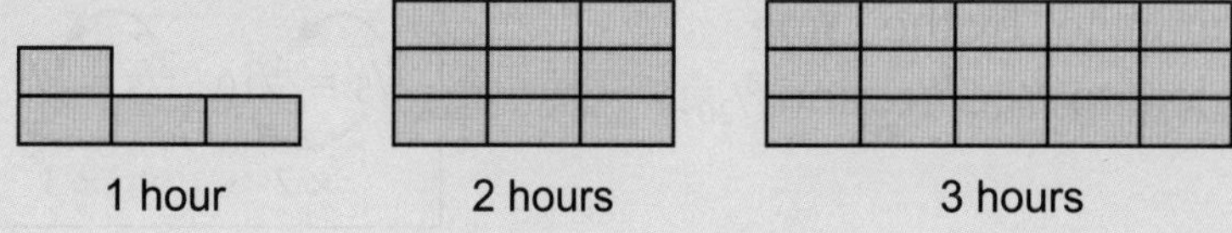

Shape sequences aren't as tricky as they look...

If you get a sequence made of shapes in your test, write out the sequence in numbers first. Then you can work out the rule in the same way that you would for a number sequence.

Fractions

Fractions are a bit tricky at first, but you'll be fine with a bit of practice.

Fractions are Parts of a Whole Number

1) A fraction looks like this:

The bottom number of a fraction is the denominator. It tells you how many equal parts something is split into.

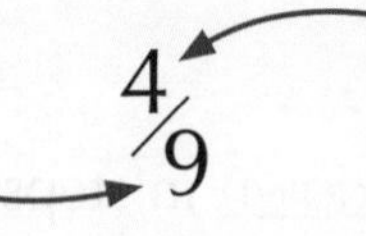

The top number of a fraction is the numerator. It tells you how many equal parts you've got.

2) Fractions can be shown using shapes.

This triangle is split into 9 equal parts. 4 out of the 9 parts are shaded. So the fraction of the triangle that's shaded is $^4/_9$.

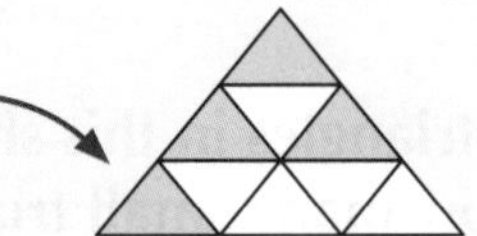

3) To find a fraction of a number (e.g. four-fifths of 15), divide the number by the fraction's denominator. Then multiply the result by the fraction's numerator.

Divide by the denominator.

$^4/_5$ of 15. 15 ÷ 5 = 3. Then, 4 × 3 = 12

Multiply by the numerator. So $^4/_5$ of 15 is 12.

Alternatively, you can multiply by the numerator then divide by the denominator.

4) You can see this more clearly with a diagram:

To find $^4/_5$ of 15 apples, start by dividing 15 by 5. That gives you 5 groups of 3 apples. So $^4/_5$ = 4 groups of 3 apples, or 12 apples.

Equivalent Fractions are Fractions that are Equal

1) For example, $^1/_4$ and $^2/_8$ are equivalent fractions because they're equal. You can show this using shapes:

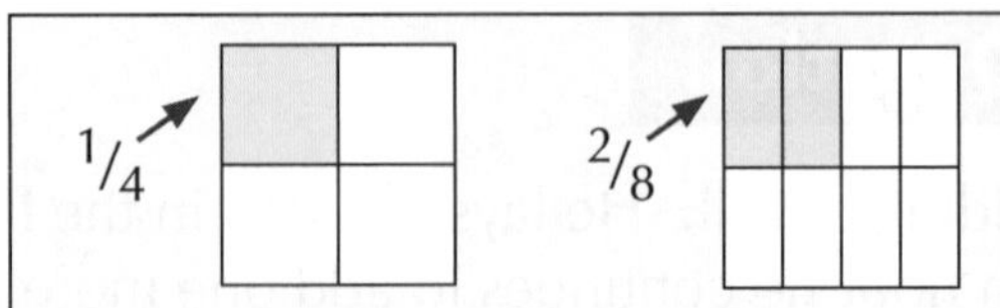

2) To find an equivalent fraction, multiply the numerator and the denominator by the same number. So $^2/_5$ is equivalent to $^4/_{10}$, $^6/_{15}$ and $^8/_{20}$.

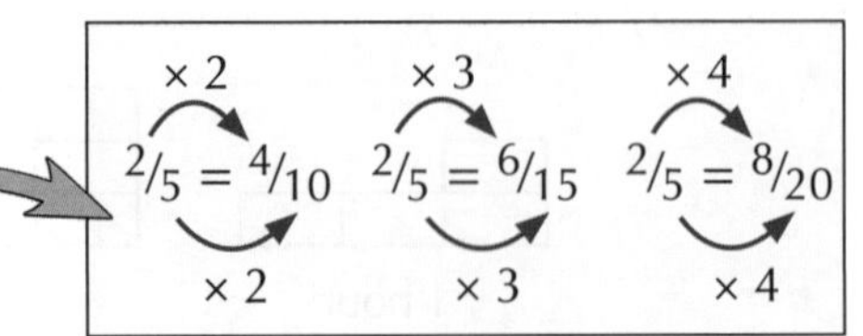

3) You can also find equivalent fractions by dividing both the numerator and the denominator by the same number. This is called simplifying a fraction. For example, $^{55}/_{100}$ is equivalent to $^{11}/_{20}$.

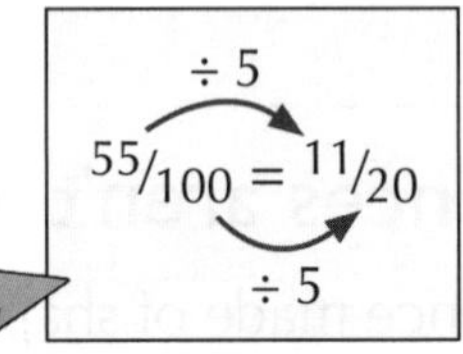

A fraction is in its 'simplest form' if you can't divide the numerator and the denominator by the same amount any more.

Fractions

Some **Fractions** are **Bigger Than 1**

1) You can write fractions that are bigger than 1 as improper fractions or mixed numbers.

2) Improper fractions have a numerator that's bigger than the denominator. For example:

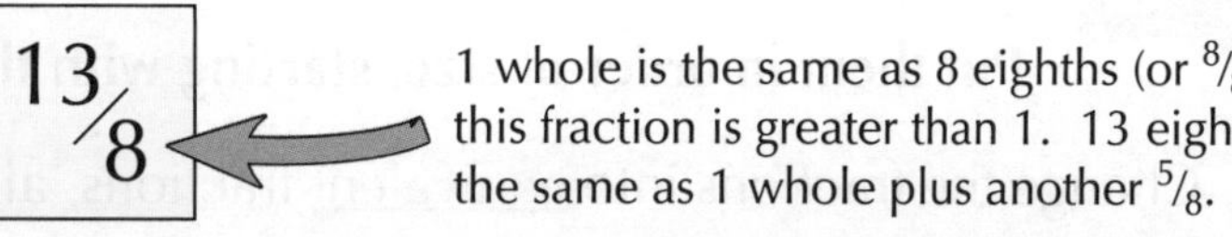

$^{13}/_{8}$

1 whole is the same as 8 eighths (or $^{8}/_{8}$) so this fraction is greater than 1. 13 eighths is the same as 1 whole plus another $^{5}/_{8}$.

3) Mixed numbers have both a whole number and a fraction. For example:

$1\,^{5}/_{8}$

This fraction is greater than 1 — there is 1 whole plus another $^{5}/_{8}$.

You can **Add, Subtract**, **Order**, **Multiply** and **Divide Fractions**

1) Adding and subtracting fractions is easy if they both have the same denominator. All you need to do is add or subtract the numerators and keep the denominator the same.

$^{2}/_{5} + ^{2}/_{5} = ^{4}/_{5}$ $\quad$ $^{4}/_{5} - ^{1}/_{5} = ^{3}/_{5}$

2) To add or subtract fractions which have different denominators, change them so they have the same denominator. You can do this by making them into equivalent fractions.

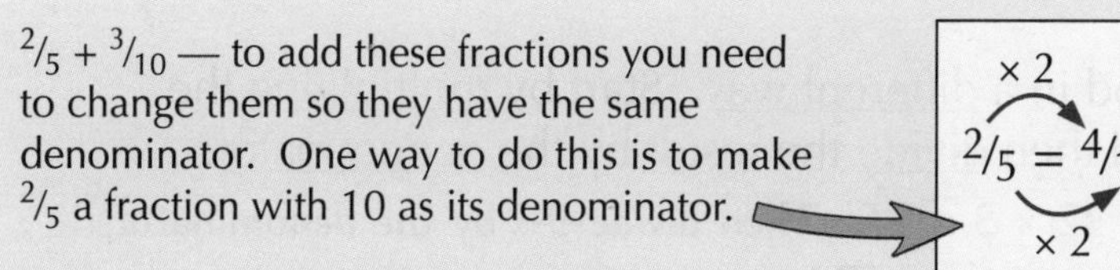

$^{2}/_{5} + ^{3}/_{10}$ — to add these fractions you need to change them so they have the same denominator. One way to do this is to make $^{2}/_{5}$ a fraction with 10 as its denominator.

$^{2}/_{5} = ^{4}/_{10}$ (× 2 top and bottom)

Both fractions now have the same denominator, so you can add them together.

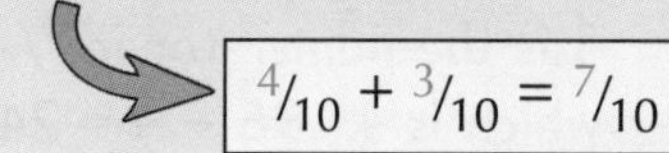

$^{4}/_{10} + ^{3}/_{10} = ^{7}/_{10}$

3) You can also use equivalent fractions to order fractions with different denominators.

To compare the fractions $^{3}/_{5}$ and $^{7}/_{10}$, you need to make their denominators the same. Make $^{3}/_{5}$ a fraction with 10 as its denominator.

$^{3}/_{5} = ^{6}/_{10}$ (× 2 top and bottom)

Now compare numerators: 7 is bigger than 6, so $^{7}/_{10}$ is bigger than $^{3}/_{5}$.

4) To multiply fractions, just multiply the numerators together and the denominators together.

$^{2}/_{5} \times ^{3}/_{7} = ^{6}/_{35}$ $\quad$ $^{2}/_{3} \times ^{2}/_{7} = ^{4}/_{21}$

5) To multiply a fraction by a whole number, multiply the numerator by the whole number. To divide a fraction by a whole number, multiply the denominator by the whole number.

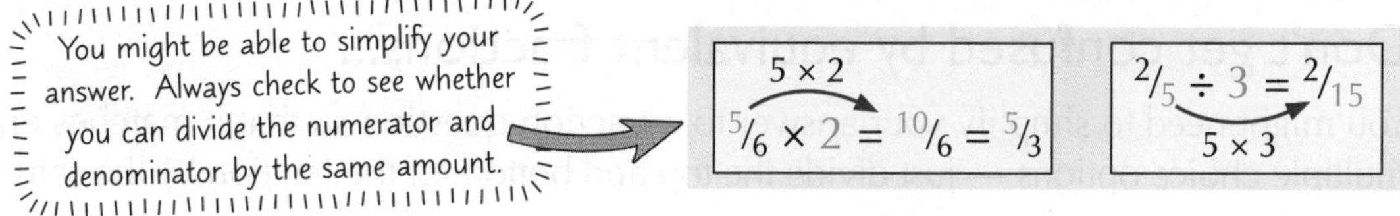

You might be able to simplify your answer. Always check to see whether you can divide the numerator and denominator by the same amount.
5 × 2
$^{5}/_{6} \times 2 = ^{10}/_{6} = ^{5}/_{3}$
$^{2}/_{5} \div 3 = ^{2}/_{15}$
5 × 3

Fractions

11+ Example Questions

Look at these fractions: $^1/_3$ $^2/_9$ $^1/_6$ $^2/_3$ $^1/_9$

Put them in order of size, starting with the smallest.

1) Change the fractions into equivalent fractions, all sharing the same denominator.
   All the denominators divide into 18: $^1/_3 = {^6/_{18}}$, $^2/_9 = {^4/_{18}}$, $^1/_6 = {^3/_{18}}$, $^2/_3 = {^{12}/_{18}}$, $^1/_9 = {^2/_{18}}$
2) Put them in order by comparing their numerators.
   $^2/_{18}$ $^3/_{18}$ $^4/_{18}$ $^6/_{18}$ $^{12}/_{18}$
3) Change them back into the original fractions.
   $^1/_9$ $^1/_6$ $^2/_9$ $^1/_3$ $^2/_3$

A coat is originally priced at £32. Its price is reduced to $^3/_4$ of the original price. What is the price of the coat now?

1) You need to find $^3/_4$ of £32. First, divide 32 by the denominator of the fraction.
   4 is the denominator in $^3/_4$. So, 32 ÷ 4 = 8. This means that $^1/_4$ of £32 = £8.
2) Now multiply 8 by the numerator.
   If $^1/_4$ = 8, then $^3/_4$ is 3 × 8 = 24.
3) The coat costs £24.
4) You could also use this method in a different way. Start by multiplying the number by the numerator and then divide the result by the denominator.
   3 is the numerator in $^3/_4$. So, 32 × 3 = 96. Then divide 96 by the denominator, which is 4. 96 ÷ 4 = 24. The coat costs £24.

Practice Questions

1) Lydia and Rose each have a pie. Their pies are exactly the same size.
   Lydia gave two fifths of her pie to Gemma. Rose gave Gemma one fifth of her pie.
   Which statement is correct?

   A Gemma has more pie than Lydia.
   B Gemma has the same amount of pie as Rose.
   C Gemma has more pie than Rose.
   D Gemma has the same amount of pie as Lydia.
   E Rose and Lydia together have exactly twice as much pie as Gemma.

2) Tia had a sack of apples. She gave Alex $^2/_3$ of the apples and kept the rest.
   Alex split his apples into 3 equal piles.
   What fraction of the sack of apples are in each of Alex's piles?

   A $^1/_3$ **B** $^1/_6$ **C** $^2/_9$ **D** $^2/_6$ **E** $^6/_9$

Don't get confused by equivalent fractions...

You might need to simplify your answer to a fraction question so that it matches one of the multiple choice options — just divide the top and bottom of the fraction by the same number.

Percentages, Fractions and Decimals

You can write a proportion of something as a decimal, a fraction or a percentage. This page will show you how percentages, fractions and decimals are related, and how to convert between them.

You can **Convert** between **Percentages**, **Fractions** and **Decimals**

Decimals can be **Converted** into **Percentages**

1) To turn a decimal into a percentage, multiply the decimal by 100, e.g. 0.53 × 100 = 53%.

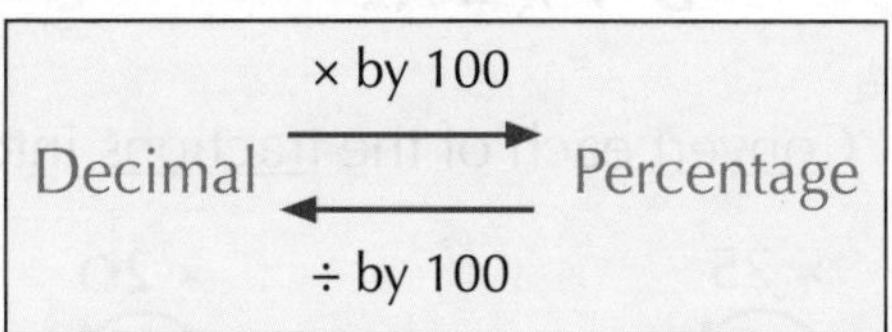

2) Divide the percentage by 100 to get back to the decimal, e.g. 72% = 72 ÷ 100 = 0.72.

Fractions can be **Converted** into **Percentages**

1) Converting fractions with 100 as the denominator into percentages is easy. The numerator is the percentage, e.g. $^{23}/_{100}$ = 23%.

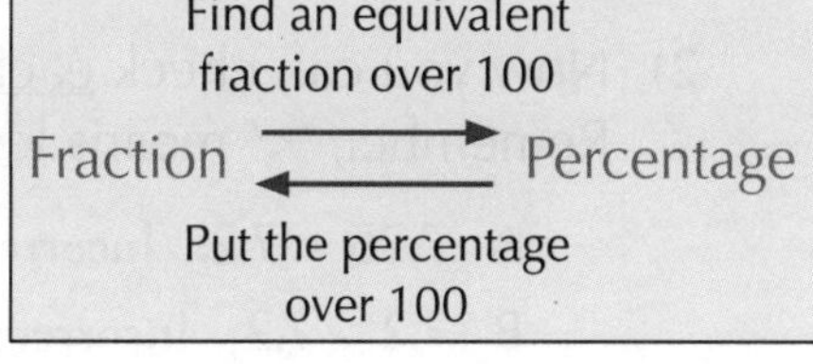

2) For other fractions, just make an equivalent fraction (see p.14) with 100 as the denominator.

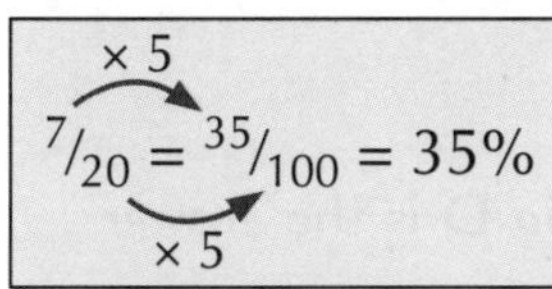

3) You can write any percentage as a fraction. Put the percentage on the top (the numerator) and 100 on the bottom (the denominator), e.g. 17% = $^{17}/_{100}$.

"Per cent" just means "out of 100" — it's usually written as %. So 17 per cent is 17 out of 100, which can also be written as 17%.

Fractions can also be **Converted** into **Decimals**

1) To convert a fraction into a decimal, you can often just find an equivalent fraction with 100 as its denominator.

Find the equivalent fraction over 100 and divide its numerator by 100

Fraction ⇄ Decimal

× by 100 and put this number over 100

2) Then divide the numerator by 100 to get the decimal.

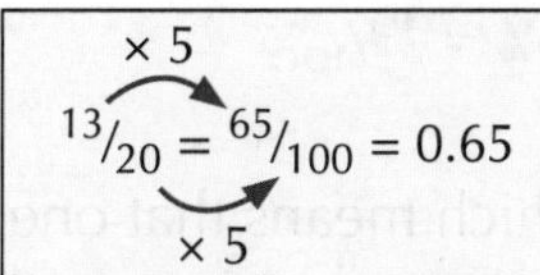

3) To convert a decimal into a fraction you just multiply the decimal by 100, then put this as the numerator above a denominator of 100. E.g. 0.29 = $^{29}/_{100}$.
(If the decimal has more than 2 decimal places, multiply by a bigger number and put that as the denominator — e.g. 0.625 × 1000 = 625, so 0.625 = $^{625}/_{1000}$)

These are very common fractions as percentages and decimals — make sure you know them:
$^{1}/_{4}$ = 25% or 0.25 $^{3}/_{4}$ = 75% or 0.75 $^{1}/_{2}$ = 50% or 0.5 $^{1}/_{10}$ = 10% or 0.1 $^{1}/_{5}$ = 20% or 0.2

Percentages, Fractions and Decimals

11+ Example Questions

EXAMPLE: **Find the correct statement.**

A $7\frac{1}{4} < 7.2$ **B** $7\frac{1}{5} > 7.2$ **C** $7\frac{1}{10} > 7.2$

D $7\frac{1}{5} = 7.2$ **E** $7\frac{1}{2} < 7.2$

1) Convert each of the fractions into a decimal so you can compare the numbers.

$7\frac{1}{4} = 7\frac{25}{100} = 7.25$ (× 25) $7\frac{1}{5} = 7\frac{20}{100} = 7.2$ (× 20) $7\frac{1}{10} = 7\frac{10}{100} = 7.1$ (× 10) $7\frac{1}{2} = 7\frac{50}{100} = 7.5$ (× 50)

2) Now you can check each statement.
Remember, '<' means less than and '>' means greater than.

A $7.25 < 7.2$. Incorrect.
B $7.2 > 7.2$. Incorrect.
C $7.1 > 7.2$. Incorrect.
D $7.2 = 7.2$. Correct. So D is the answer.
E $7.5 < 7.2$. Incorrect.

A bottle of tomato sauce contains 10% sugar.
What fraction of the tomato sauce is sugar?

A $\frac{2}{5}$ **B** $\frac{1}{10}$ **C** $\frac{1}{4}$ **D** $\frac{1}{2}$ **E** $\frac{1}{20}$

1) You might recognise that $10\% = \frac{1}{10}$. If you don't then you'll need to work it out.

Convert 10% into a fraction. $10\% = \frac{10}{100}$

2) None of the options is $\frac{10}{100}$, which means that one of them must be equivalent to it. All of the options are fractions in their simplest form, so you need to simplify $\frac{10}{100}$ to find the answer.

The numerator and the denominator are both multiples of 10 — divide them both by 10 to find the simplest form of the fraction.

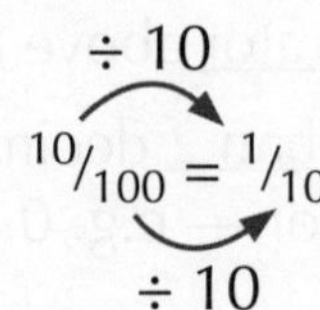

If some of the options aren't in their simplest form, simplify them first.

3) Compare your simplified fraction with the answer options — the answer is B.

Percentages, Fractions and Decimals

Which one of these is the greatest?

A $^1/_5$ of 45　B 25% of 40　C $^1/_3$ of 30　D 80% of 20　E $^3/_4$ of 20

1) Work out the value of each option which involves a fraction. To work out the fraction of a number, divide the number by the denominator and multiply it by the numerator.

   A: $^1/_5$ of 45. 45 ÷ 5 = 9. 9 × 1 = 9.

   C: $^1/_3$ of 30. 30 ÷ 3 = 10. 10 × 1 = 10.

   E: $^3/_4$ of 20. 20 ÷ 4 = 5. 5 × 3 = 15.

2) Work out the value of each option which involves a percentage. To work out the percentage of a number you could convert the percentage to a fraction. Then follow the method for working out the fraction of a number.

   B: 25% of 40 is the same as $^1/_4$ of 40. 40 ÷ 4 = 10. 10 × 1 = 10.

   D: 80% of 20 is the same as $^8/_{10}$ of 20. 20 ÷ 10 = 2. 2 × 8 = 16.

3) The answer is D because 80% of 20 is the greatest number.

Alternatively, to find a percentage of a number you can divide the number by 100 and multiply the result by the percentage you want to find.

Practice Questions

1) What percentage of the triangle on the right is shaded?

   A 10%　**B** 20%　**C** 25%　**D** 30%　**E** 40%

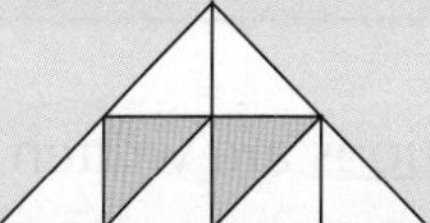

2) Marek asked all the children in Year 5 what their favourite colour was. He made a chart to show his results.

   There are 90 children in Year 5.

   How many children chose pink as their favourite colour?

   A 12　**B** 18　**C** 27　**D** 30　**E** 33

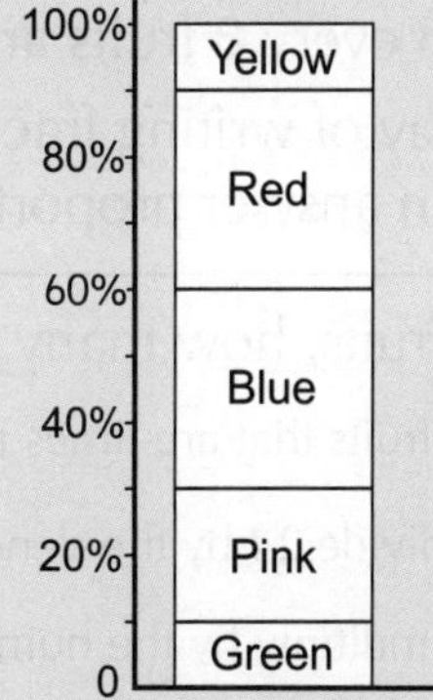

3) Which one of these is the smallest?

   A 25% of 4　**B** $^3/_4$ of 8　**C** $^2/_5$ of 10　**D** 10% of 25　**E** $^2/_6$ of 18

Practise switching between the different forms...

Memorising some common fractions as decimals and percentages will make answering these questions easier. Make sure you know the ones on the previous page really well.

Ratio and Proportion

The difference between ratio and proportion can be tricky, so read this page carefully.

Ratios Compare **One Part** to **Another Part**

1) Ratios look like this: 

You read this as '1 to 3'. It means there's one of the first type of thing for every three of the second type.

2) They are most clearly shown using shapes or objects:

The diagram shows that for every two limes there are six lemons.

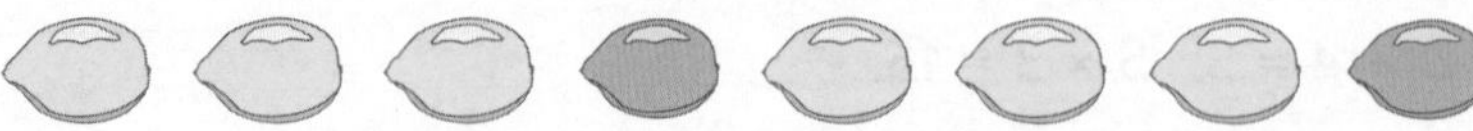

So for every lime there are three lemons. The ratio is 1 lime to 3 lemons or 1 : 3.

3) Finding equivalent ratios is a lot like finding equivalent fractions (see page 14). You have to multiply or divide all the parts of the ratio by the same number.

If there were 12 lemons, how many limes would there be?

× 4 3 lemons for every 1 lime × 4
12 lemons for every ? limes

Like with fractions, both parts of the ratio have been multiplied by the same number — so there would be 1 × 4 = 4 limes.

Proportions Compare a **Part** to the **Whole Thing**

1) Proportions are written like this: 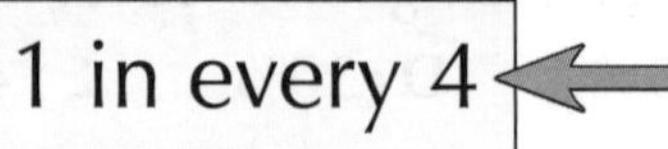

The 4 represents the whole thing and the 1 represents a part of the whole thing.

2) In the example above, 2 in every 8 fruits are limes, which is the same as 1 in every 4.
3) Proportions are another way of writing fractions. The proportion '1 in every 4' is the same as the fraction $^1/_4$. So you can answer proportion questions as you would fractions questions.

> If there were 24 fruits, how many limes would there be?
>
> The proportion of fruits that are limes is 1 in every 4, or $^1/_4$.
>
> To find $^1/_4$ of 24, divide 24 by the denominator. ⟶ 24 ÷ 4 = 6.
>
> You don't need to multiply by the numerator here, because it's 1.
>
> There would be 6 limes if there were 24 fruits.

Similar Shapes have **Side Lengths** in the **Same Ratio**

You can change the size of a shape by multiplying each side by the same number — called a scale factor. The two shapes are called similar, and have pairs of sides in the same ratio.

3 cm
A 1 cm
6 cm
B 2 cm

E.g. Shape A has been enlarged by a scale factor of 2 to give Shape B.
Shape B's sides are twice as long as Shape A's — the pairs of sides are in the ratio 1 : 2.

Ratio and Proportion

11+ Example Questions

EXAMPLE: **Divide £490 in the ratio 4 : 3.**

1) First add together the numbers in the ratio to find out how many parts £490 needs to be divided into.

   4 + 3 = 7

2) Next divide the total amount by 7 to find out how much one part is.

   £490 ÷ 7 = £70

3) Then multiply £70 by 4 to find out how much four parts are, and by 3 to find out how much three parts are.

   £70 × 4 = £280
   £70 × 3 = £210

4) The answer is £280 : £210.

EXAMPLE: **8 copies of the same magazine cost £16.40. How much will 3 copies cost?**

1) Divide the total cost by 8 to work out how much one magazine costs.

   £16.40 ÷ 8 = £2.05

2) Then multiply by three to find the cost of 3 magazines.

   £2.05 × 3 = £6.15

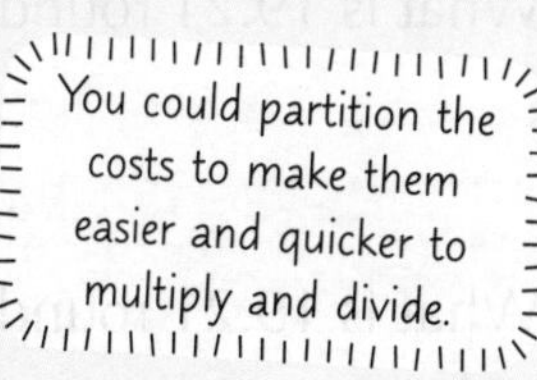

You could partition the
costs to make them
easier and quicker to
multiply and divide.

Practice Questions

1) A farmer has 48 orange Highland cows and 96 black and white cows.
   What is the ratio of orange cows to black and white cows?
   Write your answer in its simplest form.

2) Maya has a box of coloured building blocks. 5 in every 7 of them are green.
   If there are 84 blocks in total, how many green blocks are there?

Ratios are all about sharing things out...

If ratio questions are getting you in a muddle, just remember to work out how much one part of the ratio is worth. First add to find the total number of parts, then divide by the total to find the value of one part. Then, you can multiply this by the number of parts you need to get the answer.

Practice Questions

Once you're done with the Number Knowledge section, find out how much you've learned by having a go at these Practice Questions.

1. Look at the decimal number on the right. What is the value of the 9? Circle the correct answer.

   795.212

   A 9 tenths **B** 9 hundreds **C** 9 ones **D** 9 tens **E** 9 thousandths

2. Theo wrote down the distance he walked in metres on four hikes. What is the distance of his longest hike? Circle the correct answer.

   A 14 320 m **B** 13 987 m **C** 14 354 m **D** 14 263 m

3. What number is the arrow pointing to on the number line below?

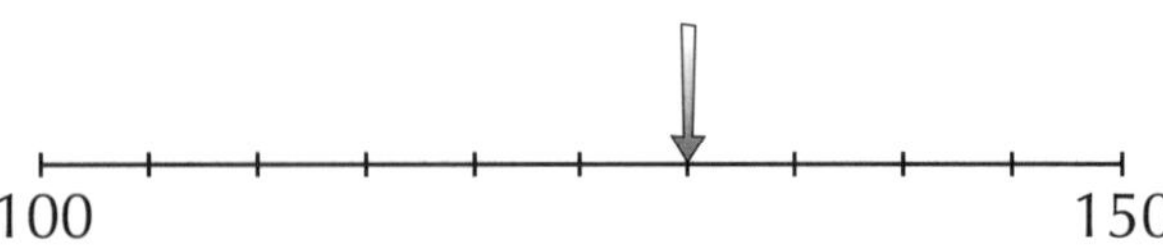

   Answer: 130

4. Which number below is closest to 5? Circle the correct answer.

   A 4.7 **B** 5.35 **C** 5.15 **D** 4.8 **E** 5.2

5. What is 19.21 rounded to the nearest ten?

   20 Answer: 20

6. What is 19.21 rounded to the nearest whole number?

   Answer: 19.00

7. There were 55 300 supporters at a wheelchair rugby match. How many supporters were there to the nearest ten thousand?

   Answer: 60 000

8. Which of the numbers below does not round to 7.1 to one decimal place? Circle the correct answer.

   A 7.12 **B** 7.15 **C** 7.05 **D** 7.09 **E** 7.08

9. What is the smallest number that rounds to 600 000 to the nearest hundred thousand?

   550 000

   Answer: 550 000

Practice Questions

10. What is the largest prime number that is smaller than 40?

Answer: 37

11. Which of the following temperatures is the lowest? Circle the correct answer.

A –4 °C **B** 0 °C **C** –12 °C **D** –14 °C **E** –9 °C

12. What is the smallest common multiple of 9 and 15?

Answer: 3

13. Which statement below is not correct? Circle the correct answer.

A $4^3 < 75$ **B** $9^2 > 81$ **C** $3^3 > 20$ **D** $7^2 < 50$

14. Verity shares a box of doughnuts equally between herself and five friends. Which of the following could be the number of doughnuts in the box? Circle the correct answer.

A 15 **B** 20 **C** 8 **D** 25 **E** 18

15. Kamal has a total of 44 gold and silver coins. The number of gold coins is a cube number and the number of silver coins is a square number. How many gold coins does he have?

27 8 36

Answer: 8

16. Zoe is thinking of a prime number. It is a common factor of 35 and 84. What number is Zoe thinking of?

Answer: 7

17. Which Roman numeral has the highest value? Circle the correct answer.

A MXVI **B** MCIX **C** CMXC **D** DCCX **E** MLXI

18. What is the greatest common factor of 40 and 72?

8 9

Answer: 8

19. What is the missing number in the sequence below?

7 15 23 31 39

Answer: 15

Practice Questions

20. How many dots will be in the next shape in this sequence?

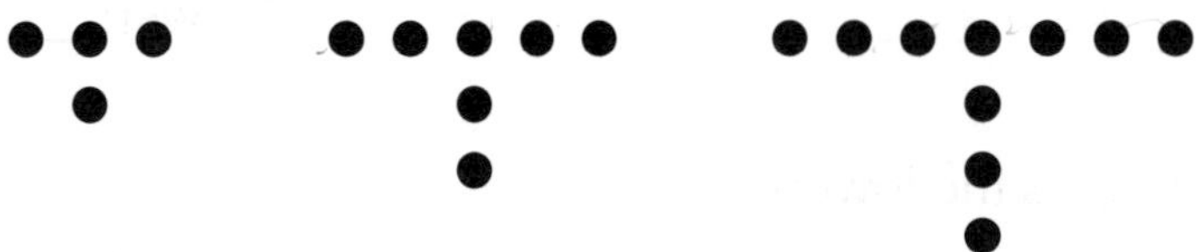

Answer: ______

21. Nazeem has 79 grapes and eats 7 every hour.
How many hours will it be before he has fewer than 50 grapes?

Answer: ______

22. How many grapes will Nazeem have left after eight hours?

Answer: ______

23. Which fraction below is not equivalent to $^{10}/_{25}$? Circle the correct answer.

A $^{12}/_{30}$ **B** $^{2}/_{5}$ **C** $^{4}/_{10}$ **D** $^{6}/_{15}$ **E** $^{30}/_{50}$

The table shows the fractions of a crossword puzzle that four children have completed.

Aidan	Beth	Cindy	Dev
$^{2}/_{5}$	$^{5}/_{6}$	$^{1}/_{3}$	$^{4}/_{9}$

24. Who has completed the most? Circle the correct answer.

A Aidan **B** Beth **C** Cindy **D** Dev

25. Cindy and Dev didn't get any of the same answers.
How much of the puzzle did they complete in total?

Answer: ______

26. How much more of the puzzle did Beth complete than Aidan?

Answer: ______

27. Izumi has read $^{7}/_{9}$ of a book. She has 12 pages left.
How many pages does the book have? Circle the correct answer.

A 42 **B** 108 **C** 84 **D** 54 **E** 24

28. What is $^{3}/_{50}$ as a percentage? Circle the correct answer.

A 30% **B** 15% **C** 6% **D** 3% **E** 60%

Practice Questions

29. What percentage of the rectangle below is shaded?

Answer: ______ %

30. A supermarket had 400 tins of tomatoes. They sold 45% of them.
How many tins of tomatoes do they have left?

Answer: ______

31. Sam used $^{7}/_{25}$ of a bag of flour to make some pasta and 24% to make a cake.
What percentage of the flour is left?

Answer: ______ %

32. Which of the following statements is not true? Circle the correct answer.

A $0.25 < 30\%$ **B** $^{1}/_{5} > 15\%$ **C** $0.9 = 90\%$ **D** $^{4}/_{5} < 0.8$ **E** $^{3}/_{10} > 0.25$

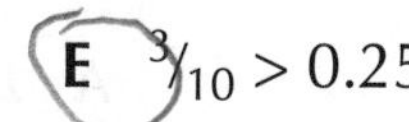

33. Divide 360 in the ratio 1 : 5.

Answer: ______ : ______

34. Look at the rectangle below. What is the ratio of a : b?

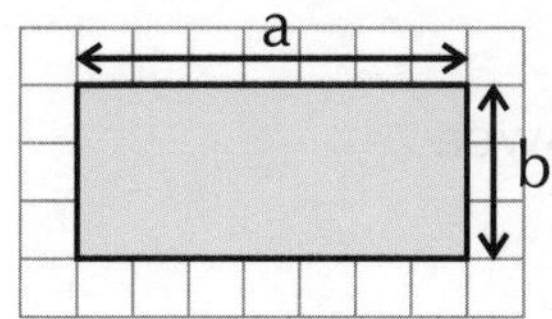

Answer: ______ : ______

In a swimming pool, there are 4 people for every 3 inflatables.

35. How many people are there if there are 12 inflatables? Circle the correct answer.

A 16 **B** 12 **C** 24 **D** 7 **E** 4

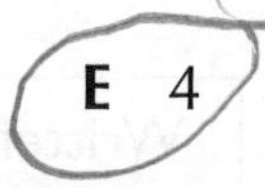

36. How many inflatables are there if there are 80 people?

Answer: ______

37. Richard has 20 identical screws in his pocket.
They have a total mass of 180 g. He uses 4 of the screws.
What is the mass of the screws he has left?

Answer: ______ g

Addition

You've been adding numbers together for years. Here are a few examples of the sorts of questions you could get in the exam, and some methods you could use to answer them.

11+ Example Questions

Eva buys an apple for 48p and an orange for 55p. How much does she spend in pounds?

1) You need to find the exact answer to this question.
2) Add the numbers together to find the answer in pence.

   48p + 55p = 103p

3) Convert this answer to pounds to find the amount Eva spends.

   103p = £1.03, so Eva spends £1.03.

Marco has £4.13, Kyle has £3.42 and Janet has £8.70. How much money do they have in total?

A £15.95 B £18.25 C £17.85 D £16.25 E £14.25

Quick Method

1) You can estimate the answer to the question by rounding the numbers to the nearest pound to make more manageable numbers.

   £4.13 is rounded down to £4.00 £3.42 is rounded down to £3.00
   £8.70 is rounded up to £9.00

2) Add the rounded numbers together to estimate the answer.

   £4.00 + £3.00 + £9.00 = £16.00

3) The answer is around £16.00. Looking at the options, the answer could be A or D.
4) As you rounded down by 55p (13p + 42p) and you rounded up by 30p, your estimate will be lower than the actual answer.
   So, the actual answer must be £16.25 — option D.

Written Method

1) An alternative method is to add the three values together in columns.

```
    4 . 1 3
    3 . 4 2
  + 8 . 7 0
  ---------
  1 6 . 2 5
  1
```

Remember to carry the digit over if the answer is more than 9.

Add together the numbers in each column starting from the right.

Make sure that you line up the place value columns and the decimal points.

2) This method gives you the exact answer, £16.25.

Addition

The table shows the amount of juice in litres sold by Cathy on her market stall over 8 weeks.

Work out the total amount of juice Cathy sold from week 3 to week 6.

Week	Amount of juice sold (l)	Week	Amount of juice sold (l)
1	43.71	5	46.30
2	46.18	6	59.12
3	82.63	7	21.14
4	34.18	8	63.94

1) For this question there are no options to choose from.
So you need to find the exact answer — you can't use rounding.

2) The question is asking for the total sales from week 3 to week 6, so find the data you need in the table.

Week 3 = 82.63 litres   Week 5 = 46.30 litres
Week 4 = 34.18 litres   Week 6 = 59.12 litres

3) Arrange the four weekly values into columns.
Add together the numbers in each column starting from the right.

```
   8 2 . 6 3
   3 4 . 1 8
   4 6 . 3 0
 + 5 9 . 1 2
 -----------
 2 2 2 . 2 3
   2 1   1
```

Use the column method to find the exact answer.

4) The total amount of juice sold from week 3 to week 6 by Cathy is 222.23 litres.

Practice Questions

1) Katie buys a cycling helmet for £13.89, a bell for £3.35 and some gloves for £12.30.
How much money does she spend?

A £31.96 **B** £29.54 **C** £32.14 **D** £28.76 **E** £26.89

2) Rafid, Freia, Martin and John take part in a relay race.
Rafid's leg took 12.37 seconds, Freia's leg took 11.88 seconds,
Martin's leg took 13.24 seconds and John's leg took 10.94 seconds.
What was their total time for the race?

Think about whether your answer makes sense...

When you've worked out an exact answer, you could check that your answer is sensible by using the rounding method to do a quick estimate. Your answer shouldn't be too far from the estimate.

Subtraction

Subtraction can get a bit tricky. All the more reason to get in lots of practice...

11+ Example Questions

Five people ran two 200 m races. Who had the greatest difference between their times for race 1 and race 2?

A Jordan
B Vanessa
C Andrei
D Rajpal
E Stacey

Name	Race 1 (s)	Race 2 (s)
Jordan	22.48	23.95
Vanessa	23.07	24.76
Andrei	22.11	23.08
Rajpal	24.04	25.67
Stacey	23.45	24.40

You could use a written method to work out the difference in time for each person, but it would take a lot of time.

1) Start by estimating the difference between the times for each person. This will mean you don't have to work out the exact time for each person.

2) Estimate the difference by rounding each time to the nearest tenth. You need to subtract their fastest time from their slowest time.

Jordan: Race 1 rounds to 22.50 and race 2 rounds to 24.00.
24.00 – 22.50 = 1.50 seconds.

Vanessa: Race 1 rounds to 23.10 and race 2 rounds to 24.80.
24.80 – 23.10 = **1.70** seconds.

Andrei: Race 1 rounds to 22.10 and race 2 rounds to 23.10.
23.10 – 22.10 = 1.00 seconds.

Rajpal: Race 1 rounds to 24.00 and race 2 rounds to 25.70.
25.70 – 24.00 = **1.70** seconds.

Stacey: Race 1 rounds to 23.50 and race 2 rounds to 24.40.
24.40 – 23.50 = 0.90 seconds.

Vanessa and Rajpal both have the greatest difference between their times, 1.70 seconds.

3) You can't tell just from rounding whether Vanessa or Rajpal has the greatest difference, so you need to find the exact difference in their times. Use the partitioning method:

Vanessa	Rajpal
23.07 = 23.00 + 0.07	24.04 = 24.00 + 0.04
24.76 – 23.00 = 1.76	25.67 – 24.00 = 1.67
1.76 – 0.07 = **1.69**	1.67 – 0.04 = **1.63**

Remember to partition the smaller number.

4) The difference between Vanessa's times is greater than the difference between Rajpal's times. Your answer is B — Vanessa.

Subtraction

Emma has £13.10. She donates £2.21 to charity.
How much money does Emma have left?

A £10.89 **B £11.81** **C £9.89** **D £11.79** **E £10.79**

Method 1

1) Partition the number that you are subtracting into its ones, tenths and hundredths:

£2.21 splits up into £2 + £0.20 + £0.01 (ones, tenths, hundredths)

2) Subtract each number one at a time:

£13.10 – £2.00 = £11.10
£11.10 – £0.20 = £10.90 ← Be careful here — you're changing the value in the ones column as well as the tenths.
£10.90 – £0.01 = £10.89 ← Your answer is £10.89 — option A.

Method 2

1) You can also subtract numbers by writing them in columns.
2) Write the number you're subtracting from first and make sure the decimal points line up.

Subtract the numbers in each column starting from the right.

$$\begin{array}{r} 1\,{}^{2}\!\not{3}\,.\,{}^{10}\!\not{1}\,{}^{1}0 \\ -\quad 2\,.\,2\,1 \\ \hline 1\,0\,.\,8\,9 \end{array}$$

If you have to subtract a bigger number from a smaller number, make an exchange from the next place value column.

Practice Questions

1) Gavin's bath holds 75.63 litres of water when it is full. Gavin pours 48.28 litres of water into the bath. How many more litres of water would he need to fill the bath?
   A 27.45 **B** 27.75 **C** 26.95
   D 28.15 **E** 27.35

2) The table shows the results of five students in two tests. Which student had the greatest increase in score between test 1 and test 2?

Name	Test 1 (%)	Test 2 (%)
Joe	57.6	61.5
Holly	60.2	63.8
Lucille	62.7	63.0
Dave	64.1	59.9
Anita	59.8	64.7

Be extra careful when the numbers have different numbers of digits...

Make sure you always line up the numbers using the place value columns or decimal points. Add zeros to the end of decimal numbers to make them have matching numbers of digits.

Multiplying and Dividing by 10, 100 and 1000

When you multiply or divide any number by 10, 100 or 1000, you just move the digits left or right.

Move digits **Left** to **Multiply** by **10, 100** or **1000**

1) If you're multiplying a number by 10, move the digits one place to the left.

2.4 × 10 = 24

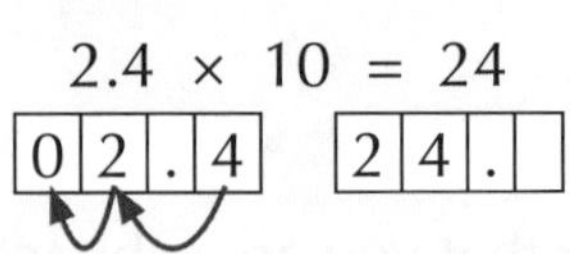

2) If you're multiplying a number by 100, move the digits two places to the left.

75.9 × 100 = 7590

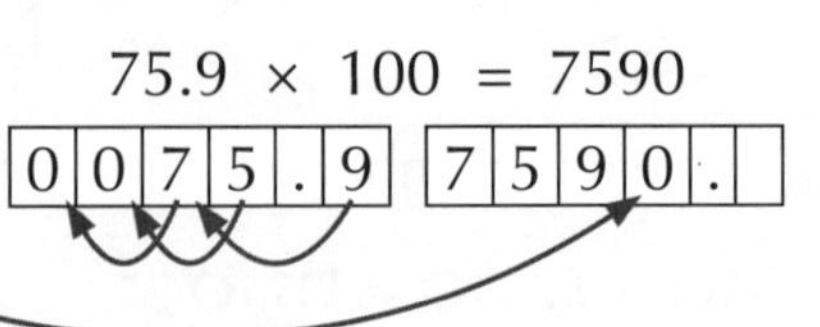

Put a zero here to fill in the gap before the decimal point.

3) If you're multiplying a number by 1000, move the digits three places to the left.

27.1 × 1000 = 27 100

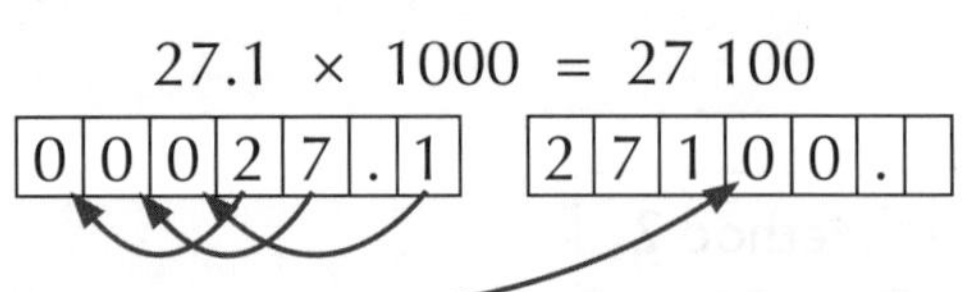

This time you need to put two zeros before the decimal point.

Move digits **Right** to **Divide** by **10, 100** or **1000**

1) If you're dividing a number by 10, move the digits one place to the right.

8.6 ÷ 10 = 0.86

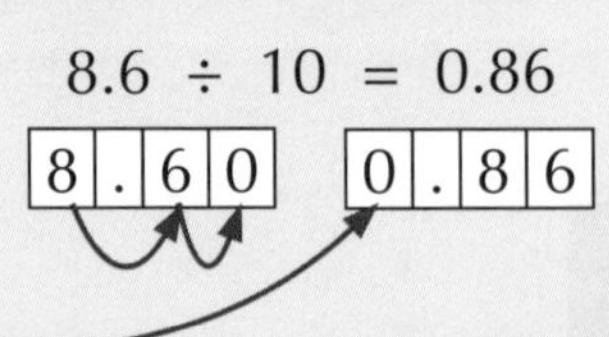

Put a zero before the decimal point to fill in the gap.

2) If you're dividing a number by 100, move the digits two places to the right.

7.5 ÷ 100 = 0.075

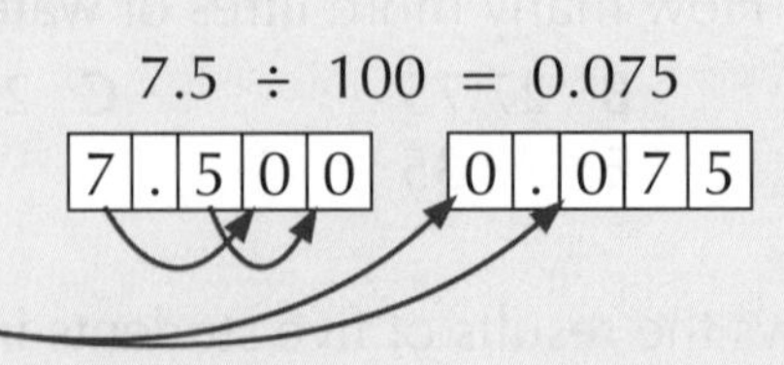

Put one zero before the decimal point and one zero after to fill in the gaps.

3) If you're dividing a number by 1000, move the digits three places to the right.

600 ÷ 1000 = 0.600 = 0.6

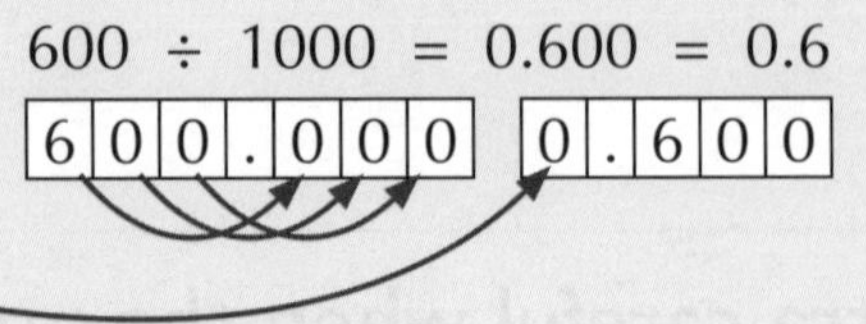

Put a zero before the decimal point to fill in the gap.

Multiplying and Dividing by 10, 100 and 1000

11+ Example Questions

Which of these calculations equals 843?

A 84 300 ÷ 10 **B** 0.843 × 1000
C 84 300 ÷ 1000 **D** 0.0843 × 1000
E 0.843 × 100

You can draw out the place value columns to help you if you're finding these calculations tricky.

1) Work out the answer to each calculation:

A Move each digit one place to the right: 84 300 ÷ 10 = 8430
B Move each digit three places to the left: 0.843 × 1000 = 843
C Move each digit three places to the right: 84 300 ÷ 1000 = 84.3
D Move each digit three places to the left: 0.0843 × 1000 = 84.3
E Move each digit two places to the left: 0.843 × 100 = 84.3

2) The correct answer is 0.843 × 1000 — option B.

301 × 10 = ... ÷ 100
Which number should fill in the blank?

1) Multiply 301 by 10 to work out the first part of the calculation.

301 × 10 = 3010 ← To multiply by ten, move each digit one place to the left.

2) The second part of the calculation must also equal 3010.
3) When you divide the missing number by 100, it will equal 3010.
So, calculate the missing number by doing the inverse operation — multiplying by 100.

3010 × 100 = 301 000 ← This time you are multiplying by 100, so each digit moves two places to the left.

4) That gives you the answer: 301 000. You can check it's correct by dividing 301 000 by 100. It should equal 3010.

Practice Questions

1) Mark has sold 1000 tickets for a raffle. The tickets were sold in books of ten.
In total, Mark collected £375 for all 1000 tickets. How much did one book cost?

A £0.37 **B** £3.75 **C** £3.57 **D** £7.35 **E** £37.50

2) 4.2 ÷ 10 = ... × 100
What number should fill in the blank?

Make sure to move the digits in the correct direction...

The options for a multiple-choice question might include the answer you would find if you were to mix up the rules for multiplying and dividing by 10, 100 or 1000.

Multiplication

There are a few ways that multiplication can be tested — these pages will show you the sorts of things that might come up, and how to tackle them.

11+ Example Questions

EXAMPLE: **A DVD costs £3.99. How much will nine DVDs cost?**

A £35.91 **B £36.00** **C £36.04** **D £35.97** **E £36.09**

Quick Method

1) Round the cost of each DVD to the nearest whole number. Then multiply by nine.

   £3.99 rounds up to £4.00. £4.00 × 9 = £36.00

   You added 1 penny for each DVD, and there were nine DVDs.

2) £36.00 is not the exact answer though. You added nine pence to this answer when you rounded the price of the DVDs. You need to subtract nine pence to reach the final answer.

   £36.00 – £0.09 = £35.91 ← Your answer is £35.91 — option A.

Written Method

1) You can multiply the numbers together in columns.
2) Make sure you line up the decimal point and the place value columns in your answer.

Starting from the right, multiply the hundredths, tenths and ones by 9.

```
   3 . 9 9
 ×       9
  3 5 . 9 1
    8   8
```

9 × 9 = 81. If the answer is more than 9, the left-hand digit is carried to the next column.

In the final column, the carried digit goes here. (9 × 3) + 8 = 35.

The carried digit gets added to the answer of the next column. Here, (9 × 9) + 8 = 89.

EXAMPLE: **What is 400 × 70?**

1) Start with a similar calculation that is easier to work out.

   4 × 7 = 28

2) Now work out how much larger the numbers in the question are than the numbers you used in the simple calculation.

   400 is 100 times larger than 4, and 70 is 10 times larger than 7.
   So the answer to 400 × 70 is 100 × 10 = 1000 times larger than 28.

3) Multiply to find the final answer.

   28 × 1000 = 28 000

Multiplication

More **11+ Example** Questions

EXAMPLE: **What is 12.4 × 6.3?**

A 0.7812 B 7.812 C 78.12 D 781.2 E 7812

1) In each option, the numbers are the same, but the decimal point is in a different place.
2) This means you can estimate the answer by rounding the two numbers in the calculation to the nearest whole number, then multiplying them together.

   12.4 is rounded down to 12. 6.3 is rounded down to 6. 12 × 6 = 72

3) The estimated answer is 72. The only option that is near to 72 is 78.12 — option C. 78.12 must be the exact answer.

526 × 24 = 12 624 ← This is a number fact.

What is 526 × 12?

Quick Method

1) Use the number fact to help you work out the answer to the question.
2) 12 is half of 24. So the answer to 526 × 12 will be half of the answer to 526 × 24.

   12 624 ÷ 2 = 6312 ⟶ 526 × 12 = 6312

Written Method

1) An alternative method would be to use long multiplication.
2) Line the numbers up in columns and put the bigger number on top.
3) Multiply each digit in the bigger number (starting from the right) with the ones and tens of the smaller number:

Multiply each digit by 2. Write the answer here.

```
    5 2 6
 ×    1 2
 --------
  1 0 5 2
      1
 --------
```

Then, multiply each number by 10. Write the answer on the line below.

```
    5 2 6
 ×    1 2
 --------
  1 0 5 2
      1
  5 2 6 0
 --------
```

4) Add your two answers together to get the final answer.

```
    5 2 6
 ×    1 2
 --------
  1 0 5 2
      1
 + 5 2 6 0
 --------
  6 3 1 2
    1
```

You may have been taught a different method for written multiplication. That's fine — just use whichever one works best for you.

Multiplication

One More **11+ Example** Question

230 × 44 = 10 120

What is 2.3 × 4.4?

1) Start by finding the relationship between the numbers in the number fact and the numbers in the question.

   230 ÷ 100 = 2.3. So, 2.3 is 100 times smaller than 230.

   44 ÷ 10 = 4.4. So, 4.4 is 10 times smaller than 44.

2) Use this to work out the relationship between the answer to the number fact and the answer to the question.

   10 × 100 = 1000.
   So, the answer is 1000 times smaller than the answer to the number fact.

3) Divide the answer of the number fact by 1000 to work out the answer to the question.

   10 120 ÷ 1000 = 10.12

There's more about how to divide by 10, 100 or 1000 on page 30.

Practice Questions

1) 3.5 × 7.9 = 27.65
   What is 350 × 79?

2) What is 6.9 × 8.2?

   A 64.40 **B** 48.18 **C** 45.95  **D** 56.58 **E** 72.52

3) Each bookshelf in a library can hold 18 books.
   How many books can be held on 53 bookshelves?

Use a number fact to make things easier for yourself...

TEST TIP

If a question gives you a number fact, it's a pretty big clue that there's a quick way to work out the answer. Look closely at how the numbers in the number fact are related to the numbers in the question. This will help you save precious time in the exam.

Division

Division is the opposite of multiplication — you're splitting a number into groups.

11+ Example Questions

Each guinea pig cage holds 3 guinea pigs.
How many cages would 124 guinea pigs need?

Quick Method

1) You need to divide 124 by 3, but 3 isn't a factor of 124.
2) Partition 124 into two numbers that are easier to work with. You need to find a number that's close to 124 and is a multiple of 3. You could split 124 into 120 and 4.
3) Start by working out how many cages you'd need for 120 guinea pigs.

   Using your 3 times table, you know that 12 ÷ 3 = 4.
   120 is 10 times bigger than 12, so 120 ÷ 3 = 40.

4) Next, work out how many cages you'd need for the remaining 4 guinea pigs. Then add your two answers together.

   4 ÷ 3 = 1 remainder 1

   40 + 1 remainder 1 = 41 remainder 1

5) You still have a remainder of 1 — so if you just have 41 cages there will be 1 poor guinea pig without a cage. You need 42 cages so that every guinea pig has a cage.

Written Method

1) You can also use a written method to divide 124 by 3.

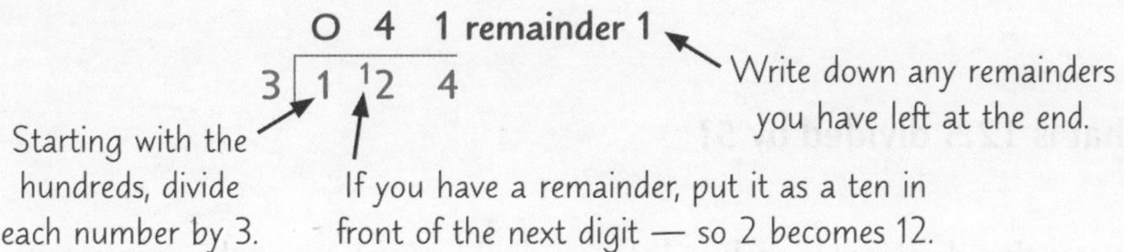

0 4 1 remainder 1
3 | 1 ¹2 4
Write down any remainders you have left at the end.
Starting with the hundreds, divide each number by 3.
If you have a remainder, put it as a ten in front of the next digit — so 2 becomes 12.

2) 41 cages will leave one extra guinea pig without a cage, so the answer must be 42.

Libby divides a number by a smaller number. Her answer has a remainder of 7.
Which of these numbers could Libby have divided by?

A 8 **B 4** **C 6** **D 5** **E 7**

There's no clear method to follow here — you need to think about it logically:

To get a remainder of 7, Libby can't have divided by a number less than 7, otherwise it could've been divided again. E.g. 4 would go into 7 once, giving a remainder of 3.

If Libby had divided by 7, then there wouldn't have been a remainder at all (because 7 ÷ 7 = 1).

Libby must have divided by a number greater than 7. So the answer must be 8 — option A.

Division

More **11+ Example** Questions

Talia ran for a distance of 2726 metres. It took her 11 minutes. To the nearest whole metre, how many metres did she run per minute?

1) You need to divide the total distance Talia ran by the length of time it took her. Long division is often worth doing when you're dividing by a two-digit number.

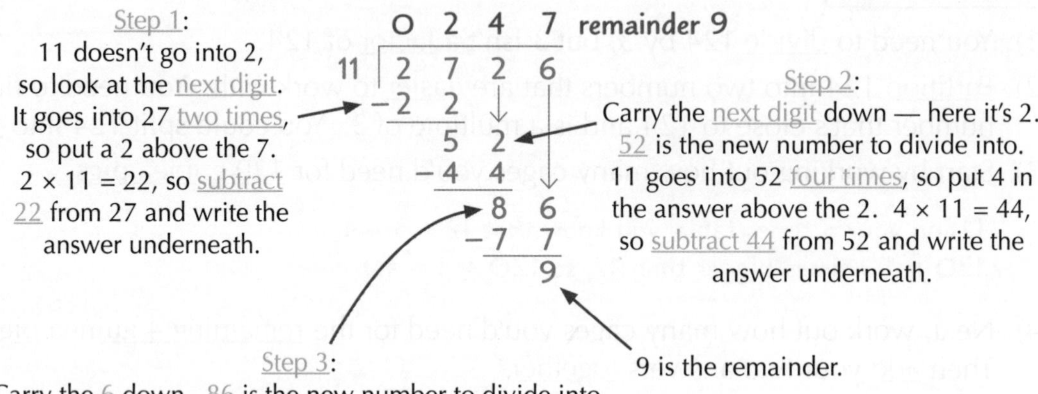

0 2 4 7 remainder 9
11 | 2 7 2 6
−2 2
5 2
−4 4
8 6
−7 7
9
Step 1:
11 doesn't go into 2, so look at the next digit. It goes into 27 two times, so put a 2 above the 7. 2 × 11 = 22, so subtract 22 from 27 and write the answer underneath.
Step 2:
Carry the next digit down — here it's 2. 52 is the new number to divide into. 11 goes into 52 four times, so put 4 in the answer above the 2. 4 × 11 = 44, so subtract 44 from 52 and write the answer underneath.
9 is the remainder.
Step 3:

Carry the 6 down. 86 is the new number to divide into. 11 goes into 86 seven times, so put 7 in the answer above the 6. 7 × 11 = 77, so subtract 77 from 86.

2) The question asks for the answer to the nearest whole number. So, 247 remainder 9 should be rounded up to 248 metres.

> If the remainder is greater than half of the number you're dividing by, it should be rounded up. If it's less, it should be rounded down.

EXAMPLE:

What is 12.5 divided by 5?

1) First, convert the decimal number into a whole number — this makes it easier to divide.

   Multiply 12.5 by 10 to make a whole number. 12.5 × 10 = 125.

2) Then, find the answer to the division.

   Find 125 ÷ 5. Partition 125 into 100 + 25 and divide each bit separately.

   100 ÷ 5 = 20, 25 ÷ 5 = 5. So 125 ÷ 5 = 20 + 5 = 25.

3) Because you multiplied 12.5 by 10 at the start, you've got to divide your answer by 10.

   25 ÷ 10 = 2.5, so 12.5 divided by 5 = 2.5

Division

EXAMPLE: **3150 ÷ 9 = 350**

What is 9450 ÷ 9?

This is similar to the method you used to answer the number fact question on page 33.

Quick Method

1) Use the number fact to help you work out the answer to the question.
2) See if you can spot how the numbers in the two calculations are related to each other. 9450 is three times larger than 3150. So, the answer to 9450 ÷ 9 will be three times larger than 350.

You could work this out by doing 300 × 3 and then 50 × 3. Then add the answers together. → 350 × 3 = 1050 → 9450 ÷ 9 = 1050

Written Method

1) You could use a written method to divide 9450 by 9.
2) Write out the division and divide each number in 9450 by 9:

```
   1 0 5 0   ← The answer is 1050.
9 |9 4 ⁴5 0
```

Divide each number by 9.

Practice Questions

1) What is 8.8 ÷ 4?
2) A soft toy costs £1.30. How many soft toys can you buy with £14.50?
3) 19 200 ÷ 16 = 1200. What is 19 200 ÷ 4?

   A 600 **B** 2400 **C** 4800 **D** 7200 **E** 9600
4) Each level on a computer game takes 8 minutes to complete. If Jamil spent 264 minutes playing the computer game, how many levels did he complete?
5) Glenda has £1680 in her bank account. She divides it equally between her 15 grandchildren. How much does each child get?

Don't panic if you can't see how to start a division question...

It's not always obvious how you should work out the answer to division questions. Think carefully about what the question is asking you to do — sometimes you'll need to partition a larger number into smaller chunks that are easier to work with.

Algebra

Algebra isn't as scary as it sounds. Make sure you're happy with the basics and then practise, practise, practise...

Algebra is using Letters to Represent Numbers

1) Algebra uses letters to represent numbers that you don't know.

This is called an algebraic equation.

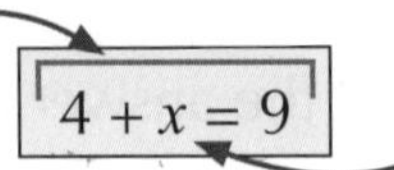

$4 + x = 9$

x represents a number that you don't know. When you add 4 to x you get 9. $4 + 5 = 9$, so $x = 5$.

2) Algebra doesn't use multiplication signs before letters. You just write the number next to the letter. For example:

$3x$ means $3 \times x$

$2ab$ means $2 \times a \times b$

$^1/_2\, x$ means $^1/_2 \times x$

3) A letter written over a number means that you have to divide by that number. For example:

$^x/_8$ means $x \div 8$

4) Algebraic expressions also use square numbers. These show that a letter is multiplied by itself.

x^2 means $x \times x$

5) Brackets are used to keep parts of an expression together. You should always work out the part in brackets first. For example:

$3(a + b)$ means $(a + b) + (a + b) + (a + b)$

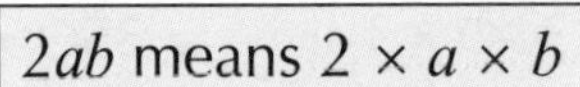

Work out the part in brackets first $(a + b)$, and then find 3 lots of the answer.

6) A formula tells you how to work out one quantity when you know a different quantity. For example, to work out how many wheels a number of cars have altogether, you could use the formula $w = 4c$, where w is the total number of wheels and c is the number of cars.

BODMAS is Really Important

1) BODMAS tells you the order in which operations should be done.

Operations are things like ×, ÷, + and –.

BODMAS = Brackets, Other, Division, Multiplication, Addition, Subtraction

Other is things like square numbers.

2) You may have to use BODMAS when working with algebraic expressions. For example, what is the value of $3(a + 5) - 7$ when a is 4?

$3(4 + 5) - 7$ — Substitute a with 4 in the expression.

$(4 + 5) = 9$ — Start off with the bit in the brackets.

$3 \times 9 = 27$ — Then multiply by 3.

$27 - 7 = 20$ — Then subtract 7.

Algebra

Do the **Opposite Operation** to solve an **Equation**

1) The values on the left-hand side of an equation equal the values on the right-hand side. You can use this to solve an algebraic equation, and find the value of the letter.
2) You need to remove parts of the equation until the letter is left on its own.
3) To remove part of an equation, do the opposite operation to both sides of the equation. For example:

+ and – are opposites, and × and ÷ are opposites.

Find x when $3x + 2 = 20$.

$3x + 2 = 20$
$-2 \quad -2$ ← The opposite of + 2 is – 2, so subtract 2 from both sides.

$3x = 18$
$\div 3 \quad \div 3$ ← x is being multiplied by 3. The opposite of × 3 is ÷ 3, so divide by 3 on both sides.

$x = 6$ ← That gives you the answer — x is 6.

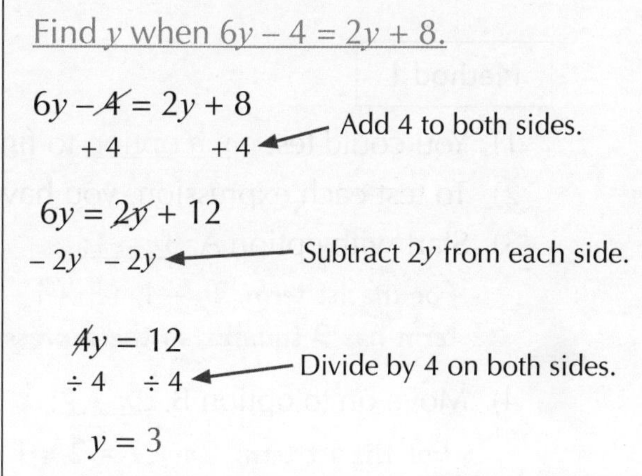

Find y when $6y - 4 = 2y + 8$.

$6y - 4 = 2y + 8$
$+4 \quad +4$ ← Add 4 to both sides.

$6y = 2y + 12$
$-2y \quad -2y$ ← Subtract $2y$ from each side.

$4y = 12$
$\div 4 \quad \div 4$ ← Divide by 4 on both sides.

$y = 3$

11+ Example Questions

A farm calculates the cost of eggs in pence (E) using this formula:

$E = 40 + 2x^2$

x is the number of eggs bought.

A man buys 9 eggs. What is the total cost in pounds?

1) The man buys 9 eggs, so change x in the formula to 9.

   $E = 40 + 2 \times 9^2$

2) Work out the calculation one part at a time. Remember to follow BODMAS.

   First, work out 9^2... → $E = 40 + 2 \times 81$ ← $9^2 = 9 \times 9 = 81$

   ... then do the multiplication... → $E = 40 + 162$ ← $2 \times 81 = 162$

   ... then work out the addition to find the cost in pence... → $E = 202$ ← $162 + 40 = 202$

   ... then divide by 100 to find the cost in pounds. → $E = 202\text{p} = £2.02$

Don't forget this last step. The question asked for the answer in pounds.

Algebra

EXAMPLE: **Gael uses squares to make the first three terms of a sequence.**

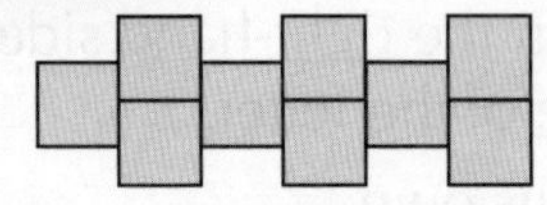

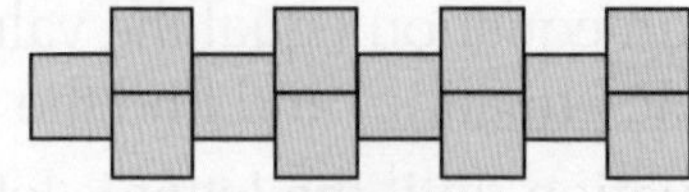

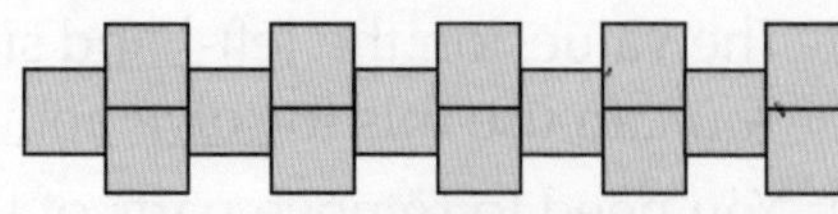

1st term **2nd term** **3rd term**

What is the correct expression for the number of squares in the *n*th term of the sequence?

A $3n - 1$ **B $2n + 7$** **C $3n + 6$** **D $n + 3$** **E $5n$**

The '*n*th term' is the name given to any term in a sequence.

Method 1

1) You could test each option to find the expression which works for the sequence.
2) To test each expression, you have to replace n with the term number of the sequence.
3) Start with option A, $3n - 1$:

   For the 1st term, $3n - 1 = 3 \times 1 - 1 = 2$. The 1st term has 9 squares, so the expression is **incorrect**.

4) Move on to option B, $2n + 7$:

   For the 1st term, $2n + 7 = 2 \times 1 + 7 = 9$. This expression is **correct** for the 1st term.
   For the 2nd term, $2n + 7 = 2 \times 2 + 7 = 11$. The 2nd term has 12 squares — **incorrect**.

5) Next, try option C, $3n + 6$:

   For the 1st term, $3n + 6 = 3 \times 1 + 6 = 9$. This expression is **correct** for the 1st term.
   For the 2nd term, $3n + 6 = 3 \times 2 + 6 = 12$. It's also **correct** for the 2nd term.
   For the 3rd term, $3n + 6 = 3 \times 3 + 6 = 15$. Bingo — it's **correct** for the 3rd term as well.

6) So, you know that the correct answer is option C — you don't have to check the other options.

Method 2

1) You can work out the expression for the nth term of the sequence.
2) Look for the relationship between the number of squares in each term.

Term Number	1	2	3
Number of Squares	9	12	15

+3 +3

The number of squares increases by 3 between each term. The sequence is following the three times table, so you need to multiply by three in the expression.

3) Start your expression with '$3n$'.

   For the 1st term, $n = 1$. So $3n = 3 \times 1 = 3$. The table says term 1 has 9 squares.
   So if you add 6, you have made a rule that works for the 1st term of the sequence, $3n + 6$.

4) Check your expression is correct by testing the other terms.

   For the 2nd term, $3n + 6 = 3 \times 2 + 6 = 12$.
   For the 3rd term, $3n + 6 = 3 \times 3 + 6 = 15$.

5) The expression works for all three terms. So the correct answer is $3n + 6$ — option C.

Algebra

At a restaurant, a hamburger costs £3 and a hotdog costs £2. Which expression gives the total cost, in pounds, of buying x hamburgers and y hotdogs?

A $2x + y$ **B** $5y - x$ **C** $3xy$ **D** $3x + 2y$ **E** $x \times y$

1) Make the expression one part at a time.
2) Start by finding the cost (in pounds) of x hamburgers:

Cost of hamburgers = $3x$ — The cost of the hamburgers is the number you're buying (x) multiplied by the price (£3). So this should be written as $3x$.

3) Next, add the cost (in pounds) of y hotdogs to complete the expression:

$3x + 2y$ — Each hotdog costs £2, so the price of y hotdogs is $2y$ pounds.

To find the total cost, add the cost of the hotdogs to the cost of the hamburgers.

4) That gives you the finished expression. The correct answer is $3x + 2y$ — option D.

Practice Questions

1) The cost (in pounds) of calling out an electrician (C) is given by the formula:
$C = 25 + 10h + p$, where h is the number of hours and p is the cost (in pounds) of any parts.
What is the cost of the electrician when they work for 3 hours and need £20 worth of parts?

2) 6, 11, 16, 21
What is the expression for the nth term of this sequence?

A $n^2 + 5$ **B** $n + 5$ **C** $5n - 1$ **D** $5n + 5$ 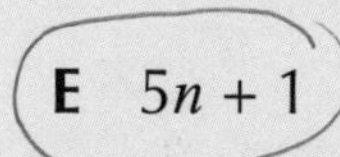 **E** $5n + 1$

3) The width of a room is 3 m. The length of the room is four times the width of the room. The height of the room is y m. Which of these is the correct expression for finding the volume of the room in m^3?

A $12y \times 4$ **B** $3y \times 4y$ **C** $12y + 3y$ 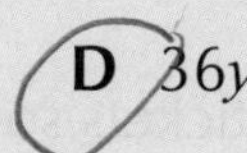 **D** $36y$ **E** $y + 36$

Volume is calculated by length × width × height.

Substitute values to check you have the right expression...

When you've written an algebraic expression, you can try it out to check it's right.
For the question above, imagine that you bought 1 hamburger and 1 hotdog. You know that the total cost will be £5 (£3 + £2 = £5), so make sure that your expression gives you 5 as the answer when x is 1 and y is 1. (3 × £1) + (2 × £1) = £3 + £2 = £5, so you have the right expression.

Practice Questions

Now you've made it all the way through the section on Working with Numbers, see how much you have learnt with these Practice Questions.

1. What is 4623 + 999?

   Answer: ________

2. A plumber has two bits of pipe measuring 8.9 cm and 7.9 cm. How many cm of pipe does she have in total? Circle the correct answer.

   A 16.18 cm **B** 16.2 cm **C** 16.8 cm **D** 17.2 cm **E** 18.2 cm

3. In a diving competition, Jane scored 8.4, 9.1, 7 and 3.7 on her first four dives. What is her total score for these dives?

   Answer: ________

4. What is 90 – 6.78? Circle the correct answer.

   A 82.32 **B** 83.22 **C** 83.32 **D** 84.22 **E** 84.32

5. What is 7450 – 2120?

   Answer: ________

Isobel has £2.18, Josh has £4.65 and Tammy has £3.22.

6. How much do they have in total? Circle the correct answer.

   A £10.05 **B** £10.95 **C** £9.95 **D** £11.05 **E** £9.90

7. How much more does Josh have than Tammy?

   Answer: £ ________

8. Monib had £50. He bought some headphones for £22.99 and a microphone for £20.50. How much does Monib have left?

   Answer: £ ________

The table shows the number of tickets sold for four shows at a theatre.

	Number of tickets sold
Show 1	4578
Show 2	2018
Show 3	3444
Show 4	6475

9. How many tickets were sold for shows 1 and 3 in total?

   Answer: ________

10. How many more tickets were sold for show 4 than for shows 2 and 3 combined?

    Answer: ________

Practice Questions

11. Kim has three oranges with a total mass of 785 g. Two of the oranges weigh 290 g and 262 g. How heavy is the third orange?

Answer: ________ g

12. What is 1468 ÷ 100?

Answer: ________

13. Circle the number that is missing from this calculation: 1000 × ____ = 57 840

A 0.5784 **B** 5.784 **C** 57.84 **D** 578.4 **E** 5784

14. Justin buys 100 bars of soap for £1.27 each. How much does he spend in total?

Answer: £ ________

15. Paul has three piles of rocks. The first pile is 100 times heavier than the second. The second pile is 10 times lighter than the third. How many times lighter is the third pile than the first?

Answer: ________

16. There are 12 marbles in a bag. Mr Fayed buys 100 bags and shares the marbles equally between 10 boxes. How many marbles are in each box?

Answer: ________

17. There are six penguins in a zoo. They each eat 4 fish a day. How many fish do they eat in total in a week?

Answer: ________

18. Which calculation gives the smallest answer? Circle the correct answer.

A 54.3 × 79 **B** 5.43 × 79 **C** 5.43 × 7.9 **D** 54.3 × 7.9

19. What is 500 × 300?

Answer: ________

20. A hot air balloon rises 1.5 metres every second. How high will the hot air balloon rise in 200 seconds?

Answer: ________ m

Practice Questions

21. Circle the number that is missing from this calculation: 120 × 9 = 3 × _____

    A 40 **B** 60 **C** 240 **D** 360 **E** 720

22. Izzy runs 140 km each month.
    How many km does she run in a year? Circle the correct answer.

    A 1400 km **B** 1540 km **C** 1680 km **D** 1740 km **E** 1780 km

23. Padma has 28 pencils. Amy has 5 times as many as Padma.
    Una has 4 times as many as Amy. How many pencils does Una have?

    Answer: ____________

24. Circle the number that is missing from this calculation: 182 ÷ _____ = 26

    A 5 **B** 6 **C** 7 **D** 8 **E** 9

25. 4865 ÷ 7 = 695. What is 48.65 ÷ 7?

    Answer: ____________

26. A 480 cm long plank of wood is chopped into 4 equal lengths.
    How long is each piece?

    Answer: ____________ cm

27. Kay shares 4325 ants equally between five ant farms.
    How many ants are in each ant farm?

    Answer: ____________

28. Oli bought 5 pastries for £3.20. How much was each pastry?

    Answer: £ ____________

29. A caretaker is putting chairs out for assembly. If he uses all the chairs he can either make 11 or 12 rows. Which of these could be the total number of chairs?
    Circle the correct answer.

    A 168 **B** 176 **C** 209 **D** 264 **E** 308

30. Leon has between 200 and 210 comic books. If he puts them into 9 equal piles there are 7 left over. How many comic books does he have?

    Answer: ____________

Practice Questions

31. If $n = 12$, work out the value of $6n + 5$.

Answer: ________

32. Which of these expressions is the same as $3(t + 4)$? Circle the correct answer.

A $3t + 3$ **B** $3t + 4$ **C** $3t + 12$ **D** $4t + 3$ **E** $4t + 12$

33. A mug can hold x ml of water and a glass can hold y ml. Which of these is the correct expression for the amount of water in ml that 7 mugs and 3 glasses can hold? Circle the correct answer.

A $3x + 7y$ **B** $7x + 3$ **C** $10(x + y)$ **D** $7x + 3y$ **E** $7x + y$

34. The first five terms of a sequence are 4, 9, 14, 19, 24...
Which of these is the correct expression for the nth term in this sequence?
Circle the correct answer.

A $4n + 5$ **B** $5n - 1$ **C** $9n - 4$ **D** $4n + 1$ **E** $5n + 4$

35. What is the value of x when $5x - 6 = 24$?

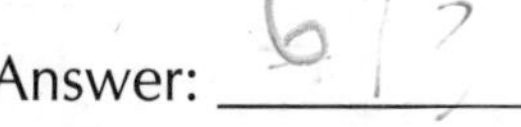

Answer: ________

36. The rule $^n/_2 + 4$ is used to generate a sequence.
What is the 100th term in the sequence?

Answer: ________

The amount you pay at a bowling alley (£B) is given by the formula: $B = 5g + p + 2$ where g is the number of games and p is the number of players.

37. How much would it cost for 3 players to play 4 games?

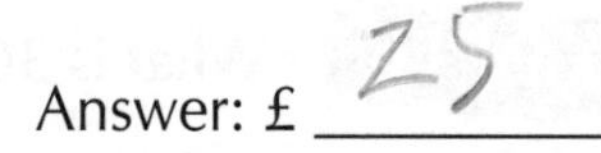

Answer: £ ________

38. If 5 players have to pay £17 in total, how many games did they play?

Answer: ________

39. An electrician charges a £30 call-out fee and £20 per hour, plus the cost of the parts they use. If they work for 3 hours and charge £195, what is the cost of the parts?

Answer: £ ________

Mixed Calculations

Mixed calculation questions will test all of your adding, subtracting, dividing and multiplying skills. But don't worry — there are some handy tricks you can learn to make them much easier.

11+ Example Questions

42 × 603 + 58 × 603 =

A 1 206   B 25 326   C 34 974   D 54 270   E 60 300

Quick Method

42 and 58 are both multiplied by 603.
You can just add 42 and 58 and multiply this number by 603 to find the answer.

42 + 58 = 100. So 42 × 603 + 58 × 603 simplifies to 100 × 603.
100 × 603 = **60 300** — so the correct answer is option E.

Written Method

1) An alternative (but slower) method would be to follow the BODMAS rule and do each multiplication before adding each of the answers.

For more on BODMAS, see page 38.

2) First, calculate 42 × 603 and 58 × 603 using a written method.

```
      6 0 3            6 0 3
  ×     4 2        ×     5 8
  ---------        ---------
    1 2 0 6          4 8 2 4
                         2
  + 2 4 1 2 0      + 3 0 1 5 0
        1                1
  ---------        ---------
    2 5 3 2 6        3 4 9 7 4
```

It doesn't matter what method you use to do these multiplications — use whichever method you find easiest. See pages 32-34 for more on written multiplication.

3) Then add together the answers to these multiplications to find the correct answer.

```
    2 5 3 2 6
  + 3 4 9 7 4
  -----------
    6 0 3 0 0
     1 1 1 1
```

So 42 × 603 + 58 × 603 = **60 300**.
The correct answer is option E.

EXAMPLE: **What is 360 ÷ (40 × 1.5)?**

1) Follow the BODMAS rule and do the calculation in brackets before the division.

Use partitioning to find 40 × 1.5. Partition 1.5 into 1 and 0.5.
40 × 1 = 40, and 40 × 0.5 = 20 (it's the same as half of 40).
Add together your results: 40 + 20 = 60.

2) Now work out 360 ÷ 60.

Both the numbers in the calculation end in a zero. This means you can simplify this calculation by dividing both numbers by 10. 360 ÷ 10 = 36, and 60 ÷ 10 = 6.

Now your calculation is just 36 ÷ 6 = **6**.

3) So the answer is 6.

Mixed Calculations

EXAMPLE: **Which of the following calculations gives the answer 88?**

A $412 + 18^2$ **B $18^2 - 412$** **C 412×18^2**
D $412 - 18^2$ **E $412 \div 18^2$**

1) All the calculations contain the same square number — 18^2.
In each case, the BODMAS rule tells you to work it out first.

Use a written method to calculate $18^2 = 18 \times 18$. ⟶

$$\begin{array}{r} 18 \\ \times\ 18 \\ \hline 144 \\ +\ 180 \\ \hline 324 \end{array}$$

2) Now check each calculation in turn. You don't have to work out each one — you can tell from a glance at the calculations if some will be far too big or too small.

A $412 + 18^2 = 412 + 324$. This will be much bigger than 88.
B $18^2 - 412 = 324 - 412$. This will be negative (so not 88).
C $412 \times 18^2 = 412 \times 324$. This will be much bigger than 88.
D $412 - 18^2 = 412 - 324$. This one looks promising, so work it out:

$$\begin{array}{r} 412 \\ -\ 324 \\ \hline 88 \end{array}$$

So the correct answer is option D.

3) If you've got time, you can check your answer by looking at the last option.

E $412 \div 18^2 = 412 \div 324$. You could estimate this as $400 \div 300 = 4 \div 3 = 1\frac{1}{3}$ — so it's certainly not 88.

Practice Questions

1) Ahmed wants to work out the cost of three oranges, two carrot cakes and one tuna roll. Which of these calculations could he do?

A $3 \times 40p + 2 \times £2 + 1 \times £1 + 5p$
B $3 \times 40p + 2 \times £2 + 1 \times £1 - 5p$
C $3 \times 40p + 2 \times £2 + 1 \times £1 + 3p$
D $3 \times 40p + 2 \times £2 + 1 \times £1 - 6p$
E $3 \times 40p + 2 \times £2 + 1 \times £1 + 6p$

Tuck Shop	
Cola	69p
Squash	49p
Orange	39p
Tuna Roll	99p
Carrot Cake	£1.99

2) Which of these calculations would give the largest answer?

A $12 \times 14 + 15 - 13$
B $13 \times 15 + 14 - 12$
C $15 \times 13 + 12 - 13$
D $14 \times 13 + 12 - 15$
E $15 \times 12 + 13 - 14$

Multiple or divide by 10, 100 or 1000 to make calculations easier...

Remember though — if you've only simplified one of the numbers, then you need to do the opposite function to your answer when you get to the end of your calculation to make it correct.

Word Problems

Word problems can be tricky — you need to read them very carefully to work out what they're asking. Then you can work out the best way to answer them quickly and correctly.

11+ Example Questions

A zoo has a total of 39 parrots and peacocks.
Which of these statements cannot be true?

A There are more parrots than peacocks in the zoo.
B There are more peacocks than parrots in the zoo.
C There are three more parrots than peacocks in the zoo.
D There are seven more peacocks than parrots in the zoo.
E There are twelve more parrots than peacocks in the zoo.

You need to test each sentence.

A The total number of parrots and peacocks in the zoo is odd (39). An odd number can't be divided by two to give two equal whole numbers, so there must be more of one bird than the other.
E.g. there could be 20 parrots and 19 peacocks — so this could be true.

B This could be true for the same reason that A could be true.

C The quickest way to work out if this is true is to use the properties of odd and even numbers. The total number of birds is odd, which means the sum of the number of parrots and peacocks must be an odd number added to an even number. The difference between an odd and an even number is always odd.
3 is an odd number, and so this could be true.

You can calculate two whole numbers with a difference of 3 that add to make 39.
Subtract 3 from the total number of birds (39 – 3 = 36). Then divide 36 by 2 (36 ÷ 2 = 18). So you have two sets of 18 — add 3 to one of these to give you 21 and 18. These are two numbers that add up to 39, but they have a difference of 3 — so this could be true.

D The difference between the numbers of parrots and peacocks is odd.
7 is an odd number — so it could be true.

You can calculate two whole numbers with a difference of 7 that add to make 39.
Subtract 7 from 39 (39 – 7 = 32). Then divide 32 by 2 (32 ÷ 2 = 16). So you have two sets of 16 — add 7 to one of these to give you 23 and 16. These are two numbers that add up to 39, but have a difference of 7 — so this could be true.

E The difference between the numbers of parrots and peacocks must be odd.
12 is even — so this **cannot be true**. So the answer is E.

Or you could try to find two whole numbers with a difference of 12 that add up to 39.
Subtract 12 from 39 (39 – 12 = 27). Then divide 27 by 2 (27 ÷ 2 = 13.5). So you have two sets of 13.5 — add 12 to one of these to give you 25.5 and 13.5. These two numbers do add up to 39, but you can't have half a peacock or parrot, so this **cannot be true**. So the answer is E.

Word Problems

Beanthwaite School ordered 6 boxes of rulers in March and 4 boxes in April. Each box contained 130 rulers.

How many rulers did the school order in total?

1) Work out the total number of boxes ordered.

   6 boxes were ordered in March and
   4 were ordered in April, so 6 + 4 = 10.

2) Multiply the total number of boxes by the number of rulers in each box.

   10 × 130 = 1300 rulers in total.

Raisa went to a restaurant with two friends.
They ordered from the menu:
3 plates of lasagne, 2 soups and 4 lemonades.

Raisa pays with a £50 note.

How much change should she receive?

Luigi's Restaurant	
Lemonade...............	90p
Soup......................	£2.50
Carbonara.............	£7.50
Pizza......................	£6.00
Lasagne.................	£8.50

1) Work out how much each item will cost. Make sure that all the amounts are in pounds.

   3 plates of lasagne is 3 × £8.50.
   Split £8.50 into £8 and £0.50:
   3 × £8 = £24 and 3 × £0.50 = £1.50.
   So 3 × £8.50 = £24 + £1.50 = £25.50

   2 soups is 2 × £2.50.
   2 × £2.5 = £5.00

   4 lemonades is 4 × 90p.
   4 × 90p = 360p
   360p = £3.60

2) Now find the total cost of all of the items.

   You could use partitioning to find the total amount.
   Add up all the pounds. 25 + 5 + 3 = £33.
   Add up all the pence. 50 + 60 = 110p = £1.10
   Now add them together. £33 + £1.10 = £34.10

For questions like this where you have lots of numbers to work with, it's helpful to make notes on some rough paper so you don't forget anything.

3) Now find the difference between the total cost of the items and £50.

   You can count on from £34.10 to £50.
   Count on to £35. £34.10 + 90p = £35
   Then count on to £50. £35 + £15 = £50
   Add the two numbers to find the difference. £15 + 90p = £15.90.

4) So the answer is £15.90.

Word Problems

More **11+ Example** Questions

I am thinking of a positive number.
If I multiply it by 3, then square it, I get 36.

What number am I thinking of?

A 2 **B** 4 **C** 6

D 8 **E** 10

You know the final answer — to find the number at the start you need to work backwards through the calculation given in the question. You can do this in two steps.

1) The number at the end is 36. To get 36 a number was squared. The only positive number that could be squared to give 36 is 6.

2) To get 6 a number was multiplied by 3. To find this number you just divide 6 by 3. $6 \div 3 = 2$.

A drinks company makes 250 litres of tropical punch each week.

Look at the ingredients used to make the punch.

The company sells the tropical punch in 50-litre barrels.

Tropical Punch	
Mango Juice	95.4 litres
Orange Juice	45.5 litres
Pineapple Juice	62.1 litres
Apple Juice	47 litres

How many litres of orange juice are in one barrel of tropical punch?

A 3.4 litres **B** 8.5 litres **C** 18.0 litres

D 9.1 litres **E** 11.6 litres

1) First you need to work out what fraction of 250 litres makes up 1 barrel of tropical punch.

   1 barrel = 50 litres. $250 \div 50 = 5$, so 1 barrel is $^1/_5$ of 250 litres.

2) There are 45.5 litres of orange juice in 250 litres of tropical punch, so you need to find $^1/_5$ of 45.5 litres.

   To find $^1/_5$ of 45.5 you need to divide 45.5 by 5.

   There are options to choose from, so you could make an estimate. $45 \div 5 = 9$, so the answer to $45.5 \div 5$ will be a little greater than 9.

   Option D is 9.1 litres — so this is the correct answer.

Word Problems

A counter is worth 5 points and has a diameter of 3.5 cm. A row of counters was lined up along a wall, with each counter touching the next. The values on the line of counters added up to 1500 points.

Find the length of the row of counters, in metres.

1) Work out how many counters there are in total.

   There are 1500 points worth of 5 point counters.
   So the total number of counters is 1500 ÷ 5.
   1500 is 100 times larger than 15, so 1500 ÷ 5 must be 100 times larger than 15 ÷ 5.
   15 ÷ 5 = 3. So 1500 ÷ 5 = 100 × 3 = 300

2) Now find the length of the line of counters.

   Each counter is 3.5 cm in diameter, and there are 300 in total — so work out 300 × 3.5.
   Partition 3.5 into 3 and 0.5:
   300 × 3 = 900
   300 × 0.5 = 150 (it's the same as half of 300).
   Then add up the result:
   900 + 150 = 1050 cm.

3) Don't forget to convert your answer into metres: 1050 cm ÷ 100 = 10.5 m.

Practice Questions

1) A bunch of seven tulips costs £4.50. A bunch of six roses costs £3.50. Lena wants 42 tulips and 42 roses. How much does she need to pay?

   A £24.50 **B** £147.00 **C** £189.00
   D £27.00 **E** £51.50

2) Benni buys 5 sandwiches that all cost the same amount. He pays with a £10 note and gets £1.50 change. How much is one sandwich? £1.70

3) Simone made bracelets to sell. Each bracelet cost her 20p to make and she sold them for 50p each. She sold 57 bracelets in total. How much money did she make, after she subtracted the cost of making the bracelets? 17.10

Word questions are often about familiar situations...

Think about what a sensible answer could be and keep it in mind when working through a problem — you'll be able to catch yourself if you stray too far off course.

Practice Questions

You've seen a wide range of Number Problems in this section.
Now it's time to put your skills to the test and have a go at these Practice Questions.

1. What is $42 \div 3 - (1 + 4)$?

Answer: ____________

2. Which of these expressions has the answer 7.5?
Circle the correct answer.

A $14 \div 2 + 3 - 1$ **B** $9 - 3 + 5 \div 2$ **C** $3 \div 2 + 3 \times 2$
D $(8 - 6) \div 2 + 5$ **E** $3 \times 1 + 12 - 9$

3. What is $28 \times 38 + 72 \times 38$?

Answer: ____________

4. Which of these expressions has the smallest answer?
Circle the correct answer.

A $90 + 30 \div 15 - 5$ **B** $90 - 30 \div 15 + 5$ **C** $90 \div 30 + 15 - 5$
D $90 + 30 - 15 \div 5$ **E** $90 - 30 + 15 \div 5$

5. What is $6000 \div (80 \times 2.5)$?

Answer: ____________

6. Daniel hires a costume for a party. He pays £5 per hour, plus a fixed fee of £10.
He hires the costume for 3 hours. Which calculation gives him the total cost?
Circle the correct answer.

A £5 × £10 + 3 **B** £5 + £10 × 3 **C** £5 × 3 + £10
D 3 × (£5 + £10) **E** £5 × 3 × £10

7. Sharla thinks of a number, n. She subtracts five, divides by two, then adds seven.
Which expression shows this? Circle your answer.

A $(n - 7) \div 2 + 5$ **B** $n - (5 \div 2) + 7$ **C** $n - 5 \div (2 + 7)$
D $n - 5 \div 2 + 7$ **E** $(n - 5) \div 2 + 7$

8. Chris has £10 of credit on a pay-as-you-go mobile phone. Calls cost 5p per minute.
After how many minutes of call time would his credit be reduced by half?

Answer: ____________ mins

Practice Questions

9. Louise thinks of a number. She squares it and then adds six. The result is 70. What number did she start with?

Answer: ____________

10. Alfie has swimming sessions on Tuesdays and Thursdays. He swims 3.5 km every session. How many weeks will it take him to swim a total distance of 140 km?

Answer: ____________

11. Mac has £5 to spend on fruit. He buys 1 pineapple, 1 watermelon, and as many kiwi fruit as he can afford. How much money does he have left? Circle the correct answer.

Fruit Prices
Pineapple............£0.95
Watermelon........£2.75
Kiwi fruit........15p each

A 5p **B** 10p **C** 15p **D** 20p **E** 25p

12. Tiana donated some jumpers and T-shirts to charity. She gave a total of 27 items of clothing. Circle the statement that cannot be true.

A Tiana donated twice as many jumpers as T-shirts.
B Tiana donated seven fewer T-shirts than jumpers.
C Tiana donated more jumpers than T-shirts.
D Tiana donated five more T-shirts than jumpers.
E Tiana donated eight fewer T-shirts than jumpers.

13. A quiz show awards 7 points for answering a hard question and 3 points for answering an easy question. Sanjay earned 149 points in total. He answered 17 easy questions. How many hard questions did Sanjay answer?

Answer: ____________

14. A set of five spoons cost £2.25. A set of four mugs costs eight times as much as the set of five spoons. How much does each mug cost? Circle the correct answer.

A £2.25 **B** £3.60 **C** £3.75 **D** £4.00 **E** £4.50

15. Aaron shares out carrots equally between his horses. Each horse ends up with 7 carrots and Aaron has 4 left over. Circle the number of carrots that Aaron could have started with.

A 21 **B** 22 **C** 24 **D** 25 **E** 26

Data Tables

Data is just any set of facts or information. It's often easier to understand and use if you organise it into a table, particularly if there's a lot of it.

11+ Example Questions

The table below shows the activities chosen by a group of people at a watersports centre. Which activity was the most popular?

Activity	Kayaking	Canoeing	Sailing	Windsurfing
Number of children	12	18	8	4
Number of adults	15	7	22	18

Add up the numbers in the column for each activity:

Kayaking: 12 + 15 = 27
Canoeing: 18 + 7 = 25
Sailing: 8 + 22 = 30
Windsurfing: 4 + 18 = 22

Sailing was the most popular activity, as the largest number of people chose it.

Frequency just means how many times something happens.

Ryan does a survey to find out how much the shops in his town charge for a can of cola. He groups his results into price bands and puts them in this table. Which of these statements is definitely true?

Price	Frequency
50p – 59p	4
60p – 69p	10
70p – 79p	12
80p – 89p	8
90p – £1.00	6

A The most expensive can of cola Ryan found costs £1.00.

B Ryan recorded the prices of 42 cans of cola.

C More than half of the cans of cola cost between 70p and 79p each.

D Three-quarters of the cans of cola cost less than 80p each.

E More than half of the cans of cola cost 70p or more each.

Look at each option and work out whether it's definitely true.

A The table only tells you that the most expensive can of cola is between 90p and £1.00. It might not be exactly £1.00 though — so you don't know if the statement is definitely true.

B To find the total number of cans of cola, add up all the frequencies in the table. 4 + 10 + 12 + 8 + 6 = 40 — so the statement isn't true.

C Half of the total number of cans is 40 ÷ 2 = 20. There are only 12 cola cans in the 70p – 79p price band — so the statement isn't true.

D One quarter of the total number of cans is 40 ÷ 4 = 10, so three quarters is 30. Add together the first three rows to find the number of cans that cost less than 80p: 4 + 10 + 12 = 26. 26 isn't three-quarters of the total number of cans — so the statement isn't true.

E Add together the last three rows of the table to find the total number of cans that cost 70p or more = 12 + 8 + 6 = 26. This is more than half of the total number of cans (20) — so this statement is **true**. E is the correct answer.

Data Tables

Years 5 and 6 are having a party. They all choose between meat pie and cheese pie. This table shows some of their choices. How many children are there in Year 5?

	Year 5	Year 6	Total
Meat pie		12	
Cheese pie	21		39
Total			64

1) This is a two-way table. There's a total for each row and column.

	Year 5	Year 6	Total
Meat pie		12	
Cheese pie	21		39
Total			64

Total number of cheese pies eaten.

Total number of pies eaten and the total number of children in Year 5 and Year 6.

This is the space for the number of children in Year 5.

Number of meat pies eaten by Year 6.

2) You don't have enough information to work out how many children there are in Year 5 straight away — you need to fill in some of the other empty boxes first.

	Year 5	Year 6	Total
Meat pie	13	12	25
Cheese pie	21		39
Total			64

First find out how many meat pies were eaten in total.
Total number – total cheese pie eaters = 64 – 39 = 25

Now you can find out how many meat pies Year 5 ate.
Total meat pie eaters – Year 6 meat pie eaters
= 25 – 12 = 13

3) Add the numbers in the Year 5 column of the table to find the number of children in Year 5.

Year 5 children = Year 5 meat pie eaters + Year 5 cheese pie eaters
= 13 + 21 = 34

	Year 5	Year 6	Total
Meat pie	13	12	25
Cheese pie	21		39
Total	34		64

Practice Questions

1) The table on the right shows the numbers of DVDs owned by some children. How many children own more than 15 DVDs?

A 9 **B** 19 **C** 28 **D** 27 **E** 13

DVDs	Frequency
0 – 5	14
6 – 10	13
11 – 15	9
16 – 20	13
21 – 25	6

Ticket	Price	Number needed	Total cost
Child	£5	32	£160
Adult	£8	4	£32
Senior Citizen		3	
		Booking Fee	£2.50
		Amount to pay	**£212.50**

2) The table on the left shows an order form for some pantomime tickets. Some boxes have been left empty. Calculate the cost of a senior citizen ticket.

Don't let unfamiliar tables put you off...

You might come across a table that looks a bit different to the ones you've seen before. Don't panic — just look at the row and column labels to work out what the table shows.

Displaying Data

Charts and graphs aren't just an excuse for a bit of colouring. They're a really important way of showing data — they can help you understand information at a glance.

Bar Charts Make it Easy to **Compare** things

Bar charts have two axes. The horizontal axis is called the *x*-axis.
The vertical axis is called the *y*-axis — it usually shows the frequency.

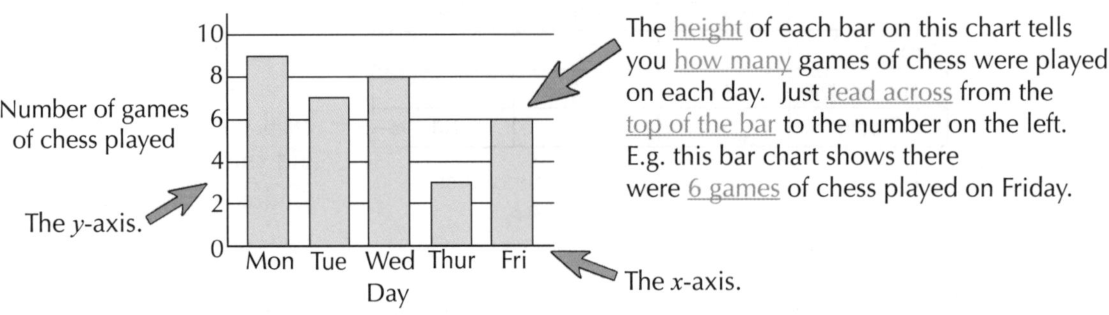

Number of games of chess played
10
8
6
4
2
0
Mon Tue Wed Thur Fri
Day
The *y*-axis.
The *x*-axis.
The height of each bar on this chart tells you how many games of chess were played on each day. Just read across from the top of the bar to the number on the left. E.g. this bar chart shows there were 6 games of chess played on Friday.

Line Graphs Often Show things that **Change over Time**

1) Line graphs show you how one thing (shown on the *y*-axis) changes as another thing changes (shown on the *x*-axis).
2) Time is often on the *x*-axis. For example, this graph shows how the temperature in an oven changes over time.

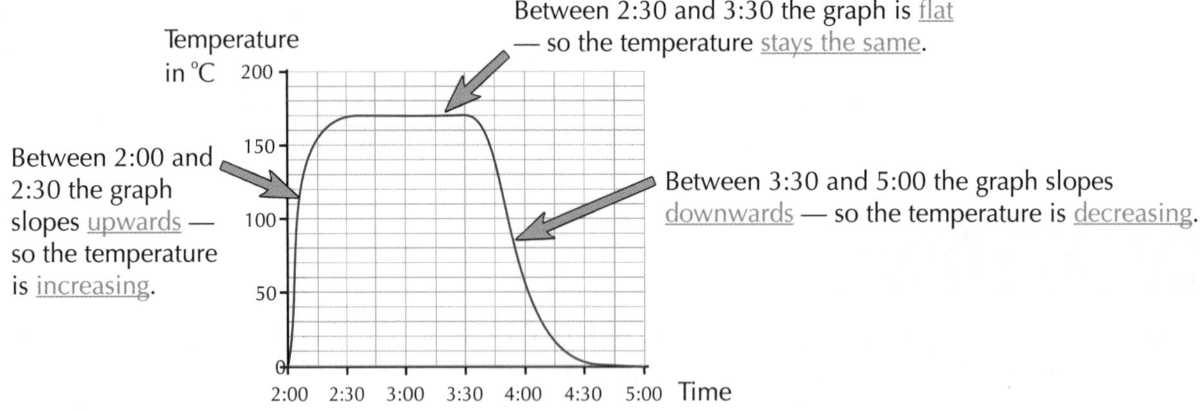

Between 2:30 and 3:30 the graph is flat — so the temperature stays the same.
Between 2:00 and 2:30 the graph slopes upwards — so the temperature is increasing.
Between 3:30 and 5:00 the graph slopes downwards — so the temperature is decreasing.

3) Here's how to read off a value from a line graph, e.g. the temperature at 3:45 from this line graph.

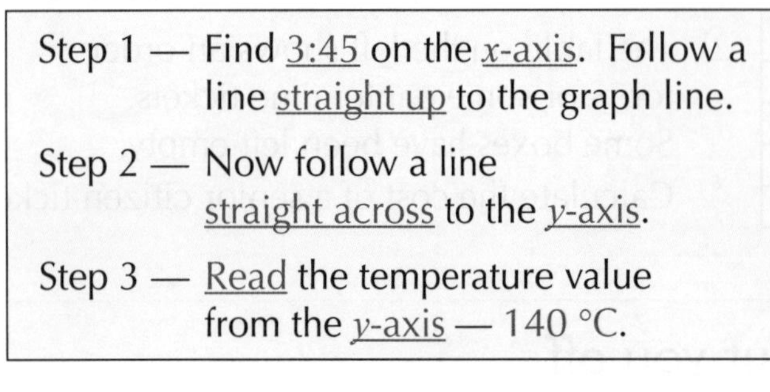

Step 1 — Find 3:45 on the *x*-axis. Follow a line straight up to the graph line.

Step 2 — Now follow a line straight across to the *y*-axis.

Step 3 — Read the temperature value from the *y*-axis — 140 °C.

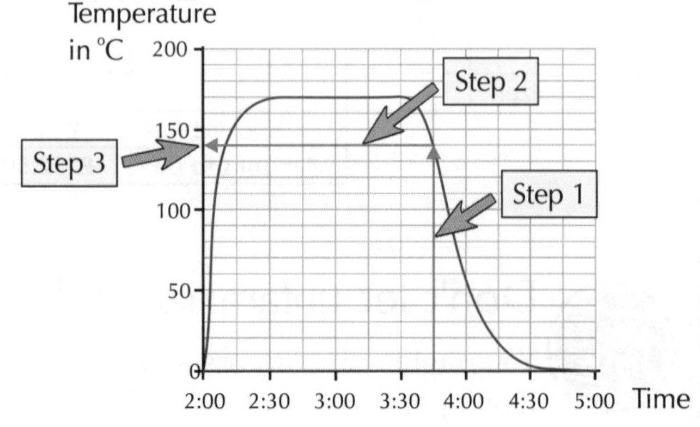

Displaying Data

Pictograms use Symbols to Show Frequency

1) In pictograms, simple pictures show numbers of things or how often something happens.
2) The key is really important — it tells you how many things each picture stands for.

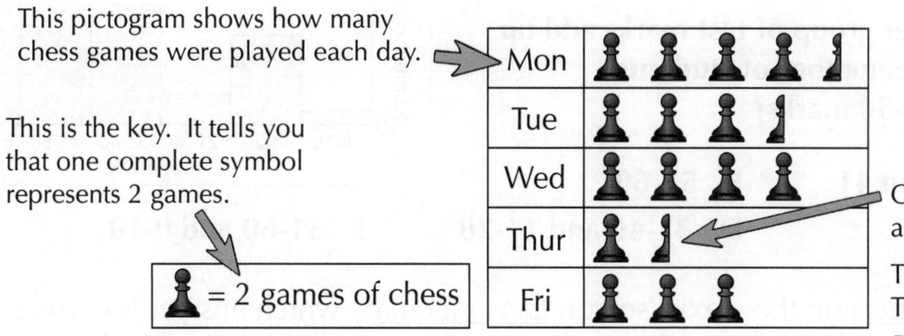
This pictogram shows how many chess games were played each day.
This is the key. It tells you that one complete symbol represents 2 games.
= 2 games of chess
Mon
Tue
Wed
Thur
Fri
One symbol = 2 games, so half a symbol = 2 ÷ 2 = 1 game.
There are 1½ symbols for Thursday, so there were 2 + 1 = 3 games played on Thursday.

Pie Charts Show Things as Proportions

Proportion just means the fraction of the total amount.

1) Each 'slice' of a pie chart is called a sector. You can work out the number of things shown by each sector on a pie chart.
2) For example, the pie chart below shows what 60 four-year-old boys said they wanted to be when they grow up. You can find how many boys said each thing by working out what fraction a sector is of the whole pie.

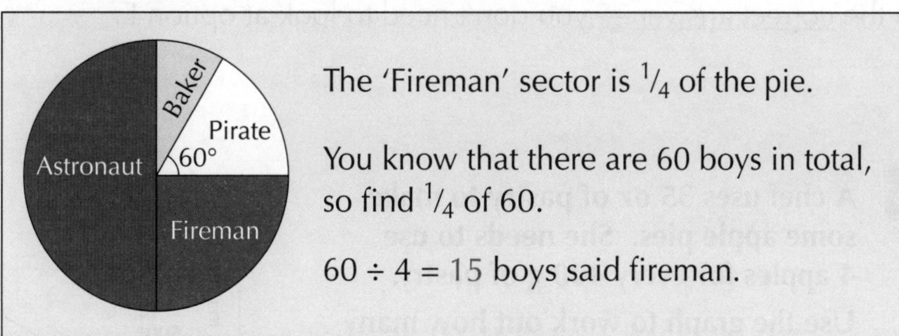
Baker
Pirate
60°
Astronaut
Fireman

The 'Fireman' sector is $^1/_4$ of the pie.

You know that there are 60 boys in total, so find $^1/_4$ of 60.

$60 \div 4 = 15$ boys said fireman.

You can also use the number of degrees (see p.68) that make up a sector to work out how many boys said each thing.

The 'Pirate' sector has an angle of 60°.

The pie chart is a circle, so the total angle of all the sectors is 360°.

The fraction of the whole pie made up by the pirate sector is $^{60°}/_{360°} = ^1/_6$ (÷ 60 top and bottom)

So the number of boys that want to be a pirate is $^1/_6$ of $60 = 60 \div 6 = 10$.

Baker
Pirate
60°
Astronaut
Fireman

Displaying Data

11+ Example Questions

EXAMPLE:

The bar chart shows the scores a class of students got in a maths test. Which other group of test marks add up to the same number of students that got 41-50 marks?

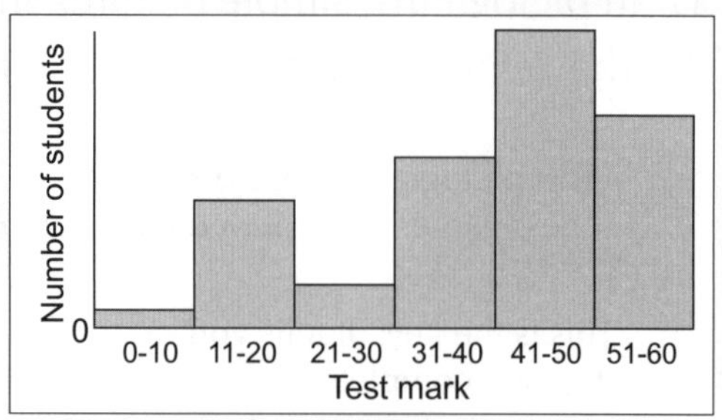

A Less than 41 **B 51-60**

C 11-20 **D 31-40 and 11-20** **E 51-60 and 0-10**

1) There are no numbers on the y-axis, so you can't calculate which answer is correct. You need to go through the options and visually compare the heights of the bars.

A This is the height of the 0-10, 11-20, 21-30 and 31-40 bars added together. This would add up to make a much greater number of students than the 41-50 bar — incorrect.

B The 51-60 bar on its own is a smaller number than the 41-50 bar — incorrect.

C The 11-20 bar on its own is a much smaller number than the 41-50 bar — incorrect.

D The height of the 31-40 bar added to the height of the 11-20 bar would make the same number of students as the 41-50 bar — correct.

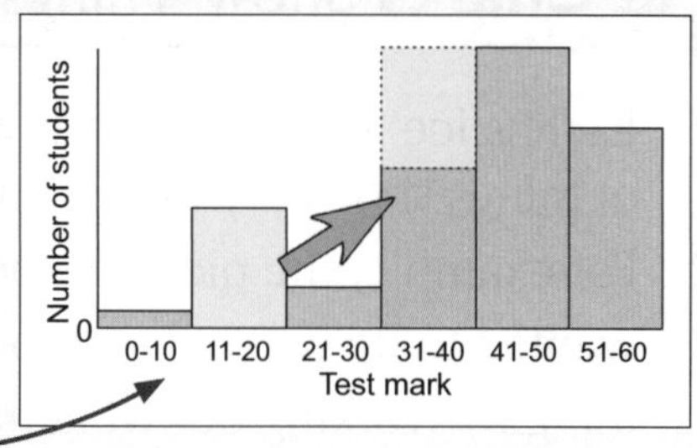

2) D is the correct answer — you don't need to look at option E.

EXAMPLE:

A chef uses 35 oz of pastry to make some apple pies. She needs to use 4 apples for every 400 g of pastry. Use the graph to work out how many apples she needs if she uses all the pastry to make apple pies.

1) Read off how much 35 oz of pastry is in grams from the graph.

35 oz = 1000 g.

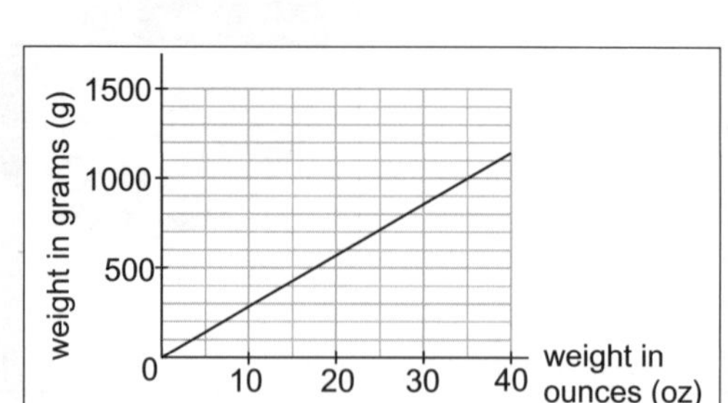

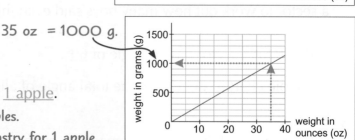

2) Find the amount of pastry used for 1 apple.

For 400 g of pastry you need 4 apples.

So she uses 400 ÷ 4 = 100 g of pastry for 1 apple.

3) She needs 1 apple for every 100 g of pastry and she's using 1000 g of pastry.

1000 ÷ 100 = 10 — she needs 10 apples.

Displaying Data

The pictogram shows the number of differently shaped sweets in a bag. How many more animal shaped sweets than fruit shaped sweets are there in the bag?

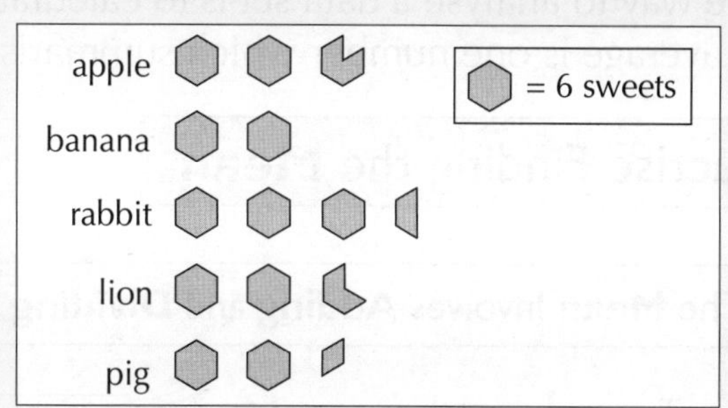

1) First work out how many sweets are animal shaped (i.e. either a rabbit, a lion or a pig).

   There are 7 whole symbols for the animal sweets. $7 \times 6 = 42$ sweets.

   The rabbit shape also has $^3/_6$ of a symbol on the end = 3 sweets, the lion shape has $^4/_6$ of a symbol on the end = 4 sweets and the pig shape has $^2/_6$ of a symbol on the end = 2 sweets.

   Add these together to get the total number of animal shaped sweets.

   $42 + 3 + 4 + 2 = 51$ sweets.

2) Now use the same method to work out how many fruit shaped sweets there are.

   There are 4 whole symbols for fruit shaped sweets. $4 \times 6 = 24$ sweets.

   The apple shape also has $^5/_6$ of a symbol on the end = 5 sweets.

   Total number of fruit shaped sweets = $24 + 5 = 29$ sweets.

3) Then subtract to find the difference between the two.

   There are $51 - 29 = 22$ more animal shaped sweets than fruit shaped sweets.

The table shows the ingredients in 300 ml of a salad dressing. Ben wants to draw a pie chart to show the proportion of each ingredient in the dressing. What angle would the vinegar sector of the pie chart have?

Ingredient	Amount
Vinegar	50 ml
Olive oil	200 ml
Lemon juice	50 ml

1) First find what fraction of the dressing is made up of vinegar.

   50 ml out of 300 ml is vinegar.

   The fraction of the total dressing that's vinegar is $^{50}/_{300} = {}^1/_6$

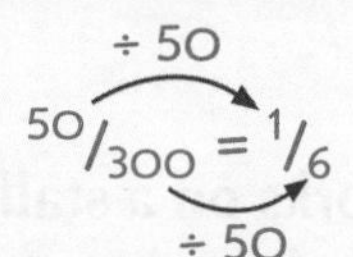

Divide the numerator and the denominator by 50 to simplify.

2) The total angles in a pie chart are 360°, so find $^1/_6$ of 360°.

   $^1/_6$ of $360° = 360° \div 6 = 60°$.

Practice Question

1) A class of children were asked what their favourite colour is. Two children chose brown. This was represented on a pie chart by a 20° sector. How many children are in the class?

There are lots of different ways of displaying data...

Make sure you can interpret all these graphs and charts — any type could come up in your test.

Analysing Data

One way to analyse a data set is to calculate the mean, a type of average.
An average is one number which summarises a whole set of numbers.

Practise Finding the **Mean**

The **Mean** Involves **Adding** and **Dividing**

1) To work out the mean: 
   - Add up all the numbers in the data set.
   - Divide the total by how many numbers there are.

2) So to work out the mean of the data set on the right, first add up all the numbers: 13 + 8 + 7 + 4 + 11 + 2 = 45.

   13, 8, 7, 4, 11, 2

3) There are six numbers, so divide the total by six: 45 ÷ 6 = 7.5.

11+ Example Questions

Safiya records how long she exercises each day for 5 days:

24 mins	25 mins	35 mins	39 mins	32 mins

What is the mean time she spends exercising?

1) Add together all the times.
   24 + 25 + 35 + 39 + 32 = 155 mins

2) She records her times on five different days, so divide the total by five.
   The mean time she spends exercising is 155 ÷ 5 = 31 mins

Marcus works on a stall that sells fruit smoothies.
The table below shows the price of each type of smoothie.

Banana	£2.70
Mango	£3.10
Strawberry	£2.50
Raspberry	£2.70

What is the mean price of a smoothie from Marcus's stall?

1) Add together the prices of all the smoothies.
   £2.70 + £3.10 + £2.50 + £2.70 = £11

2) There are four different types of smoothie, so divide the total by four.
   The mean price of a smoothie is £11 ÷ 4 = £2.75

Analysing Data

EXAMPLE: **The bar chart shows five children's marks in three tests.**

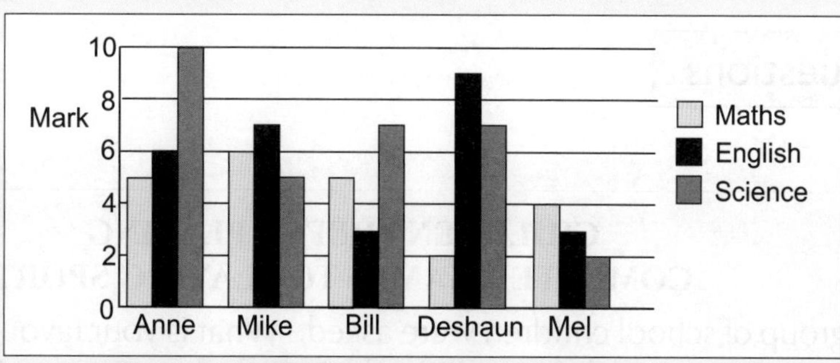

Which child had the highest mean mark across all the tests?

1) Add together each child's marks and divide them by three to find each mean mark.

Anne: (5 + 6 + 10) ÷ 3 = 7 Mike: (6 + 7 + 5) ÷ 3 = 6 Bill: (5 + 3 + 7) ÷ 3 = 5
Deshaun: (2 + 9 + 7) ÷ 3 = 6 Mel: (4 + 3 + 2) ÷ 3 = 3

2) Compare the means — the highest is 7, so the answer is Anne.

EXAMPLE: **Derek has a set of five numbers. He calculates that the mean of his numbers is 11.5.**

8	13	18	7.5	11

He forgets one of his numbers. The mean of the four numbers he can remember is 12.5. Which number has he forgotten?

1) First work out the total of the numbers he can remember.

If the mean of the four numbers he can remember is 12.5, he must have divided a number by 4 to get 12.5. So multiply 12.5 by 4 to find the total. 12.5 × 4 = 50.

2) Then work out the total of the original five numbers.

8 + 13 + 18 + 7.5 + 11 = 57.5

3) Subtract the total of the four numbers he can remember from the original total.

57.5 – 50 = 7.5 — the number he forgot was 7.5.

Practice Question

1) The data set on the right shows how many tea bags were used in the Smith household each day. What was the mean number of tea bags used per day?

Mon	Tue	Wed	Thur	Fri
22	23	17	17	26

Remember to divide by how many numbers there are...

It's really important that you learn the 2-step method to find the mean.
Once you know it, you can use it as normal or reverse it to find a missing number.

Misleading Data

People often use data to try to prove a point they're making. However, you have to think really hard about data to make sure it's not being twisted to make you believe something that's not true.

11+ Example Questions

CHILDREN PREFER PLAYING COMPUTER GAMES TO PLAYING SPORT

A group of school children were asked, 'What is your favourite weekend activity?'. 20% of them said 'playing computer games', while only 1 in 4 children said their favourite activity was 'playing sport'.

Why is this newspaper article misleading?

A The article doesn't say what other activities the children picked.

B According to the numbers given in the article, more children said they liked playing sport than playing computer games.

C The article doesn't tell you how many boys and girls were in the group asked.

D The figures in the article show that fewer children chose sport than computer games.

E The article doesn't tell you what sports or computer games the children like to play.

1) Read the article and work out what the article is claiming to be true.

The headline says that children prefer playing computer games to playing sport.

2) Look carefully at any figures you're given, to see if they back up what the article is claiming. Put the figures into the same form (e.g. fractions, decimals or percentages) to compare them.

20% of children said their favourite activity was playing computer games.
1 in 4 children said playing sport — which is the same as 25%.

25% is greater than 20%, so more children said playing sport than playing computer games.

3) Look at the options to see which one is correct.

Options A, C, and E are all true, but they don't mean that the article is misleading.

Option D is incorrect — the figures show that more children chose sport than computer games.

Option B is correct. The article is misleading because it says that fewer people picked sport than computer games, when the figures show that more people picked sport than computer games.

Misleading Data

This graph is used to show the increase in the number of chickens eaten by the population of a country between 2018 and 2019.

Why is the graph misleading?

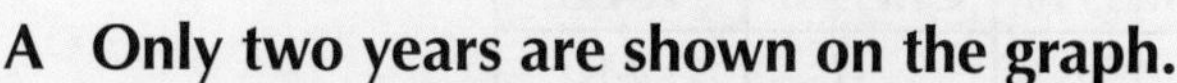

A Only two years are shown on the graph.
B The scale on the vertical axis is uneven.
C The graph doesn't show how many turkeys were eaten.
D We are not told which country the data is about.
E The chicken picture for 2019 is more than double the area of the 2018 picture.

1) The graph is a type of bar chart, but it uses pictures of chickens instead of bars. The height of each picture tells you how many chickens were eaten.

   It shows that 30 million chickens were eaten in 2018, and 60 million chickens were eaten in 2019.

2) Look at each answer and decide if it's a good reason why the graph is misleading.

   A: The graph is only about 2018 and 2019, so it's not misleading that only two years are shown.

   B: This isn't true. The values are evenly spaced.

   C: It doesn't matter how many turkeys are eaten — the graph is about chickens.

   D: You haven't been led to believe that the data is about anywhere in particular, so this isn't the answer.

   E: From reading the graph you know that about twice as many chickens were eaten in 2019 than 2018. The trouble is, the area of the chicken for 2019 is about 4 times as big as the area of the chicken for 2018. This means that at a glance, the graph makes it look like the difference between the years was far greater than it actually was. E is the correct answer.

Practice Question

1) A newspaper report with a graph has the headline:
   Sales of pencils plummet. Why is the report misleading?

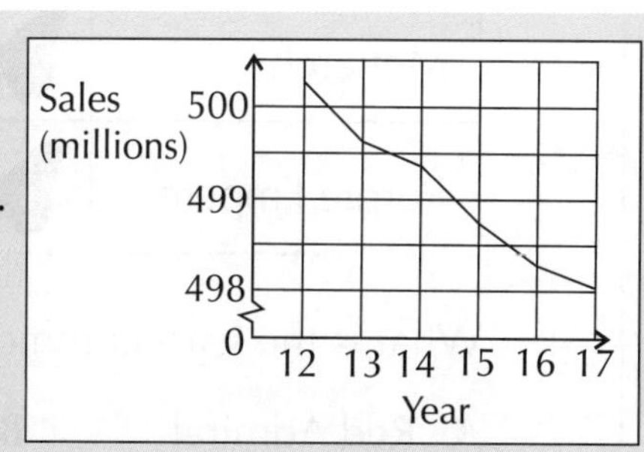

   A There are no crosses on the graph to mark the plotted points.
   B The graph does not show how many pens were sold.
   C The y-axis doesn't start on zero so it makes the drop in sales look worse than it is.
   D The graph doesn't show what happened before 2012.
   E The pencil manufacturers want you to go and buy more pencils.

Misleading graphs try to make you think the wrong thing...

Watch out for graphs that have part of the y-axis missing (shown by a zigzag line). E.g. These bar charts show the same data, but the second one makes the difference in the heights of the bars look much bigger than the first.

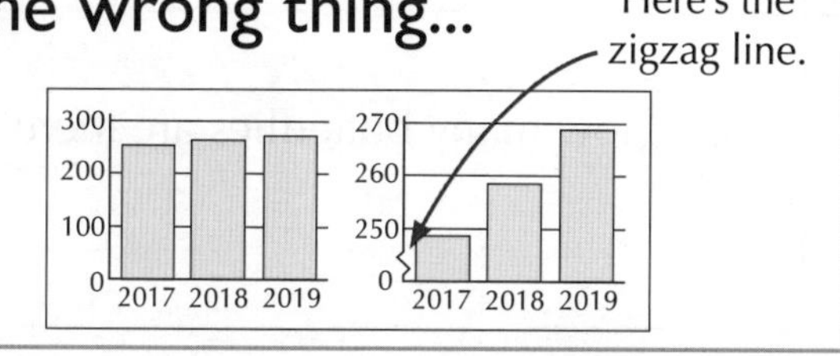

Practice Questions

Try out your Data Handling skills on these Practice Questions.

The pupils in Year 6 are split into two classes, A and B. They were asked to choose between swimming, cricket and gymnastics. The results are shown in the table below.

	Class A	Class B	**Total**
Swimming	12		21
Cricket	6		10
Gymnastics		12	
Total	28		

1. How many pupils in Class B chose swimming?

   Answer: ______

2. Which activity was the most popular? Circle the correct answer.

   A Swimming **B** Cricket **C** Gymnastics

3. How many pupils are there in Year 6 in total?

   Answer: ______

The pictogram below shows the number of different types of butterfly in a butterfly house.

Red Admiral	
Tortoiseshell	
Monarch	
Purple Emperor	

Key: = 4 butterflies

4. What is the least common type of butterfly? Circle the correct answer.

   A Red Admiral **B** Tortoiseshell **C** Monarch **D** Purple Emperor

5. How many more Tortoiseshell butterflies than Red Admiral butterflies are there?

   Answer: ______

6. How many butterflies are there in total?

   Answer: ______

Practice Questions

The bar chart on the right shows the number of books borrowed from a library each day for five days.

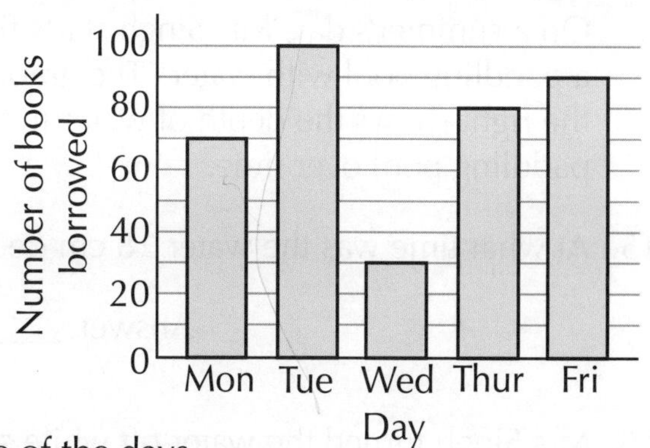

7. How many more books were borrowed on Tuesday than on Monday?

   Answer: ______

8. The library was only open for half a day on one of the days. Which day was this most likely to be? Circle the correct answer.

   A Monday **B** Tuesday **C** Wednesday **D** Thursday **E** Friday

9. What was the mean number of books borrowed in a day?

   Answer: ______

Violet is going on holiday to America. The graph on the right shows the conversion between pounds (£) and American dollars ($).

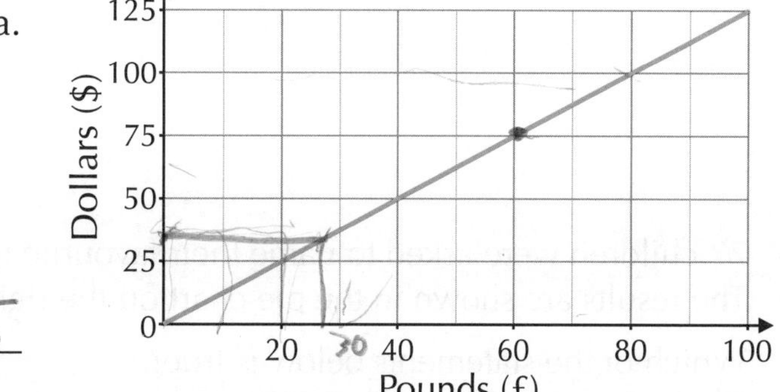

10. How many dollars is £60 worth?

    Answer: $ ______

11. In total, she took $400 with her. How much is this in pounds?

    Answer: £ ______

12. At the end of the holiday, Violet had $27 left. Which is the most expensive souvenir she could afford? Circle the correct answer.

    A A hoodie costing £30 **B** A vase costing £27 **C** A scarf costing £19

Some children were asked what they had eaten for breakfast that morning. The results are shown in the pie chart on the right.

Fruit
Toast
Cereal
120°
Yoghurt

13. What is the angle for the 'Fruit' sector? Circle the correct answer.

    A 45° **B** 60° **C** 360° **D** 120° **E** 90°

14. 20 children had cereal for breakfast. How many children were asked in total?

    Answer: ______

Practice Questions

On a summer's day, Mrs Singh starts filling a paddling pool with water. The graph on the right shows the depth of water in the paddling pool over time.

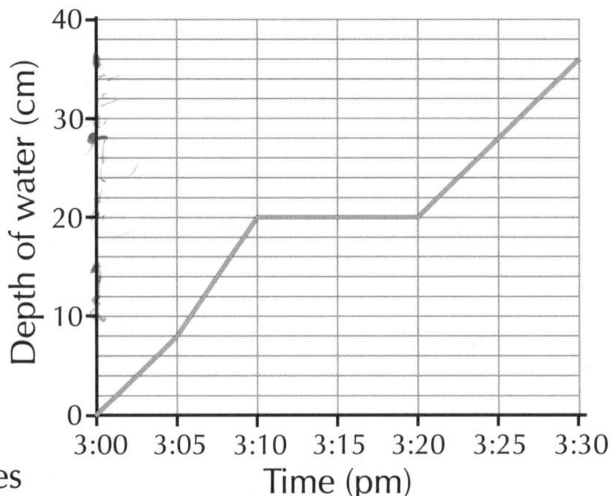

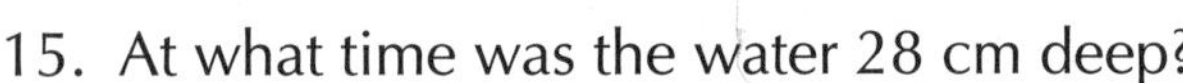

15. At what time was the water 28 cm deep?

Answer: ______

16. Mrs Singh turned the water off while she answered the phone. Between which two times was the water turned off? Circle the correct answer.

A 3:00 pm and 3:30 pm **B** 3:10 pm and 3:15 pm
C 3:05 pm and 3:10 pm **D** 3:10 pm and 3:20 pm

17. How deep was the water at 3:30 pm?

Answer: ______ cm

18. 72 children were asked to name their favourite type of flower. The results are shown in the pie chart on the right.

Which of the statements below is true?
Circle the letter next to the correct answer.

A Irises were the least popular type of flower.
B More children chose lilies than tulips.
C 18 children chose roses.
D The same number of children chose daisies and bluebells.
E 9 children chose daisies.

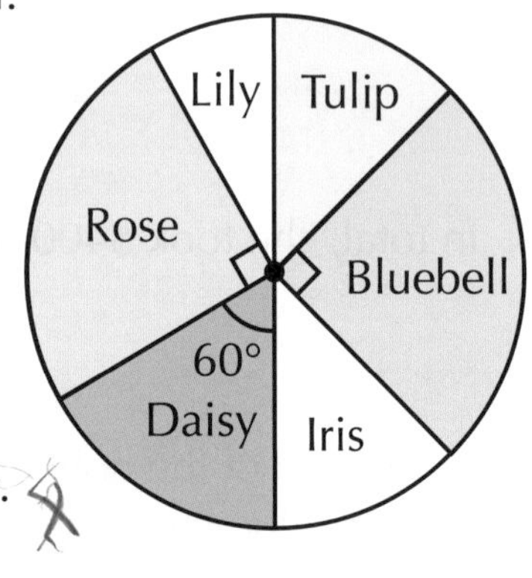

19. Dina records the amount of money she spends on comics each month. The amounts for five of the last six months are shown below:

£4.80 £5.40 £3.90 £6.20 £4.30

Dina has forgotten how much she spent in the other month, but she knows that the mean amount spent over the six months was £4.50. How much did she spend in the missing month?

Answer: £ ______

Practice Questions

Gleb measured the temperature and wind speed at 12 noon every day for a week.
His results are shown in the table below.

	Mon	Tues	Wed	Thurs	Fri	Sat	Sun
Temperature (°C)	11	9	8	10	12	13	14
Wind speed (mph)	9	11	7	14	8		

20. What was the mean temperature that week?

Answer: _______ °C

21. The mean wind speed for the whole week was 9 mph. The wind speed on Sunday was 6 mph more than the wind speed on Saturday. What were the wind speeds on Saturday and Sunday?

Answer: Saturday: _______ mph, Sunday: _______ mph

Detached	
Semi-detached	
Terraced	
Bungalow	

Key:
= 10 houses

22. The pictogram above shows the different types of houses in a village.
Why is the pictogram misleading? Circle the letter next to the correct answer.

A Bungalows could be detached, semi-detached or terraced.
B It doesn't include flats.
C It doesn't say which village it is.
D The pictures are arranged differently, and are different sizes and shapes.
E It doesn't say how many people live in each house.

23. The misleading bar chart below shows the results of a school council election.

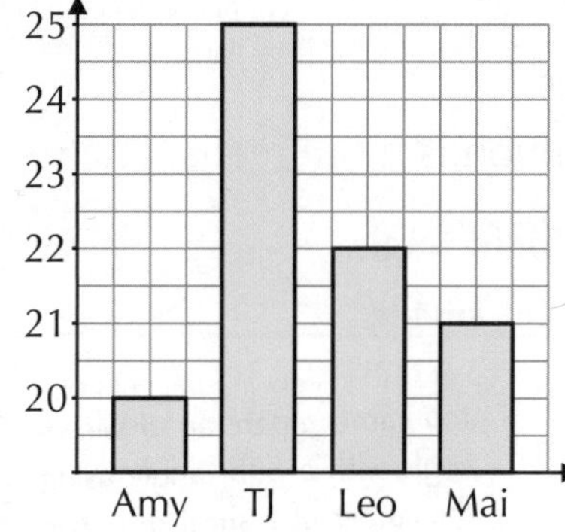

Which of the following statements is true?
Circle the letter next to the correct answer.

A TJ received twice as many votes as Leo.
B Mai received $^2/_3$ of the number of votes that Leo received.
C Amy received half as many votes as Mai.
D Amy received $^4/_5$ of the number of votes that TJ received.
E Leo received 3 times as many votes as Amy.

Angles

The three main types of angle you need to know are right angles, acute angles and obtuse angles.

Angles are Measured using Degrees (°)

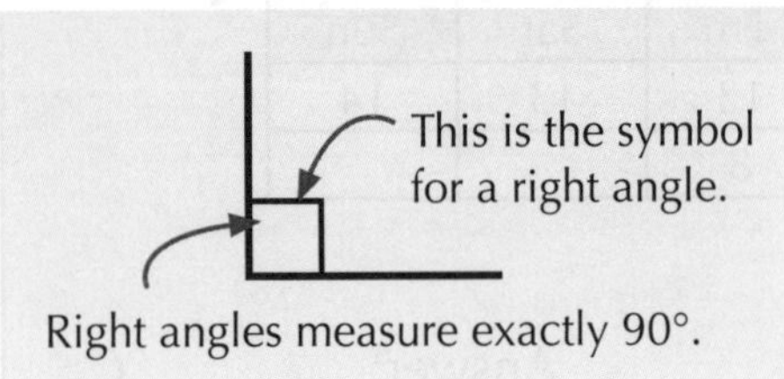

Right angles measure exactly 90°.

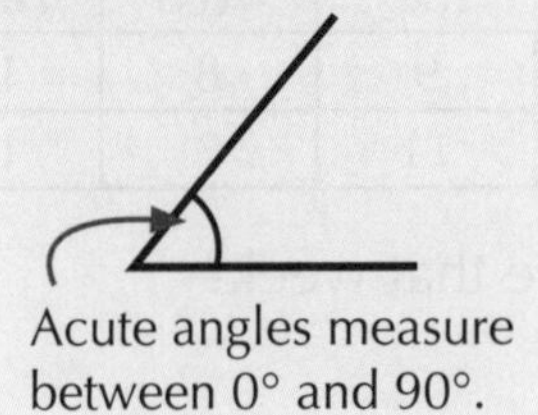
Acute angles measure between 0° and 90°.

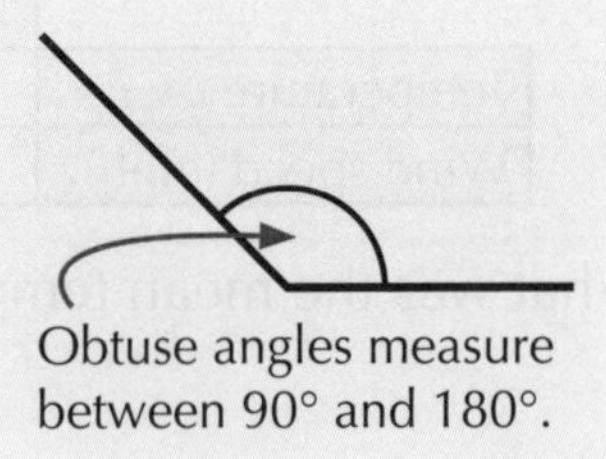
Obtuse angles measure between 90° and 180°.

You need to know these Rules about Angles

Angles around a Point Add Up to 360°

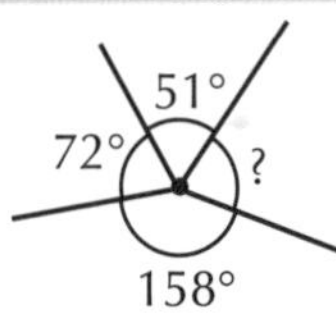

The four angles total 360°.
So the missing angle is
360 – 51 – 72 – 158 = 79°.

Angles on a Straight Line Add Up to 180°

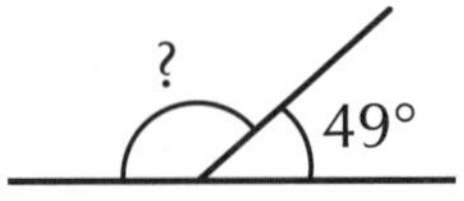

The two angles total 180°.
So the missing angle is
180 – 49 = 131°.

Angles in a Triangle Add Up to 180°

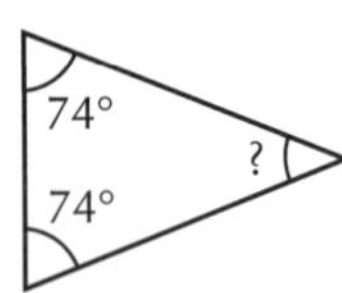

The three angles total 180°.
So the missing angle is
180 – 74 – 74 = 32°.

Angles in a Quadrilateral Add Up to 360°

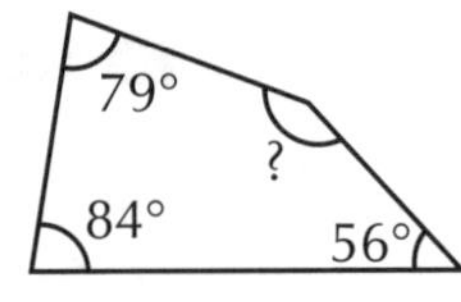

The four angles total 360°.
So the missing angle is
360 – 84 – 79 – 56 = 141°.

11+ Example Questions

Estimate the size of angle x.

A 90° B 30° C 105° D 75° E 120°

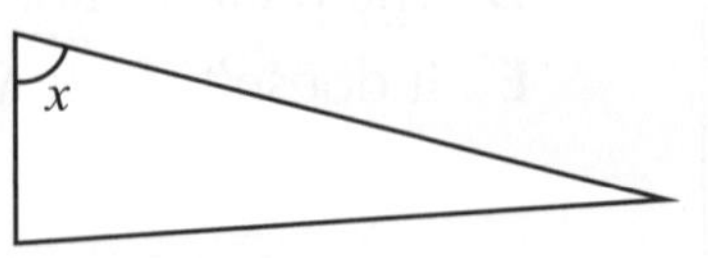

You can't do a calculation here — you don't know the sizes of the other angles.

1) It's smaller than 90°, so it must be an acute angle.
That means option A is incorrect — it's a right angle.
Options C and E are also incorrect — they're obtuse angles.
2) That leaves options B and D. You need to decide which option is more realistic.

If the angle was 30°, it would be three times smaller than a right angle.
When you compare angle x to a right angle, it's only a little bit smaller.
So, the angle must be 75° — it's the most realistic option.

3) The correct answer is option D — 75°.

You can compare an unknown angle with a right angle using the corner of a sheet of paper.

Angles

What is the size of the angle marked a between the two hands on this clock?

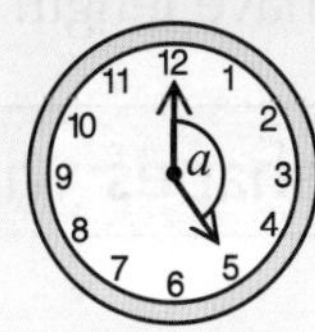

1) The total angle around the centre point of the clock is 360°.
2) There are 12 hours equally spaced apart on the clock. Work out the size of the angle between each hour.

Divide the total angle by the number of hours. ⟶ 360 ÷ 12 = 30° ⟶ The angle between each hour on the clock is 30°.

3) Work out how many hours apart the two hands are.

The minute hand is at 12 and the hour hand is at 5. They are 5 hours apart.

4) Multiply the number of hours by 30° to find the value of the missing angle.

5 × 30 = 150°. Angle a is 150°.

Ted made the following pattern using a rectangle and a triangle. What is the size of angle x?

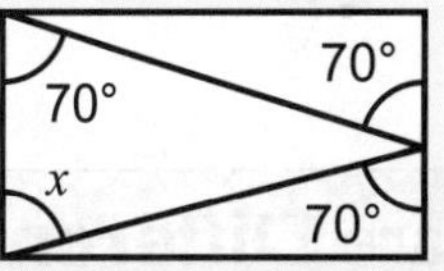

1) Work out the size of the other angle in the triangle.

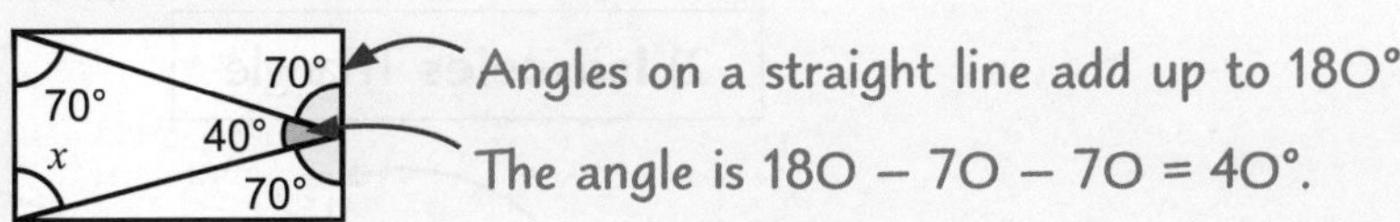

2) The three angles in a triangle add up to 180°. Use this rule to work out the size of x:

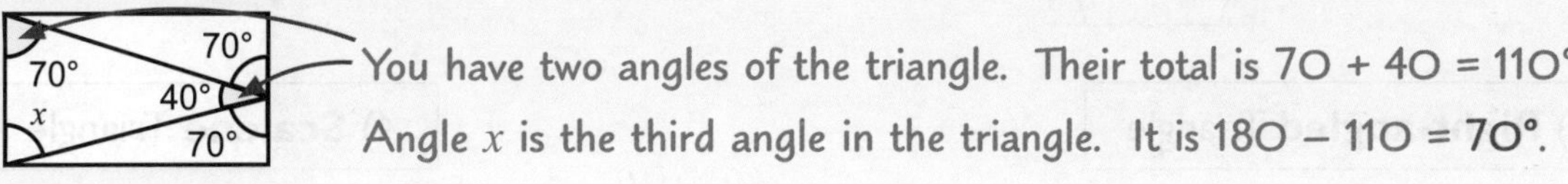

70°
70°
40°
x
70°
You have two angles of the triangle. Their total is 70 + 40 = 110°.
Angle x is the third angle in the triangle. It is 180 – 110 = 70°.

Practice Questions

1) Estimate the size of angle c.

A 100° **B** 125° **C** 10°
D 45° **E** 90°

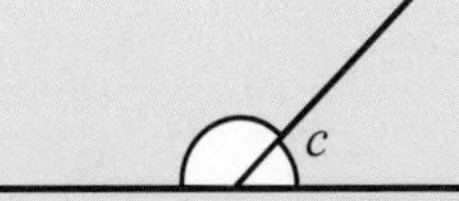

2) What is the size of the angle between the north-east and south points on this compass?

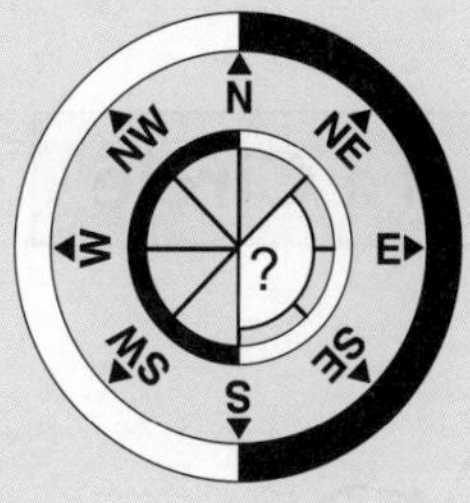

Think about the total number of points on the compass.

Look out for triangles and quadrilaterals in a busy diagram...

It can be hard to know where to start when you have to find a missing angle. Spotting triangles and quadrilaterals in the diagram is a good first step, since you know what their angles add up to.

2D Shapes

2D shapes are flat — they have length and width but no depth.

Parallel lines have exactly the same slope.

Quadrilaterals are shapes with Four Sides

Square

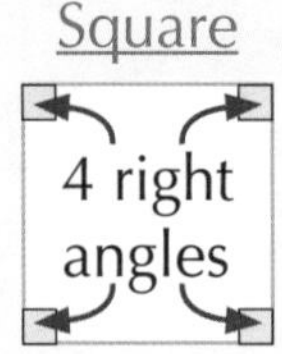

4 equal sides and
2 pairs of parallel sides

Trapezium

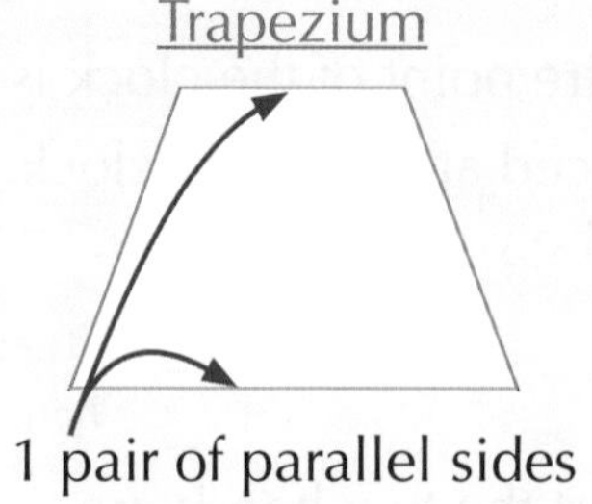

1 pair of parallel sides

Parallelogram

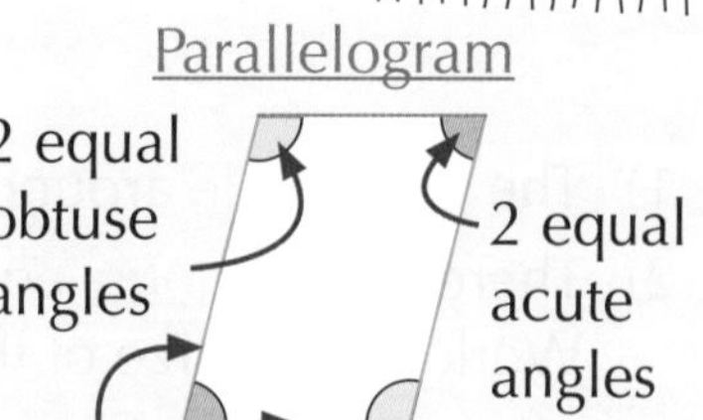

2 pairs of equal sides and
2 pairs of parallel sides

Rectangle

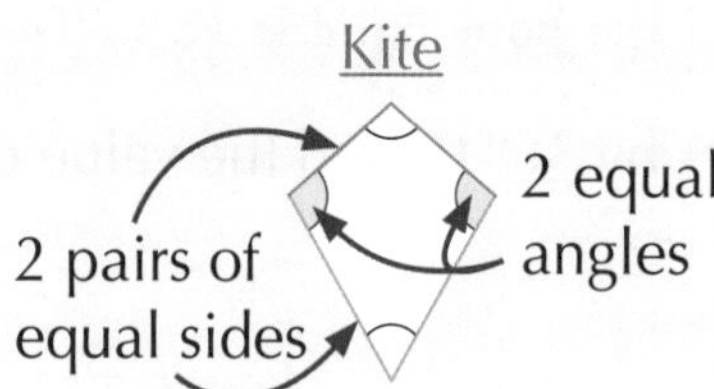

2 pairs of equal sides and
2 pairs of parallel sides

Kite

Rhombus

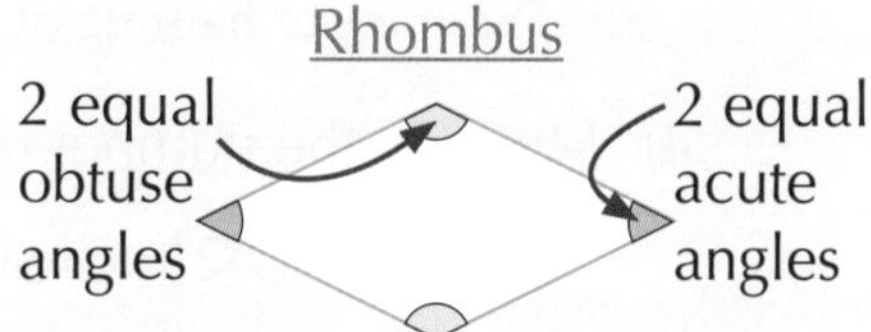

4 equal sides and
2 pairs of parallel sides

There are Different Types of Triangle

The angles in a triangle add up to 180° (see page 68).

1) Equilateral Triangle

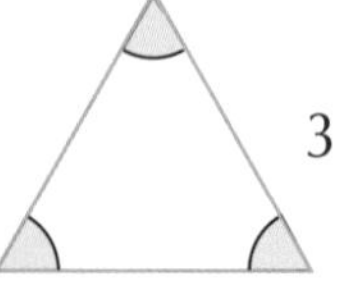

2) Isosceles Triangle

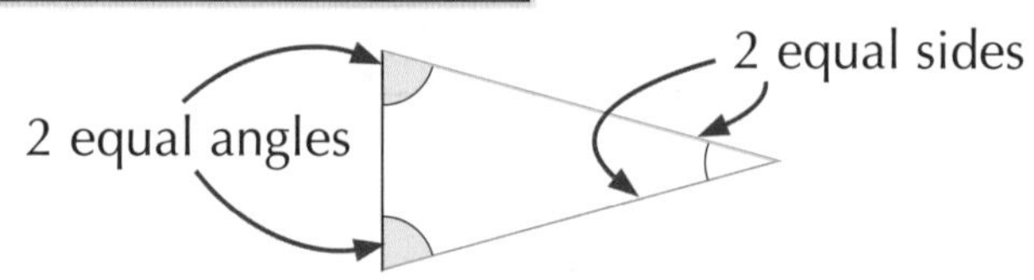

3) Right-angled Triangle

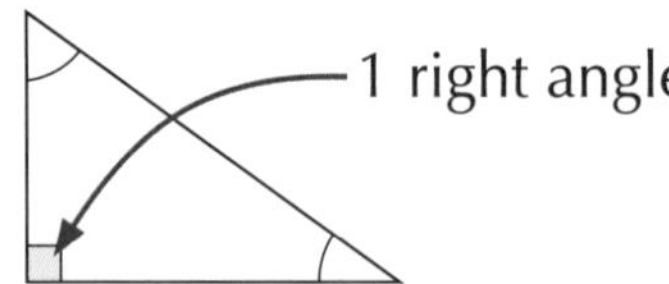

Right-angled triangles can be isosceles or scalene, but they always have a right angle.

4) Scalene Triangle

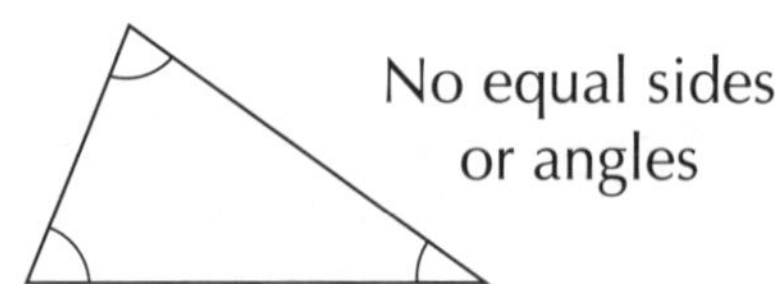

Know the Parts of a Circle

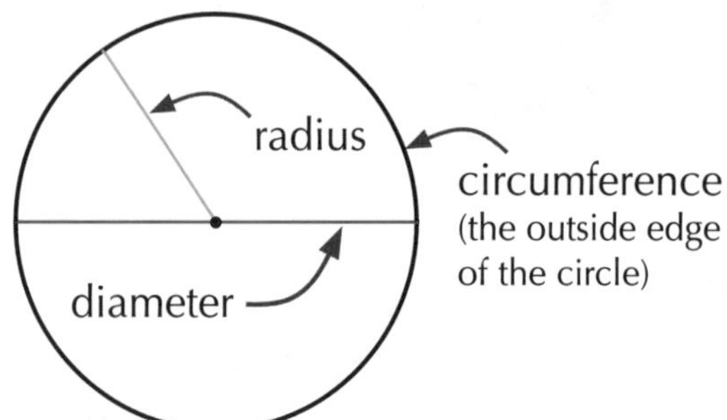

The Diameter is Twice the Radius

You can use this rule to work out the diameter or the radius.

The radius of this circle is 6 cm.
So the diameter = 2 × 6 = 12 cm

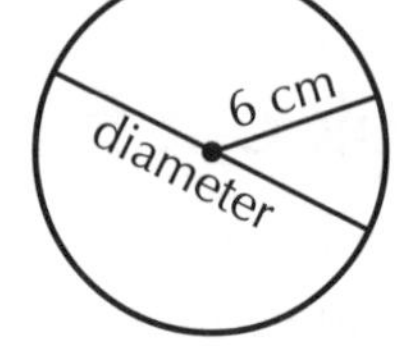

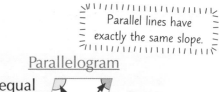

2D Shapes

Regular Polygons have Equal Sides and Angles

A polygon is a 2D shape with straight lines.

Regular Pentagon	Regular Hexagon	Regular Heptagon	Regular Octagon
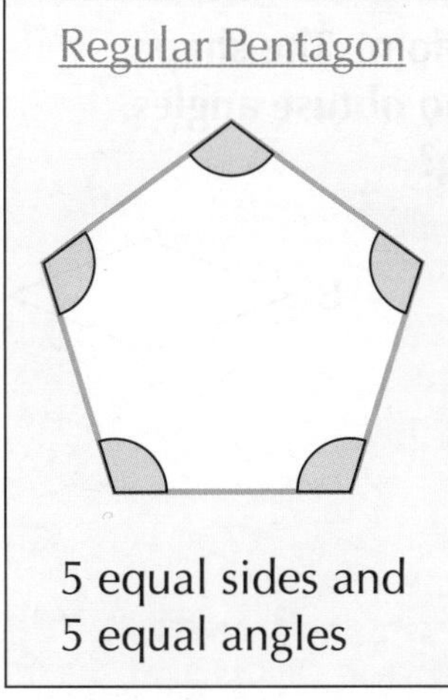	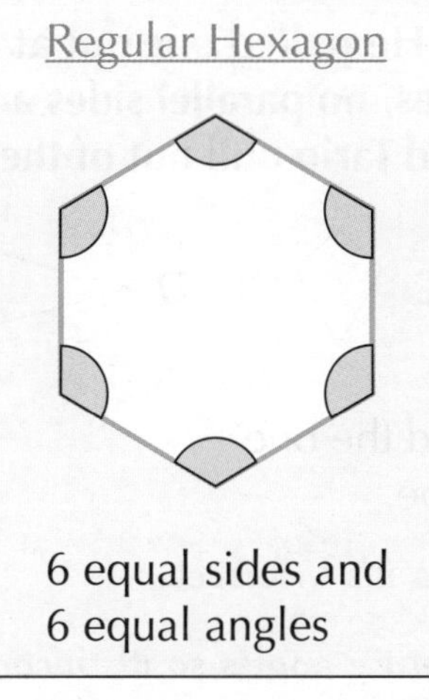	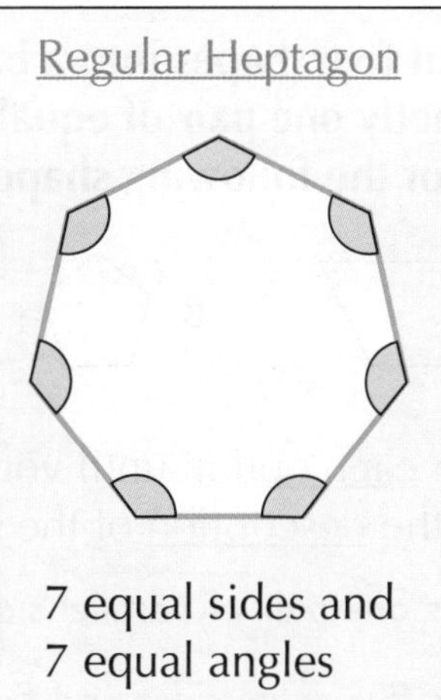	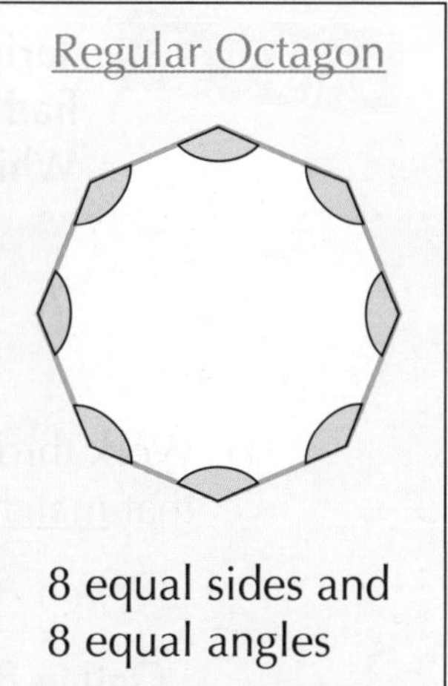
5 equal sides and 5 equal angles	6 equal sides and 6 equal angles	7 equal sides and 7 equal angles	8 equal sides and 8 equal angles

Irregular polygons have at least one side or angle that's different in size. E.g. an irregular pentagon has five sides but at least one of the sides or angles is different to the others.

11+ Example Questions

Which of the following shapes should be placed in area Z of the Venn diagram?

A Square
B Rectangle
C Rhombus
D Isosceles Triangle
E Trapezium

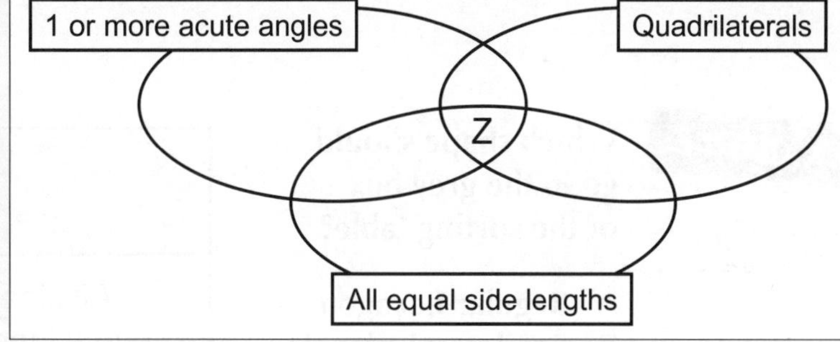

1) Area Z is in the centre of the Venn diagram. You need to find the option that's a quadrilateral with 1 or more acute angles and all equal side lengths.

2) First, eliminate any options that aren't quadrilaterals.

   An isosceles triangle has 3 sides so it's not a quadrilateral. The answer isn't option D.

3) Next, eliminate the options that don't have all equal side lengths.

   Rectangles and trapeziums don't have all equal side lengths.
   The answer isn't option B or E.

4) That leaves A and C. Eliminate the option that doesn't have 1 or more acute angles.

   A square has 4 right angles. The answer isn't option A.

5) The correct answer must be a rhombus — option C.
   It's a quadrilateral with 2 acute angles and 4 equal sides.

2D Shapes

More **11+ Example** Questions

Tariq put five shapes into a bag. He pulled one out at random. The shape had exactly one pair of equal sides, no parallel sides and no obtuse angles. Which of the following shapes did Tariq pull out of the bag?

A  **B** **C**  **D** **E** 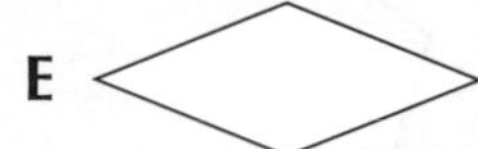

1) Work through each option until you find the one that matches the description of the shape.

   Option A has one pair of parallel sides so it's incorrect.

   Option B has five equal sides and five obtuse angles so it's incorrect.

   Option C has two pairs of equal sides and two obtuse angles so it's incorrect.

   Option D has **one pair of equal sides, no parallel sides** and **no obtuse angles.**

2) Option D matches the description of the shape that Tariq chose — this is the correct answer.
3) You can check option E to make sure you haven't made a mistake.

   Option E has four equal sides, two pairs of parallel sides and two obtuse angles so it's incorrect.

Which shape should go in the grey box of the sorting table?

A Regular hexagon
B Equilateral triangle
C Regular pentagon
D Parallelogram
E Rectangle

	At least one obtuse angle	No obtuse angles
All sides equal lengths		
Exactly two pairs of equal length sides	(grey box)	

1) First rule out the shapes that don't fit in the 'at least one obtuse angle' column.

   Equilateral triangles and rectangles don't have any obtuse angles so you can rule out B and E.

2) Then rule out the shapes that don't fit in the 'two pairs of equal length sides' row.

   Regular hexagons and regular pentagons both have all equal length sides — you can rule out A and C.

3) So, the only shape that fits in the 'at least one obtuse angle' column and the 'two pairs of equal length sides' row is a parallelogram. The correct answer is option D.

2D Shapes

Fran has a box containing identical rhombus tiles. One of the tiles is shown. What is the size of angle c?

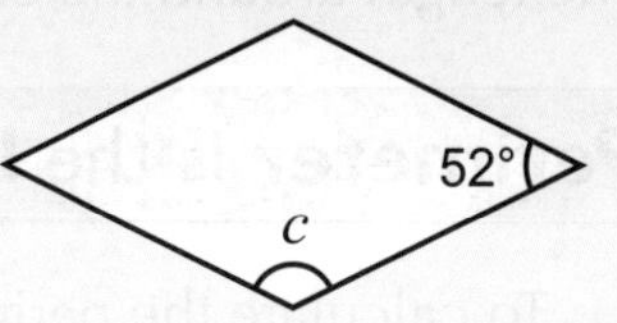

1) Start by working out the size of the other acute angle.

A rhombus has two equal acute angles. So, this angle is also 52°.

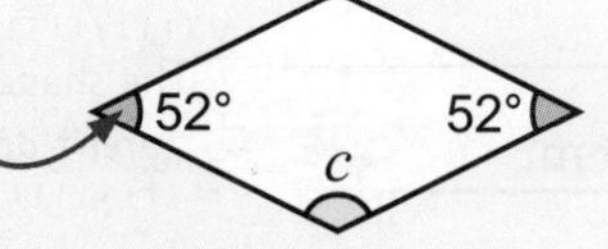

There's more about acute angles and obtuse angles on page 68.

2) Work out the total size of the two obtuse angles.

A rhombus is a quadrilateral, so the total size of the angles is 360°. This means that the total size of the two remaining angles is 360 – 52 – 52 = 256°.

3) You can now calculate the size of angle c.

A rhombus has two equal obtuse angles, so the size of angle c is 256° ÷ 2 = 128°

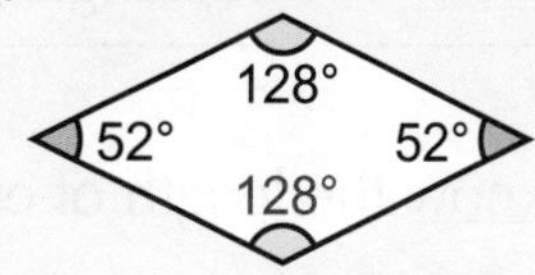

Practice Questions

1) Rhona is describing a triangular tile to her friends. She says that it has no right angles, no equal sides and no equal angles. What is the shape of the tile that Rhona is describing?
   A Equilateral triangle
   B Isosceles triangle
   C Scalene triangle
   D Right-angled triangle

2) Which shape should go in the grey box of the sorting table?
   A Trapezium
   B Square
   C Rectangle
   D Equilateral triangle
   E Rhombus

	All equal angles	Angles aren't all equal
All equal side lengths		
Side lengths aren't all equal		

3) Naomi is thinking of a shape. She gives David some clues about it:
   - The shape has no obtuse angles.
   - The shape has no right angles.
   - Two of its sides are equal in length.

   What shape is Naomi thinking of?

4) Lucas draws the biggest circle possible on a square piece of paper, as shown on the right. What is the radius of the circle he has drawn?

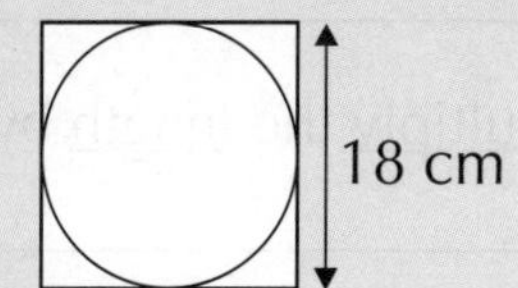

Don't just memorise the properties of 2D shapes...

It's tempting to think you're all set once you've learnt the properties on pages 70 and 71. You'll need to know how to apply these properties in the test though, so make sure you're comfortable with questions like the examples above before you move on.

2D Shapes — Area and Perimeter

The length around the edge of a shape is its perimeter. The space covered by a shape is its area.

Perimeter is the Length Around a Shape

1) To calculate the perimeter of a shape, add up the length of every side of the shape.

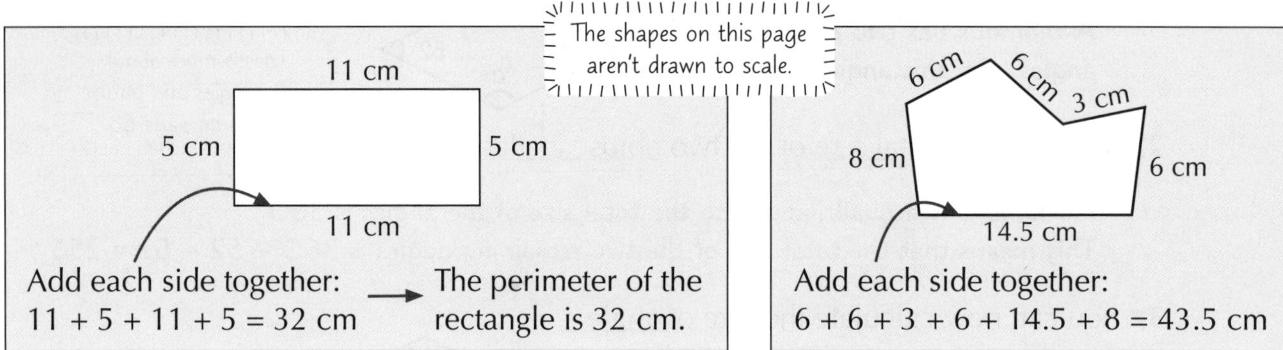

Add each side together: 11 + 5 + 11 + 5 = 32 cm → The perimeter of the rectangle is 32 cm.

Add each side together: 6 + 6 + 3 + 6 + 14.5 + 8 = 43.5 cm

2) Sometimes you don't know the length of every side. You need to work out the missing lengths.

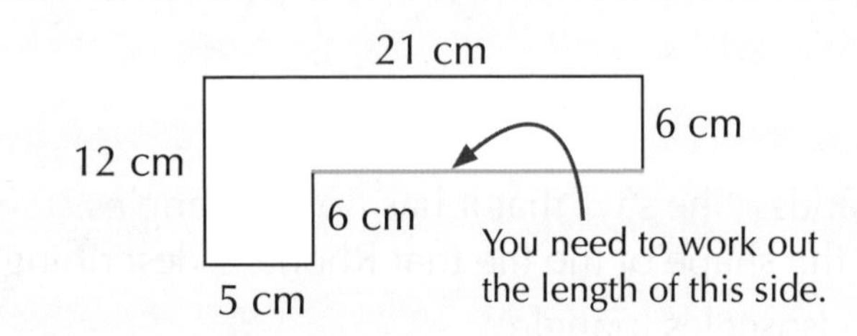

The two shorter horizontal sides equal the length of the longer side opposite. So the missing side is 21 cm – 5 cm = 16 cm.

Now add the sides together to find the perimeter: 21 + 6 + 16 + 6 + 5 + 12 = 66 cm.

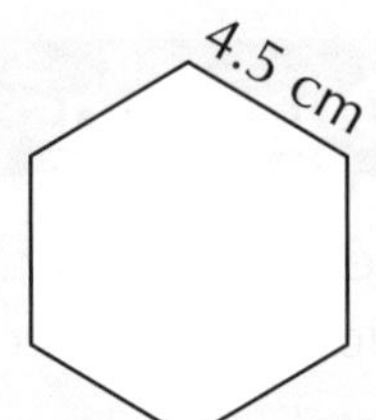

This is a regular hexagon so all of the sides are equal.

Add them together to find the perimeter: 4.5 + 4.5 + 4.5 + 4.5 + 4.5 + 4.5 = 27 cm (or 4.5 × 6 = 27 cm).

Area is the Space Inside a Shape

Finding the **Area** of a **Square** or **Rectangle**

Multiply the length by the width to work out the area of a square or rectangle.

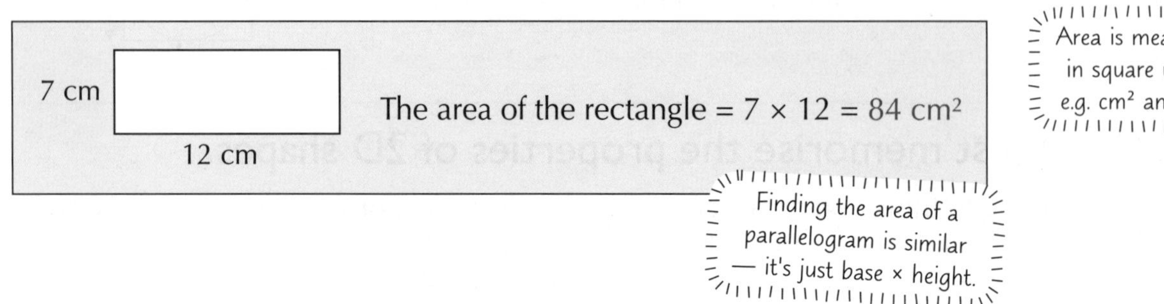

The area of the rectangle = 7 × 12 = 84 cm²

Area is measured in square units, e.g. cm² and m².

Finding the area of a parallelogram is similar — it's just base × height.

2D Shapes — Area and Perimeter

Finding the **Area** of a **Triangle**

Calculate the area of a triangle by multiplying half of the base length by the height.

You might see this as the formula: **area = ½ × base × height**

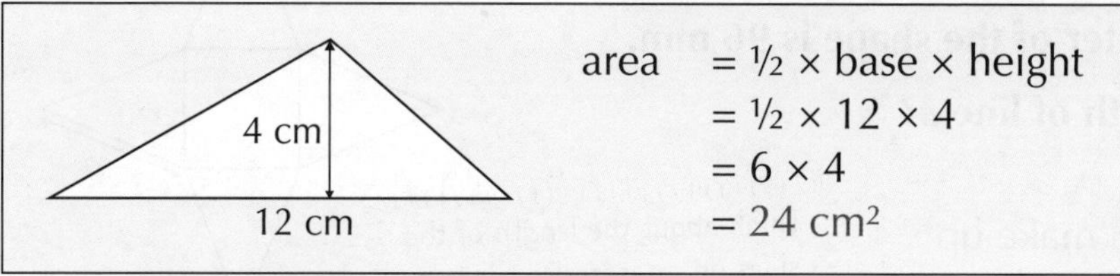

Finding the **Area** of **Other Shapes**

Sometimes you need to split a more complex shape into smaller shapes to calculate its area.

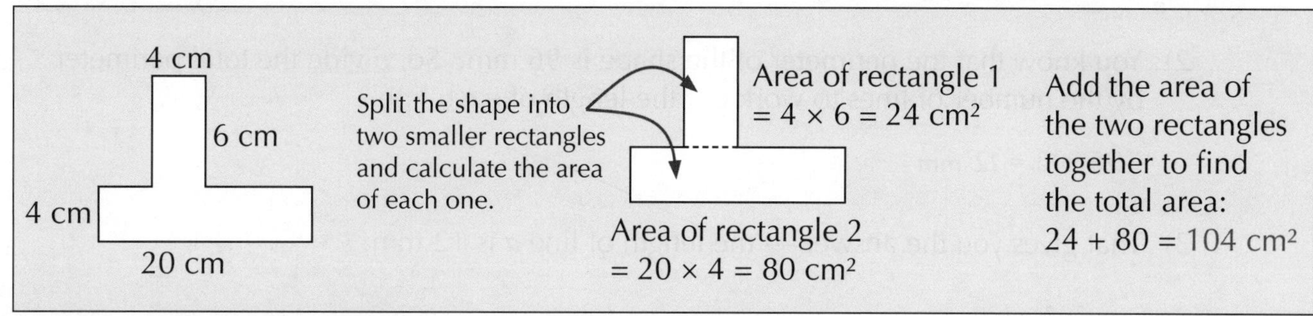

4 cm
6 cm
4 cm
20 cm
Split the shape into two smaller rectangles and calculate the area of each one.
Area of rectangle 1 = 4 × 6 = 24 cm²
Area of rectangle 2 = 20 × 4 = 80 cm²
Add the area of the two rectangles together to find the total area:
24 + 80 = 104 cm²

11+ Example Questions

Yasmin used 5 identical rectangular tiles to make the shape shown. The length of each tile is 16 cm and the width of each tile is 8 cm.

What is the perimeter of the arrow shape that's been made inside the grey tiles?

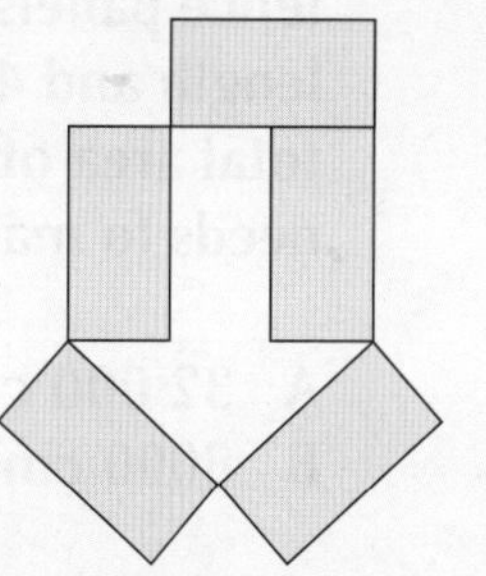

1) Work out the length of each part of the shape.

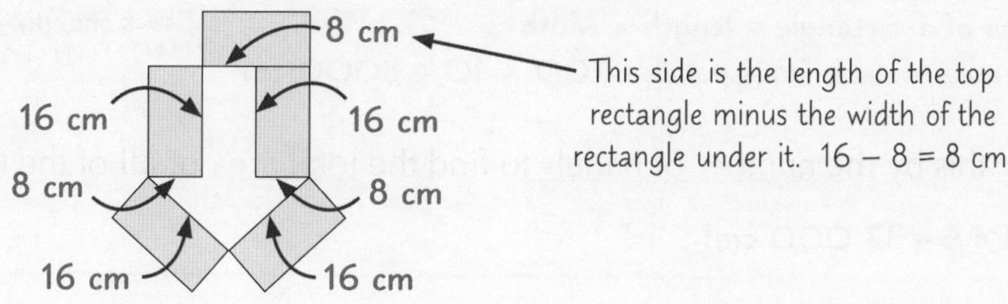

2) Add each side together to find the perimeter.

8 + 16 + 8 + 16 + 16 + 8 + 16 = **88 cm**

2D Shapes — Area and Perimeter

More **11+ Example** Questions

Marcelo made this shape using one square and four identical isosceles triangles.

The total perimeter of the shape is 96 mm.

What is the length of line *a*?

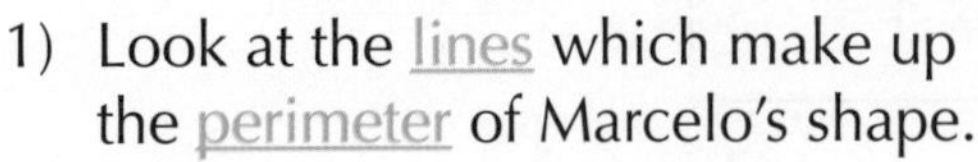

1) Look at the lines which make up the perimeter of Marcelo's shape.

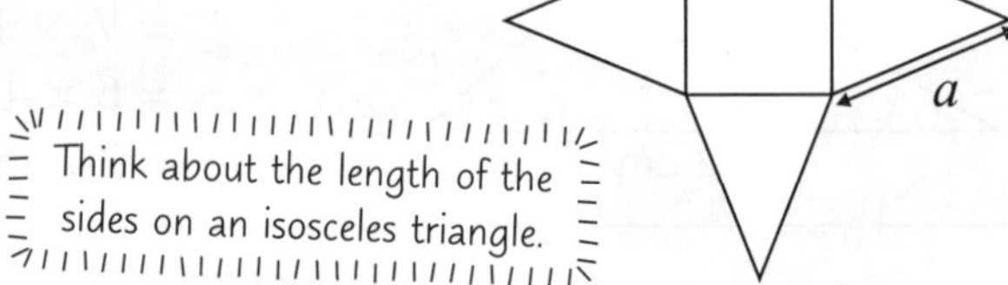

Think about the length of the sides on an isosceles triangle.

The perimeter of the shape is made using the two equal sides of four isosceles triangles.
There are eight lines that make up the perimeter of the shape.
The isosceles triangles are identical, so all eight lines must be the same length.

2) You know that the perimeter of the shape is 96 mm. So, divide the total perimeter by the number of lines to work out the length of each line.

   96 ÷ 8 = 12 mm

3) That gives you the answer — the length of line *a* is 12 mm.

Mabel is building a new run for her rabbits. The run is made up of four rectangular fence panels which are each 200 cm in length and 40 cm in width. What is the total area of the fence panels that Mabel needs to make the run?

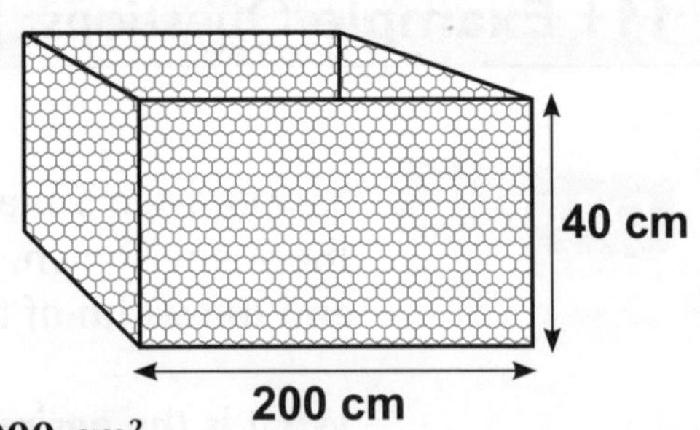

A 32 000 cm²   **C** 40 000 cm²   **E** 16 000 cm²
B 8000 cm²   **D** 24 000 cm²

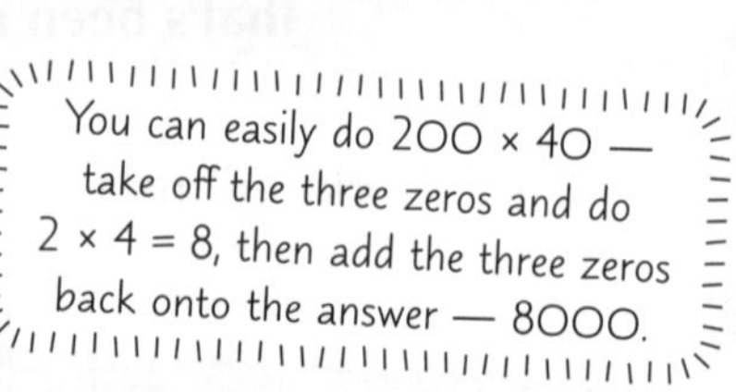

You can easily do 200 × 40 — take off the three zeros and do 2 × 4 = 8, then add the three zeros back onto the answer — 8000.

1) Start by finding the area of each rectangular panel.

   The area of a rectangle = length × width
   So the area of each fence panel = 200 × 40 = 8000 cm²

2) Multiply this by the number of panels to find the total area of all of the fence panels.

   8000 × 4 = 32 000 cm²

3) The total area of the fence panels used by Mabel is 32 000 cm².
   So the correct answer is option A.

2D Shapes — Area and Perimeter

The diagram shows the downstairs of Stephen's house. Stephen wants to lay a new carpet in his living room and his dining room. What is the area of carpet that Stephen needs?

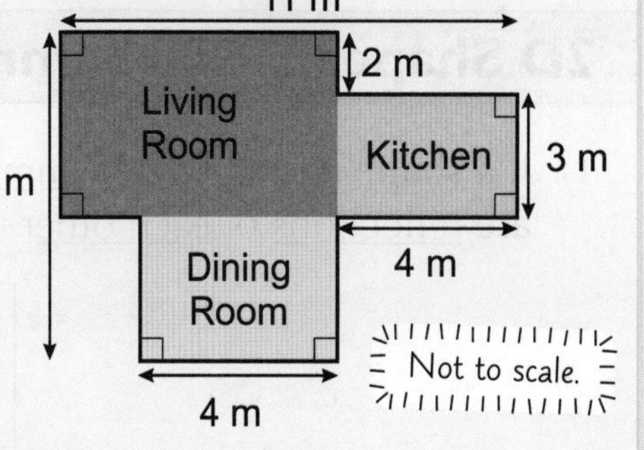

A 35 m² **C 99 m²** **E 51 m²**
B 16 m² **D 63 m²**

1) You need to work out the areas of the living room and dining room separately, and then add them together.
2) Start by working out the unknown lengths.

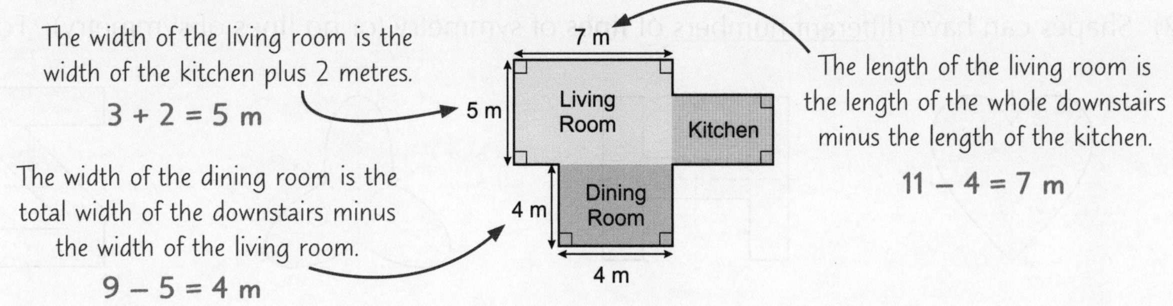

The width of the living room is the width of the kitchen plus 2 metres.
3 + 2 = 5 m
The width of the dining room is the total width of the downstairs minus the width of the living room.
9 – 5 = 4 m
7 m
5 m
Living Room
Kitchen
4 m
Dining Room
4 m
The length of the living room is the length of the whole downstairs minus the length of the kitchen.
11 – 4 = 7 m

3) Next, work out the area of the living room and the area of the dining room.

Area of the living room = 7 × 5 = 35 m²
Area of the dining room = 4 × 4 = 16 m²

4) Add the two areas together to find the total area of carpet that Stephen needs.

35 + 16 = 51 m² — option E is correct.

Practice Questions

1) This shape is made from two identical regular hexagons joined together. The total perimeter of the shape is 75 cm. How long is side *Z*?

2) Calculate the area of this shape.

A 48 cm² **B** 72 cm² **C** 64 cm²
D 132 cm² **E** 96 cm²

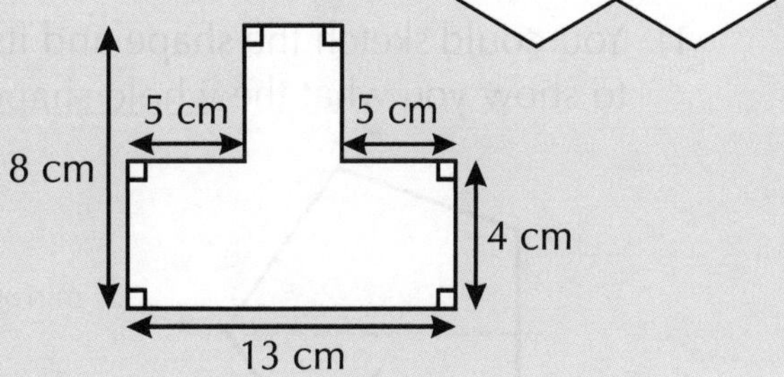

Only use the outside edges of the shape to work out the perimeter...

If the shape you need to find the perimeter of is made up of smaller shapes joined together (like the example on the previous page), you don't need to use the joined edges in your calculation.

Symmetry

Symmetrical shapes can be split into two identical halves. These halves are reflections of each other.

2D Shapes can be Symmetrical

1) If a shape has a line of symmetry, it means that both parts of the shape on each side of the line are reflections of each other.

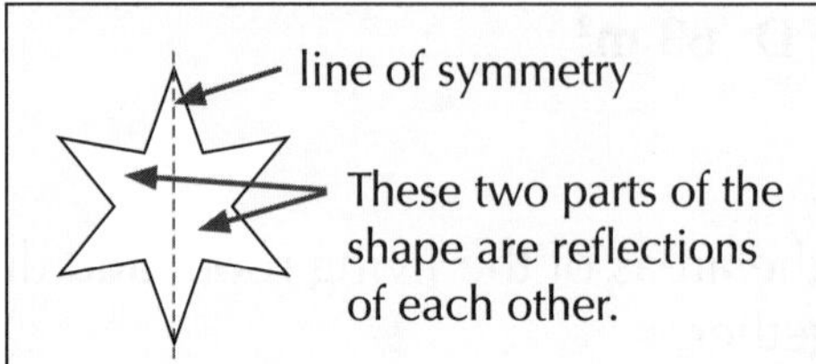
line of symmetry
These two parts of the shape are reflections of each other.

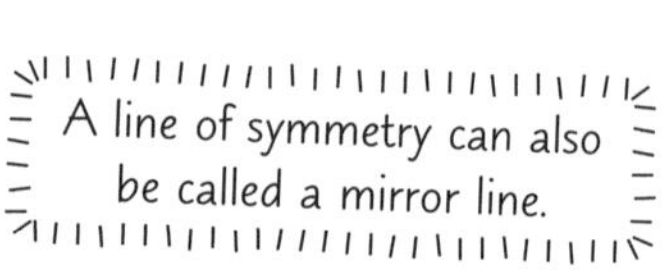
A line of symmetry can also be called a mirror line.

2) Shapes can have different numbers of lines of symmetry (or no lines of symmetry). For example:

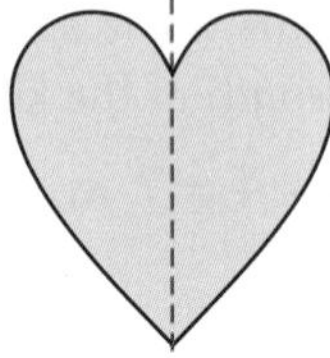

1 line of symmetry

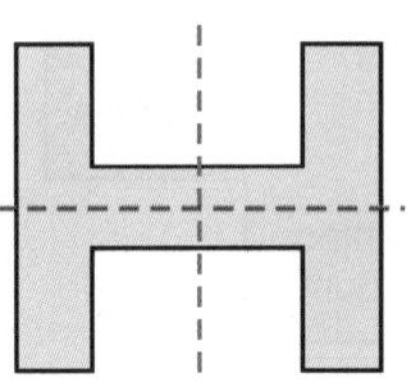

2 lines of symmetry

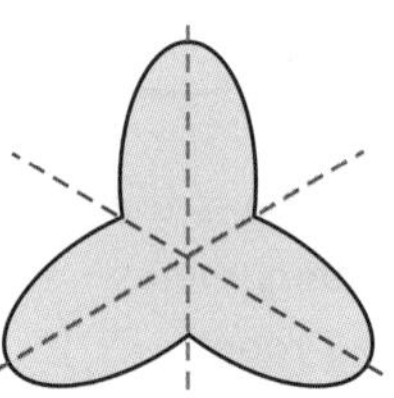

3 lines of symmetry

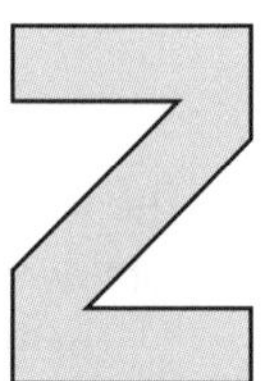

No lines of symmetry

11+ Example Questions

EXAMPLE:

Charlene has drawn half of a shape. She reflects it in the mirror line to make a whole shape. What is the name of the whole shape?

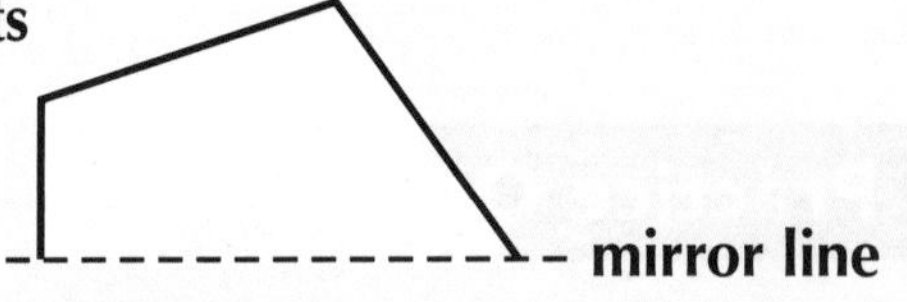
mirror line

A Rhombus **B Parallelogram** **C Pentagon**
D Hexagon **E Kite**

1) You could sketch the shape and its reflection on some rough paper to show you what the whole shape will be.

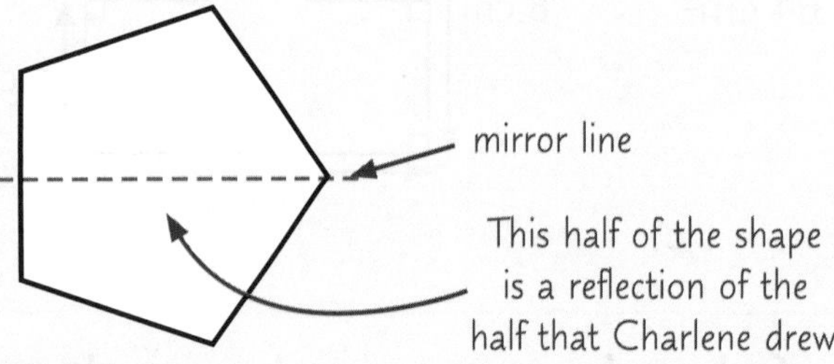
mirror line
This half of the shape is a reflection of the half that Charlene drew.

2) The whole shape has five sides. This means that it's a pentagon — option C.

Symmetry

How many lines of symmetry does this shape have?

1) Start by looking for any horizontal or vertical lines of symmetry.

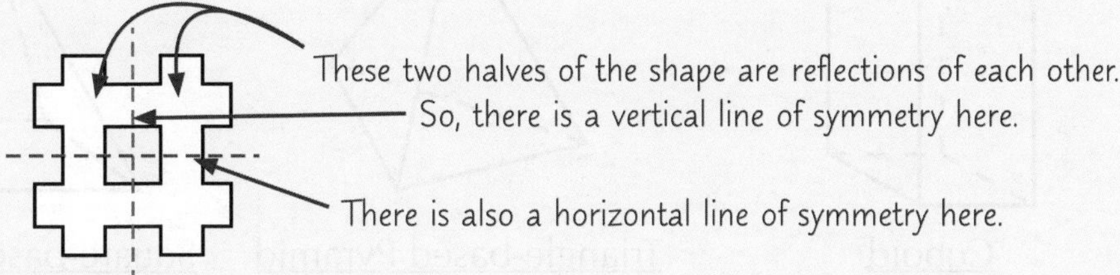

2) Next, look for any diagonal lines of symmetry.

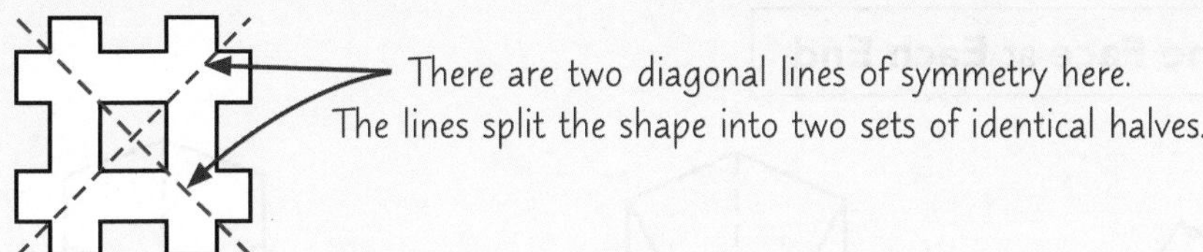

There are two diagonal lines of symmetry here.
The lines split the shape into two sets of identical halves.

3) The shape has four lines of symmetry in total.

Practice Questions

1) What whole shape would you see when this half shape is reflected in the mirror line?

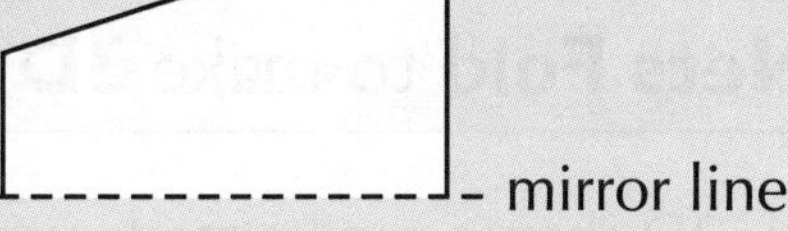

A Trapezium **B** Parallelogram **C** Rhombus
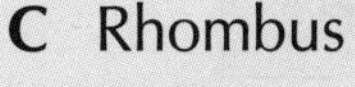
D Pentagon **E** Hexagon
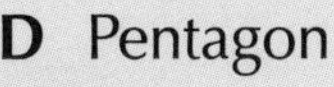

2) Elsa drew the following shape. How many lines of symmetry does it have?

Make good use of your scrap paper...

If you're stuck in the exam, you can draw the shape on a scrap piece of paper and fold it in half. Unfold the paper and look to see whether the two halves of the shape on either side of the fold line are symmetrical. If they are, the fold line is a line of symmetry.

3D Shapes

3D shapes are different from 2D shapes — they have length and width, but they also have depth.

Know these common **3D Shapes**

Cubes and **Cuboids** have **Six Faces**

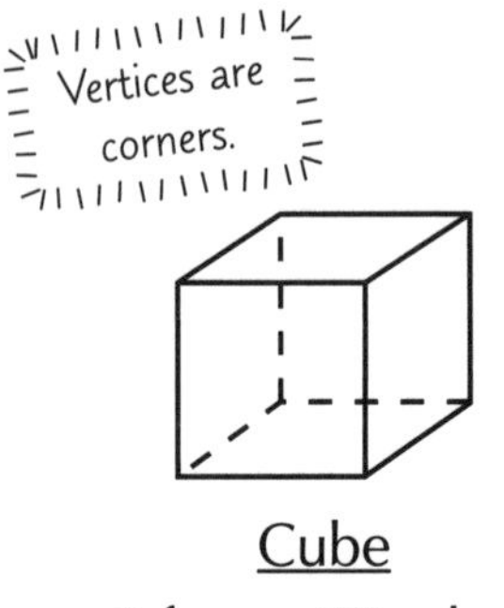

Cube
6 faces, 12 edges and 8 vertices

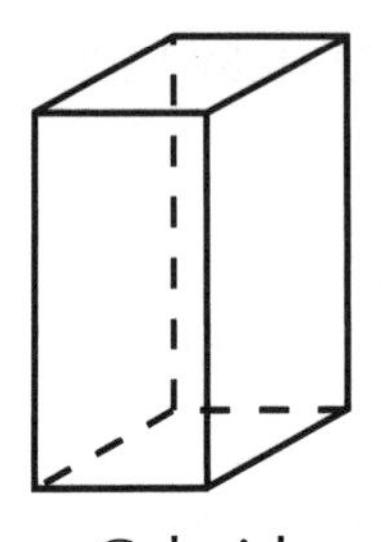

Cuboid
6 faces, 12 edges and 8 vertices

Pyramids have **Triangular Faces** that join at a **Point**

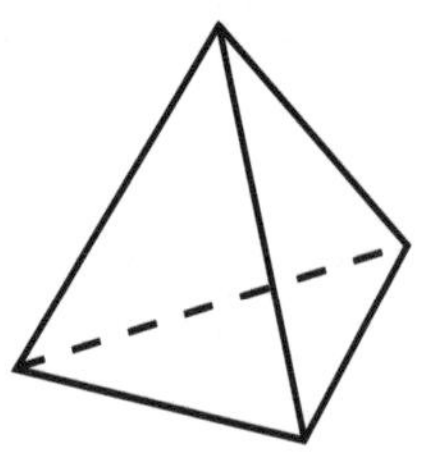

Triangle-based Pyramid
4 faces, 6 edges and 4 vertices

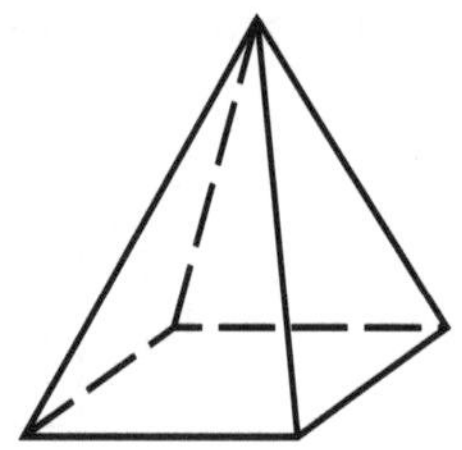

Square-based Pyramid
5 faces, 8 edges and 5 vertices

Prisms have the **Same Face** at **Each End**

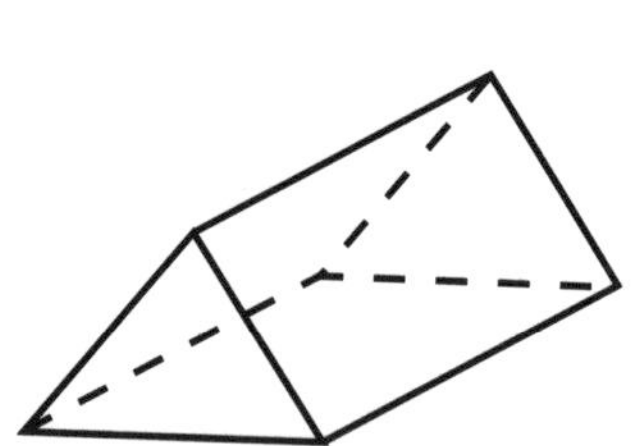

Triangular Prism
5 faces, 9 edges and 6 vertices

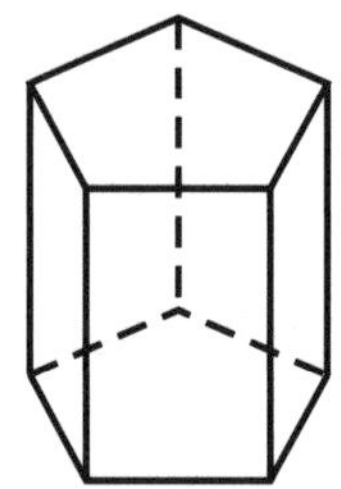

Pentagonal Prism
7 faces, 15 edges and 10 vertices

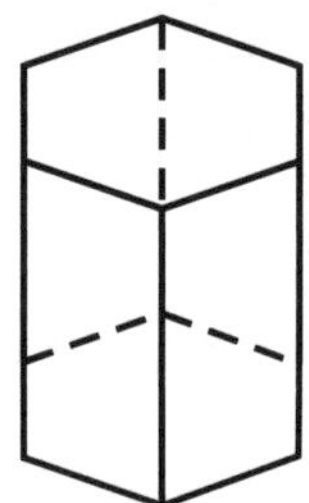

Hexagonal Prism
8 faces, 18 edges and 12 vertices

Nets Fold to make **3D Shapes**

1) 3D shapes can be made using a net. A net is a 2D shape which can be folded to make a 3D shape.
2) The shapes that make up the net become the faces of the 3D shape.
3) There's often more than one net that you can use to make a 3D shape.

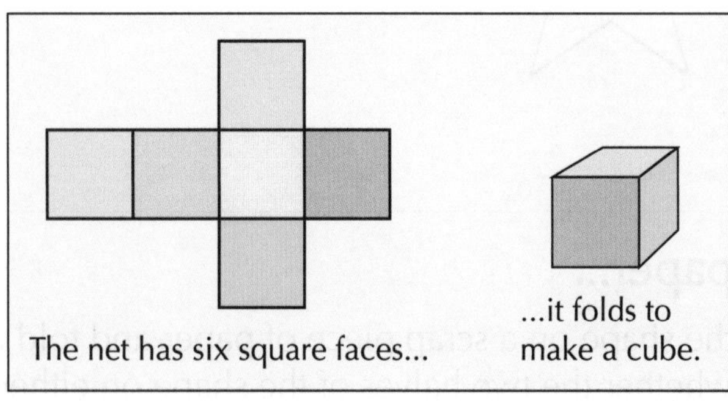

The net has six square faces... ...it folds to make a cube.

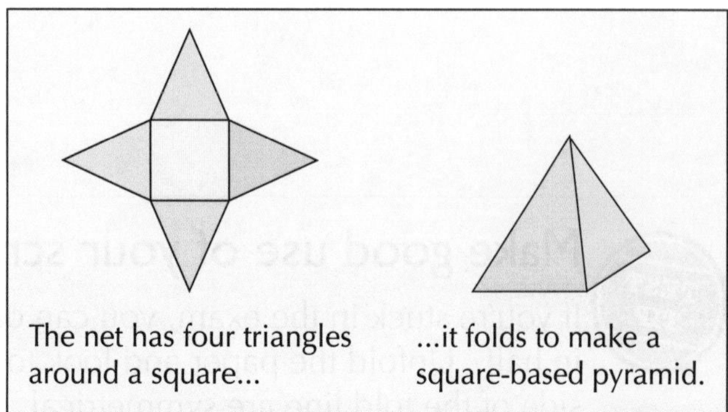

The net has four triangles around a square... ...it folds to make a square-based pyramid.

3D Shapes

Volume of Cubes and Cuboids = Length × Width × Height

1) Volume is the amount of space inside a shape.
2) You can work out the volume of a cube or a cuboid by multiplying the length, width and height together.

Volume is measured in cubed units — e.g. m^3 or cm^3.

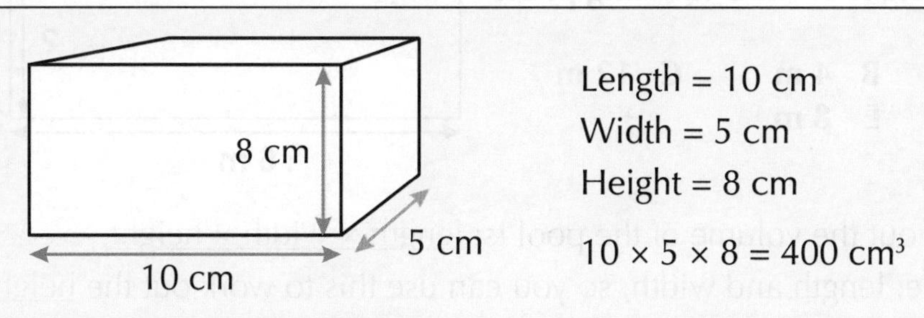

11+ Example Questions

Sunita has made this net. What shape will be made when the net is folded?

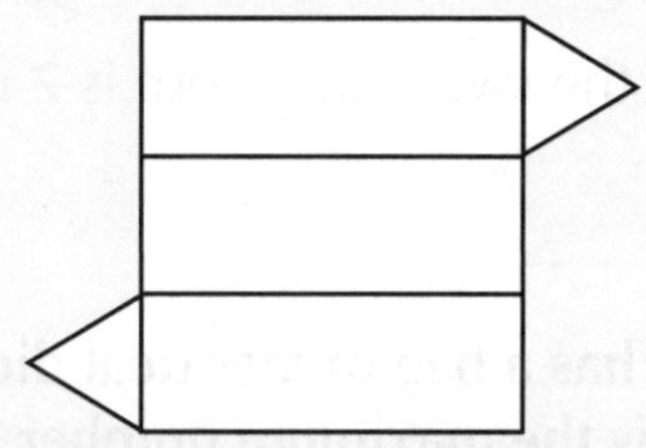

Method 1

Imagine the net being folded up. Work out which edges will join to each other.

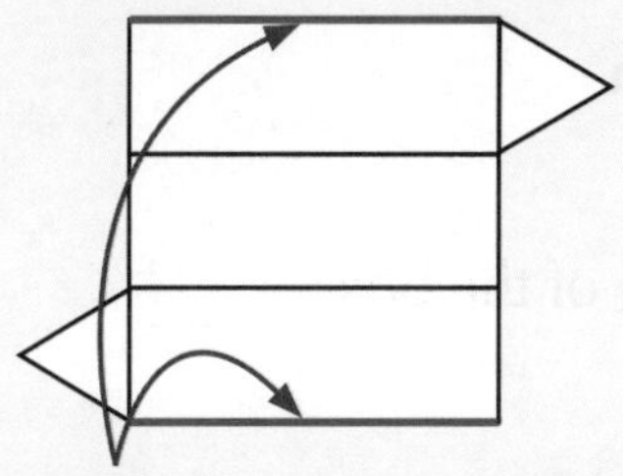

These two edges will join together when the net is folded.

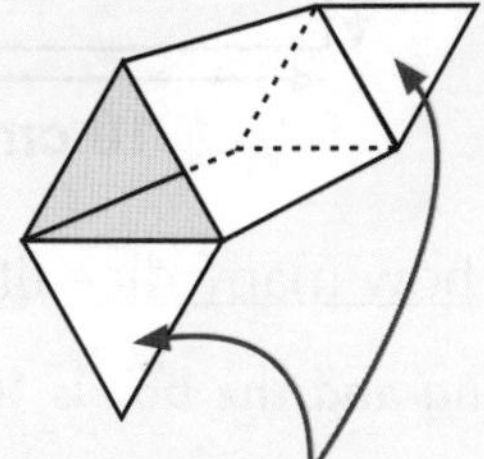

Fold in the triangular faces at each end of the shape.

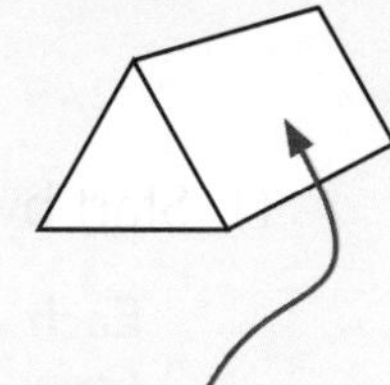

The finished shape is a **triangular prism**.

Method 2

You could also work out the final shape by looking at the number of faces and the shape of the faces.

There are two identical triangular faces at each end of the shape.

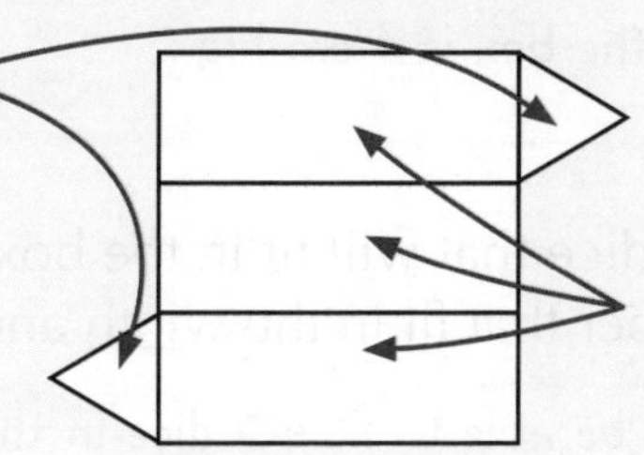

There are three rectangular faces to join to the triangular ends. So, the finished shape will be a **triangular prism**.

3D Shapes

More **11+ Example** Questions

Chloe's swimming pool is shown.
It can hold 48 m³ of water when full.
What is the height of the swimming pool?

A 1.5 m **B 4 m** **C 12 m**
D 2 m **E 8 m**

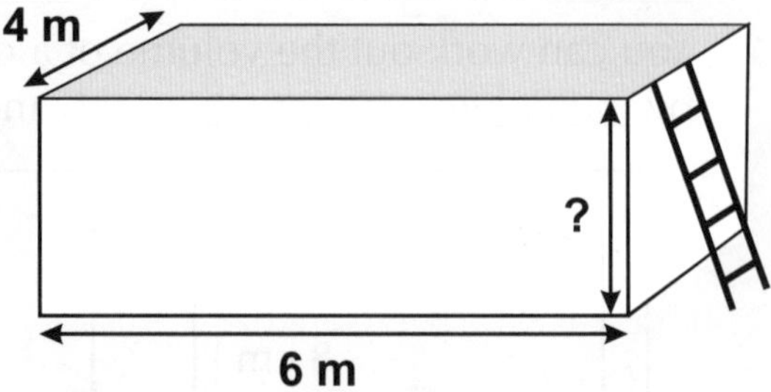

1) The formula to work out the volume of the pool is: length × width × height.
2) You know the volume, length and width, so you can use this to work out the height.

length × width × height = 48 m³
6 × 4 × height = 48 m³
24 × height = 48 m³
So height = 48 ÷ 24 = 2 m.

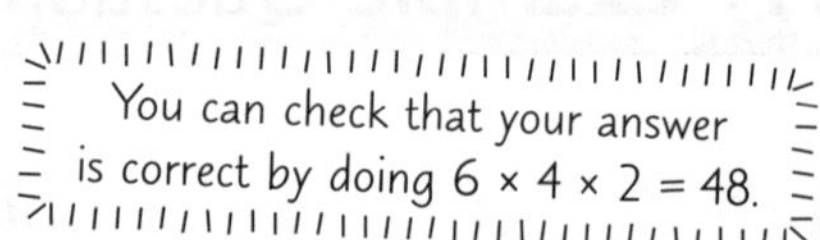

You can check that your answer is correct by doing 6 × 4 × 2 = 48.

3) The height of the swimming pool is 2 m — option D.

EXAMPLE:

Oscar has a bag of identical dice of side 2 cm.
What is the maximum number of dice that he can fit in this box?

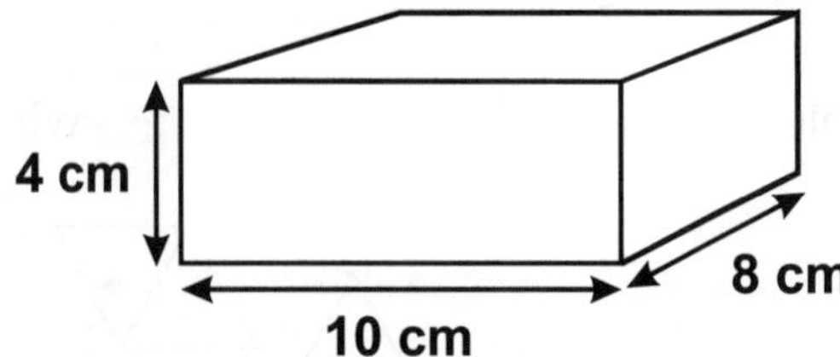

1) Start by working out how many dice fit along the length of the box.

Each dice is 2 cm long and the box is 10 cm long.
10 ÷ 2 = 5 dice.

2) Next, work out how many dice fit along the width of the box.

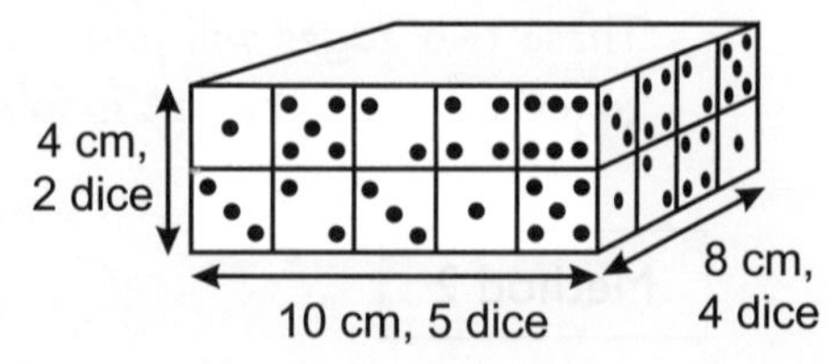

Each dice is 2 cm wide and the box is 8 cm wide.
8 ÷ 2 = 4 dice.

3) Then, work out how many dice fit up the height of the box.

Each dice is 2 cm high and the box is 4 cm high.
4 ÷ 2 = 2 dice.

4) To find the total number of dice that will fit in the box, multiply the number of dice that fit in the length by the number that fit in the width and the number that fit up the height.

5 × 4 × 2 = 40. Oscar will be able to fit 40 dice in the box.

3D Shapes

Joel folds this net to make a pentagonal prism. Which corner is going to join to corner X?

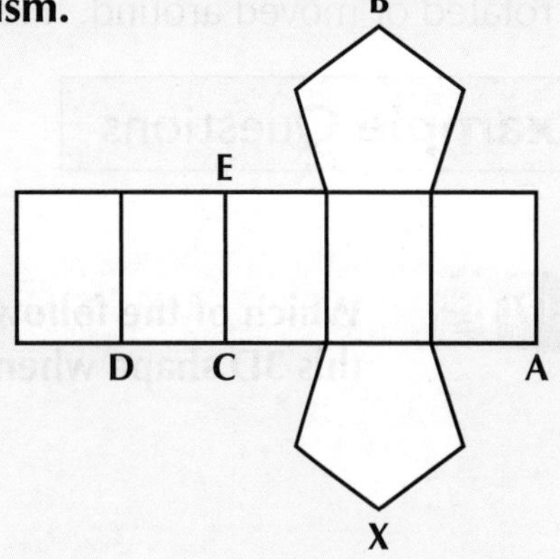

1) You need to imagine how the net will be folded to make the pentagonal prism.

2) Each corner of the two pentagons will join with a corner of a rectangle.

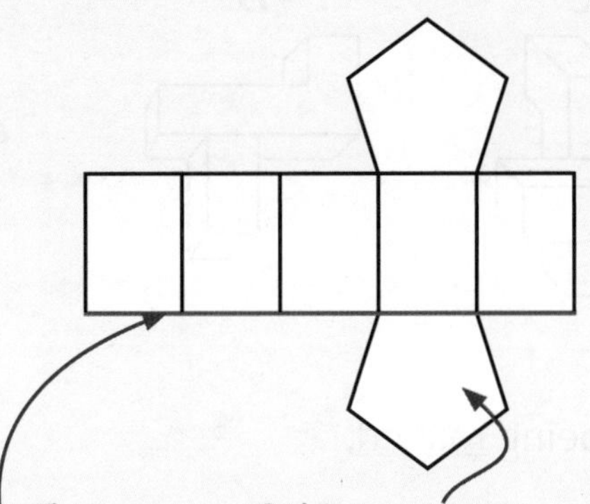

The corners of this pentagon are going to join with the corners on this line. So the correct answer must be A, C or D.

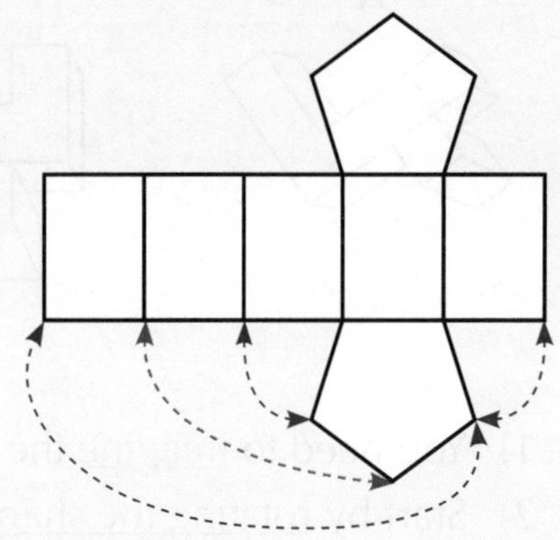

Corner X is going to join to corner D. So, the correct answer is option D.

Practice Questions

1) Which of these nets will not fold to make a cube?

A 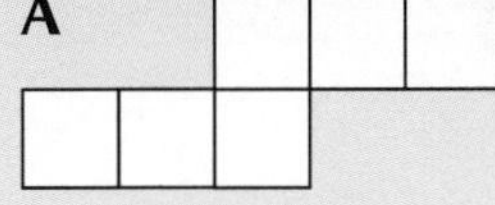

B 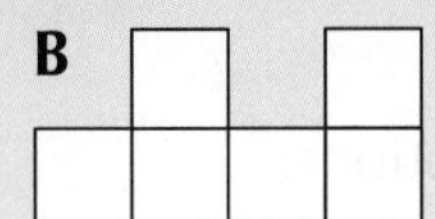

C 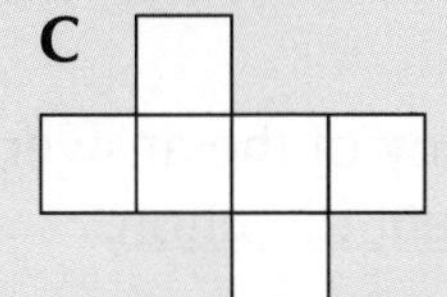

D 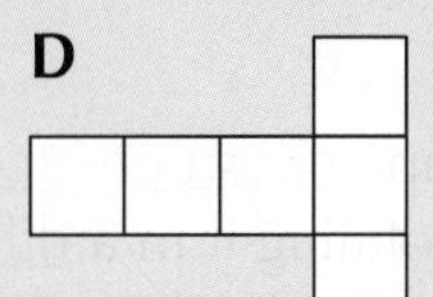

E 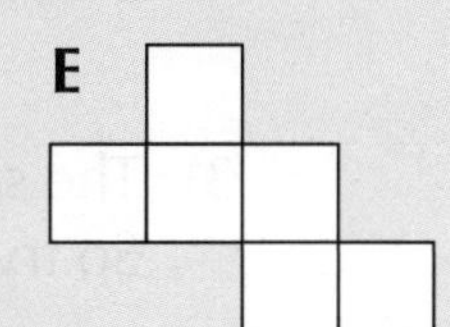

2) Vegetable stock cubes have sides that are 1 cm long. How many vegetable stock cubes will fit in a box that is 4 cm long, 8 cm wide and 2 cm high?

3) Frankie has made this net. What shape will be made when the net is folded?

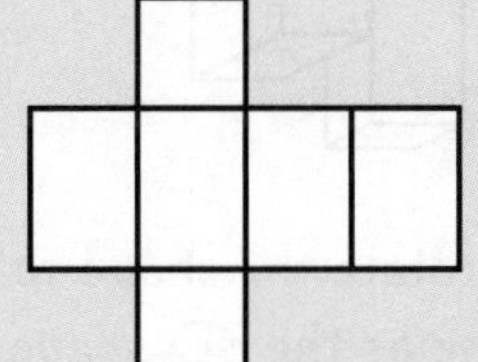

Make sure you're comfortable with sketching 3D shapes...

If you're asked about the properties of 3D shapes, it might help to draw them — it's easier to count the faces, edges or vertices that way. It's easy to miss one if you're just imagining the shape.

Shape Problems

Some questions will ask you to picture in your head what shapes will look like when they're flipped, rotated or moved around. Here are some sample questions to help you get the idea.

11+ Example Questions

Which of the following options shows this 3D shape when it has been rotated?

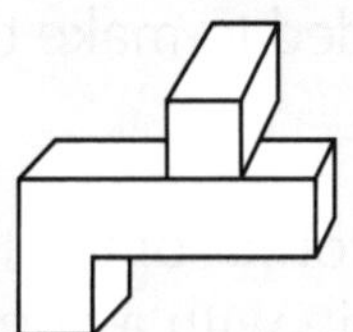

A

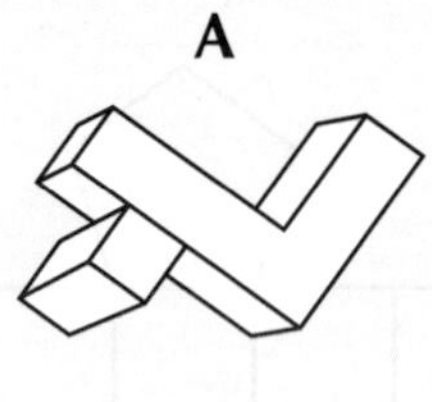

B

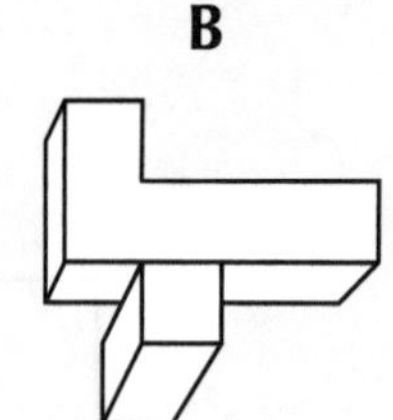

C

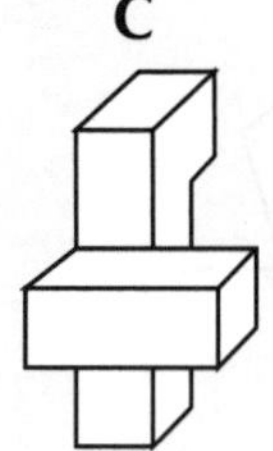

D

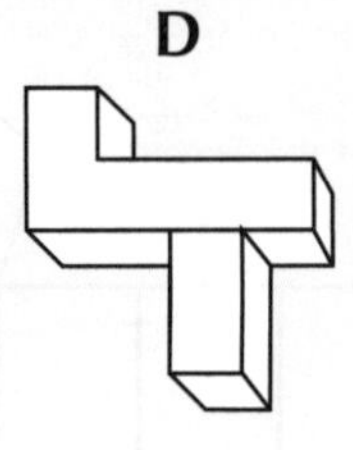

E

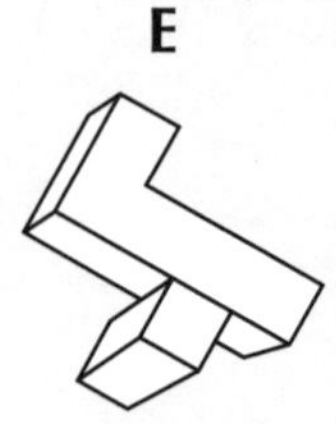

1) You need to imagine the original 3D shape being rotated.
2) Start by rotating the shape in one direction.

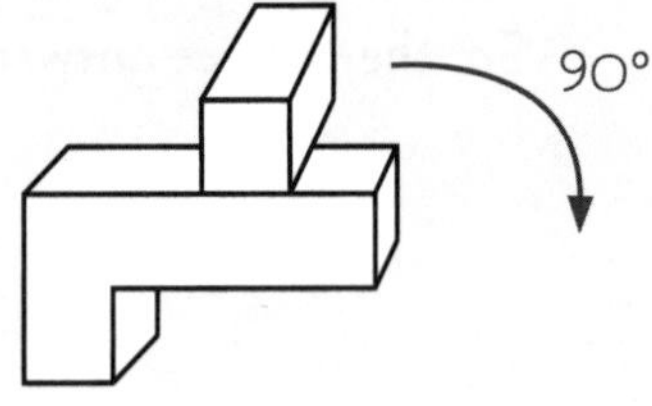

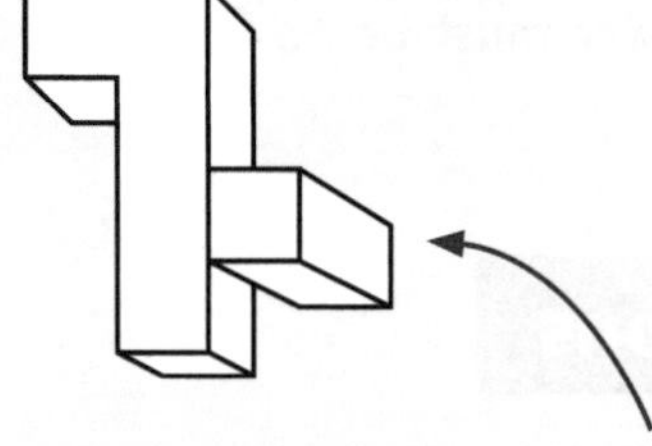

When you rotate the shape 90° in a clockwise direction, it looks like this.

3) The shape doesn't match any of the answer options.
   So try rotating it in a different direction.

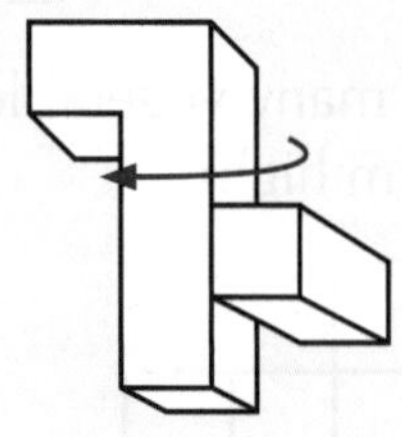

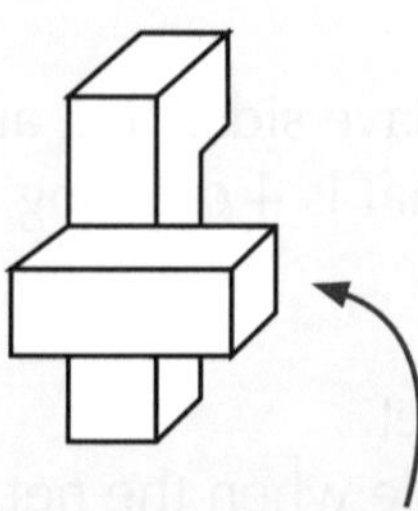

If you then rotate the shape to the left by 90°, this is what it looks like.
It is the same as the 3D shape given in option C, so the two shapes must be identical.

4) That gives you the answer. The correct answer is option C.

Shape Problems

Lily has two blocks made out of square tiles. She fits them together to make some new shapes. She does not overlap the two blocks. Which of the following shapes can Lily not make?

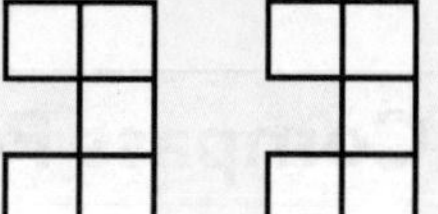

A

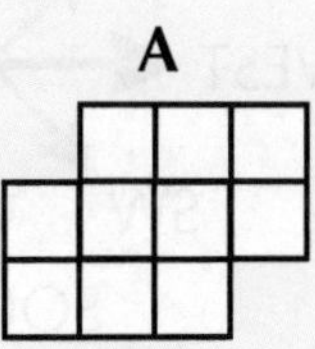

B

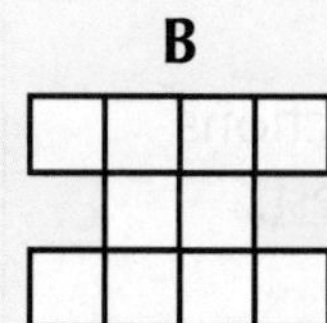

C

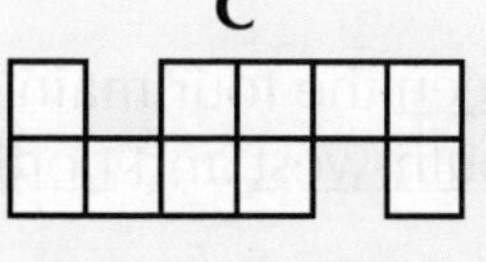

D

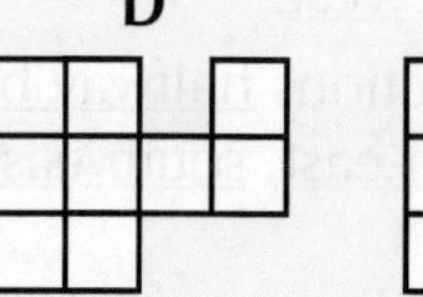

E

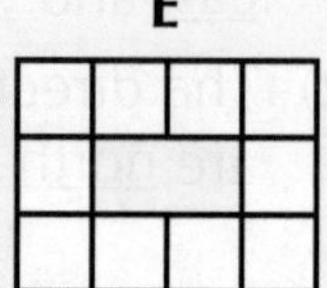

1) Look at each answer option and see if it can be made from Lily's blocks.
2) You need to imagine rotating the blocks to see if they can make the shapes.

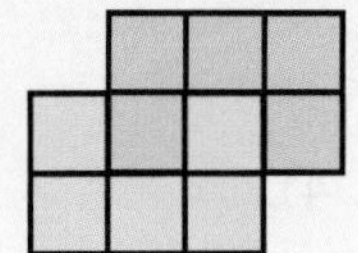

Shape A can be made from Lily's blocks.

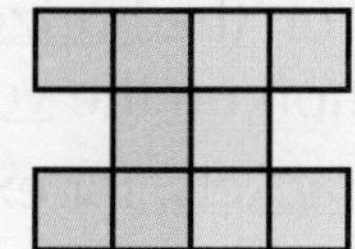

Shape B can be made from Lily's blocks.

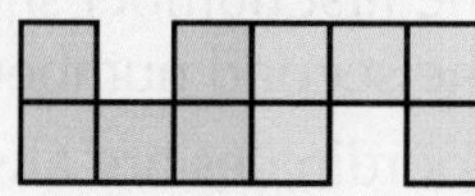

Shape C can be made from Lily's blocks.

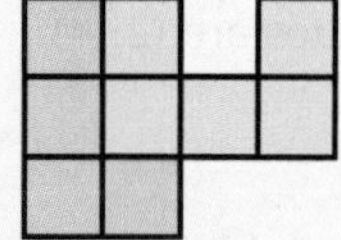

Shape D can't be made from Lily's blocks. The two blocks would have to overlap to make this shape.

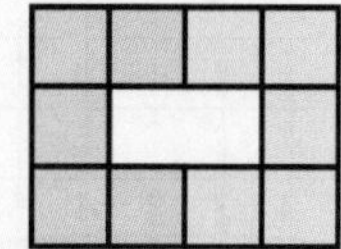

Shape E can be made from Lily's blocks.

3) Option D is the correct answer — it can't be made from the blocks used by Lily.

Practice Question

1) The diagram shows how a logo on a window appears when viewed from the front. Which of the following options shows the same logo when viewed from the back?

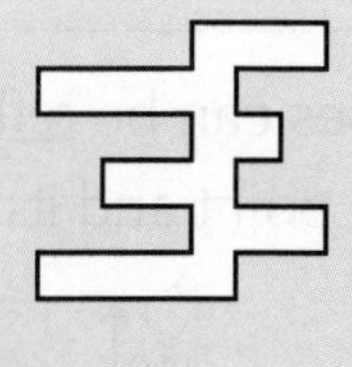

A

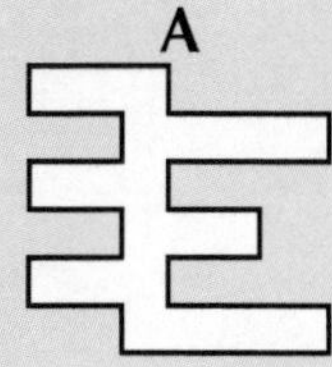

B

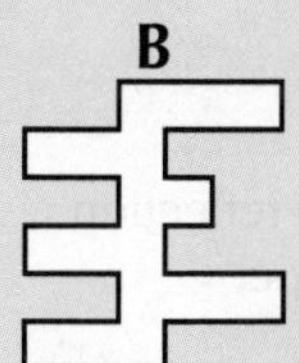

C

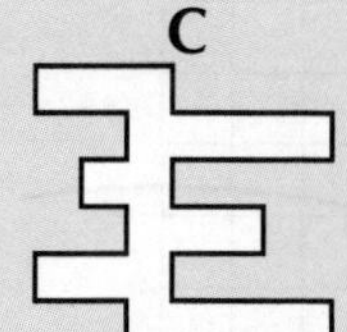

D

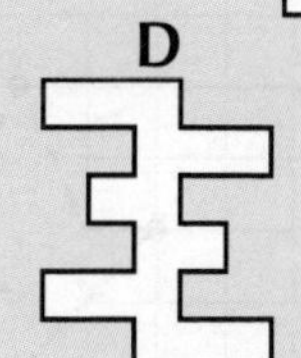

E

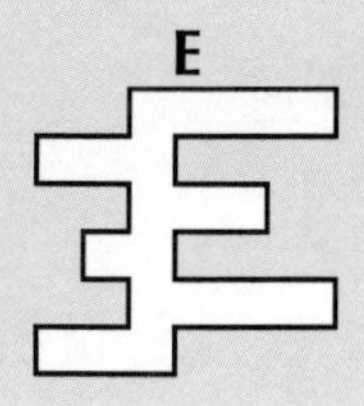

You can draw it out if you get stuck...

For questions like the example above, you could sketch the options on a rough piece of paper. Then try to shade in the two blocks to see if both of them fit into the shape.

Coordinates

Coordinates are pairs of numbers that help you to find points on a grid.

Compass Points tell you about Direction

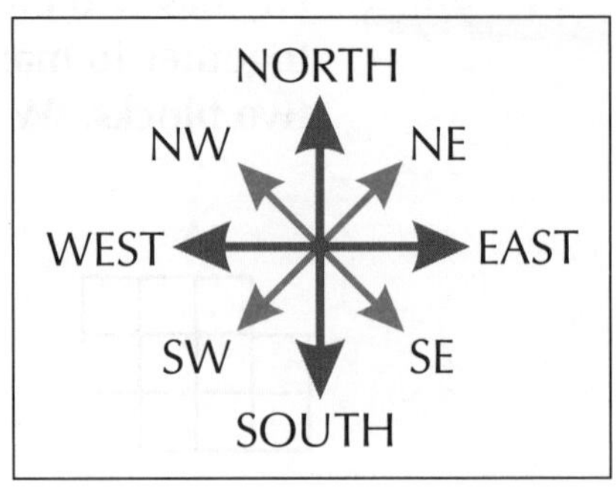

1) The four main compass directions are north, south, east and west.
2) The directions halfway between the four main directions are north-east, south-east, south-west and north-west.

Coordinates show a Point on a Grid

1) Each point on a grid has two numbers to show its position. These are coordinates.
2) The first number shows the position on the horizontal x-axis.
   The second number shows the position on the vertical y-axis.
3) Coordinates are always written in brackets, for example (0, 0) or (5, 4).

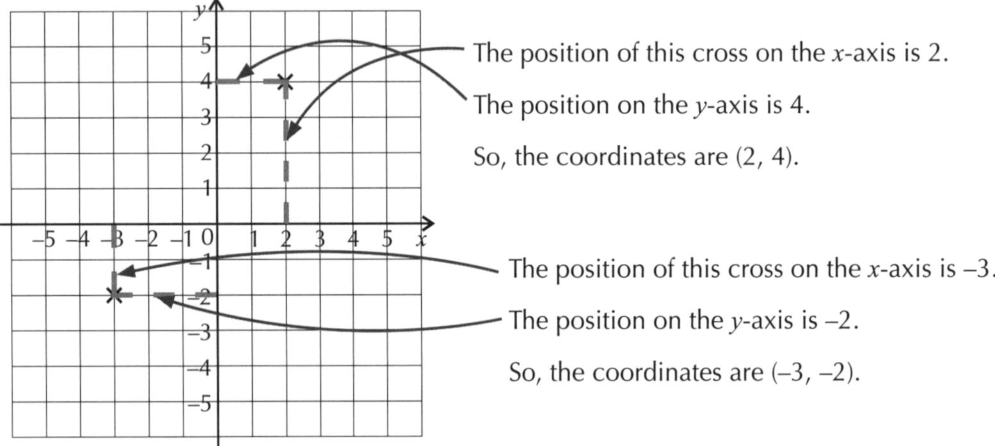

The position of this cross on the x-axis is 2.
The position on the y-axis is 4.
So, the coordinates are (2, 4).
The position of this cross on the x-axis is –3.
The position on the y-axis is –2.
So, the coordinates are (–3, –2).

Shapes can be Transformed on a Coordinate Grid

Reflection in a Line

1) Shapes can be reflected across a mirror line on a coordinate grid.
2) Each point and its reflection are exactly the same distance from the mirror line.

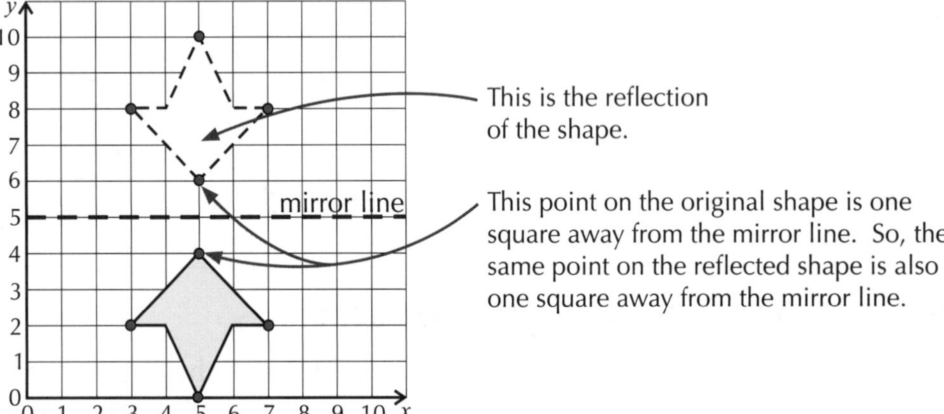

mirror line
This is the reflection of the shape.
This point on the original shape is one square away from the mirror line. So, the same point on the reflected shape is also one square away from the mirror line.

Coordinates

Translation is Sliding a Shape

Translation is when a shape is moved from one place to another, without being flipped or rotated.

This shape has been translated by moving it 5 squares right and 4 squares down:

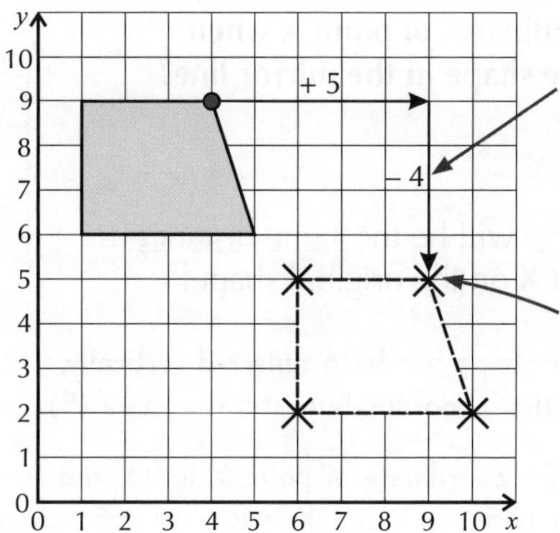

For the red point (4, 9), the x-coordinate on the translated shape will be 5 greater, and the y-coordinate will be 4 less.

The x-coordinate of this corner will be 4 + 5 = 9 and the y-coordinate will be 9 – 4 = 5 — (9, 5).

When you translate a shape, the new shape should look exactly the same as the original.

11+ Example Questions

EXAMPLE: **A rectangle was drawn on a coordinate grid. What are the coordinates of corner A?**

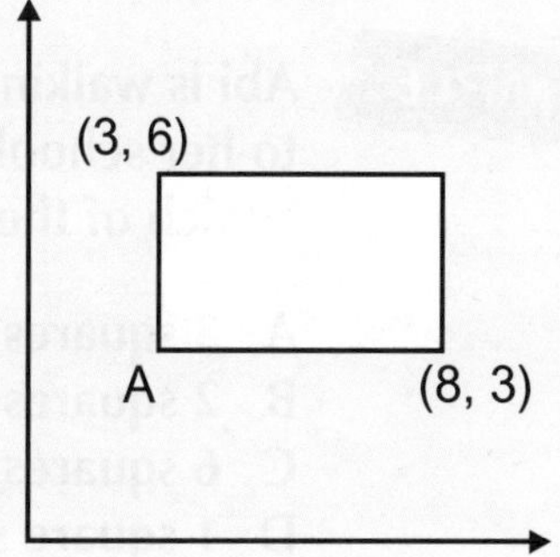

1) You can use the coordinates you've been given to work out the coordinates of corner A.

These two corners are on the same position on the x-axis. The x-axis coordinate of the top corner is 3, so the x-axis coordinate of A is also 3.

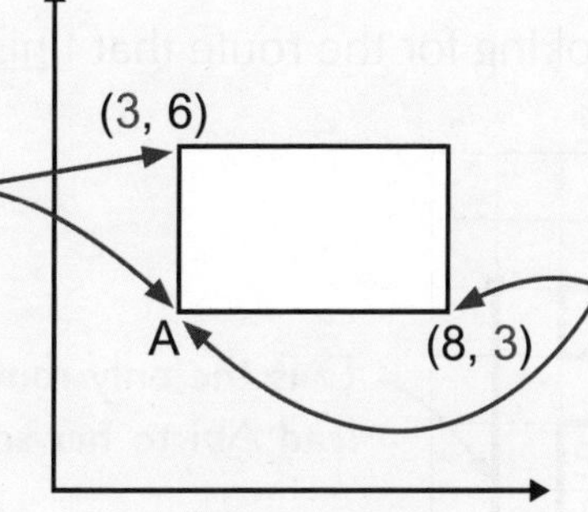

These two corners are on the same position on the y-axis. The y-axis coordinate of the right-hand corner is 3, so the y-axis coordinate of A is also 3.

2) That gives you the x-axis and y-axis coordinates. So, the coordinates of corner A are (3, 3).

Coordinates

More **11+ Example** Questions

Gurbaj drew this shape on a coordinate grid. What are the coordinates of point X when Gurbaj reflects the shape in the mirror line?

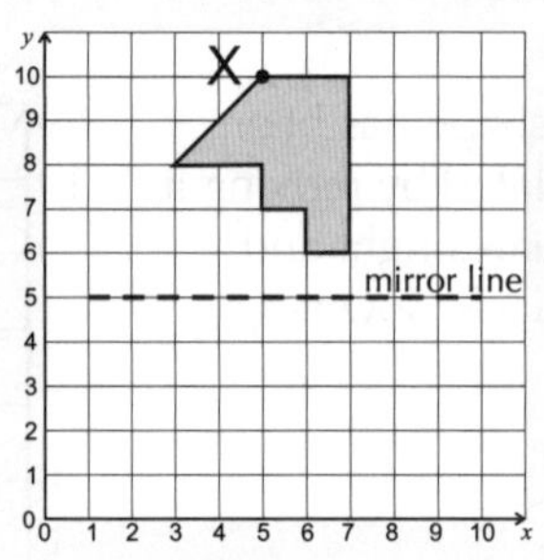

Point X on the reflected shape will be the same distance from the mirror line as point X on the original shape.

If you're allowed to write on the exam paper, you could draw the reflection of the shape.

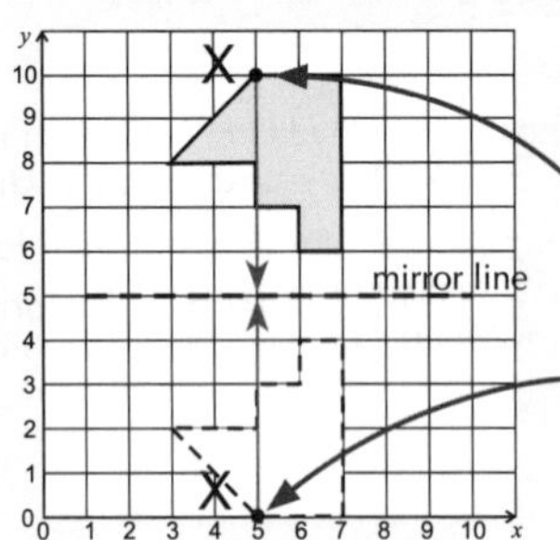

The shape has been reflected vertically, so the x-coordinate is still the same (5).

The y-coordinate of point X is 10, and the y-coordinate of the mirror line is 5. So, point X is $10 - 5 = 5$ squares away from the mirror line.

The reflected point X will also be 5 squares away from the mirror line. So, the y-coordinate will be $5 - 5 = 0$.

The coordinates of the reflected point X are (5, 0).

EXAMPLE:

Abi is walking from her house at point Z to her school at point W. Which of the following could describe her route?

A 3 squares north, 4 squares east, 1 square north
B 2 squares east, 4 squares north, 2 squares east
C 6 squares north, 3 squares east, 1 square south
D 1 square south, 5 squares east, 5 squares north
E 4 squares east, 2 squares north, 3 squares west

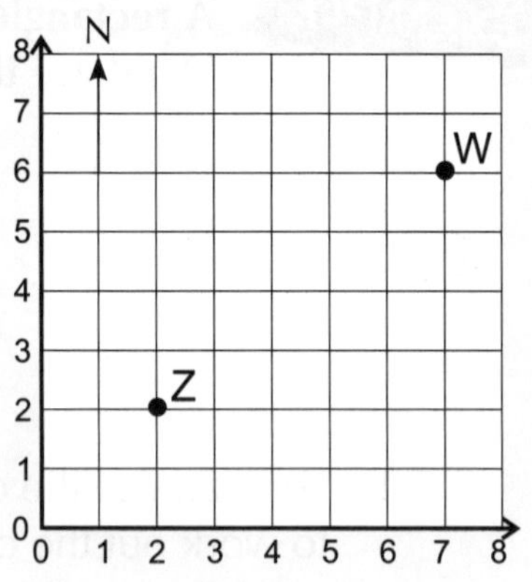

1) Starting at point Z, follow each route on the grid.
2) Remember, you're looking for the route that finishes at point W.

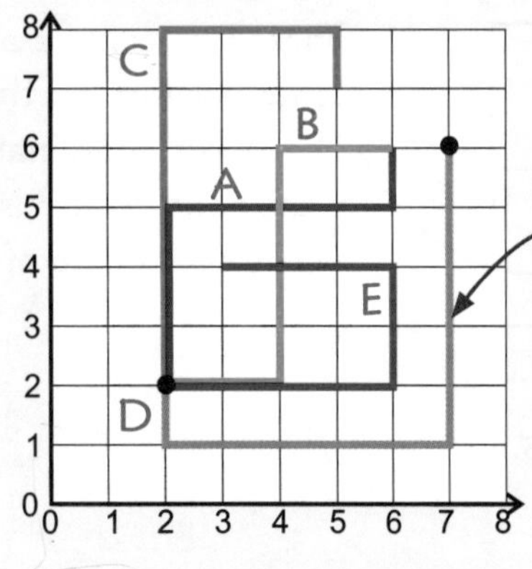

D is the only route that will lead Abi to her school.

So, option D is the correct answer.

Coordinates

Yohan draws a square on a grid. The coordinates of the four corners are (3, 5), (7, 5), (3, 9) and (7, 9). Which of the following points is inside Yohan's square?

A (7, 3) **B (6, 4)** **C (9, 8)** **D (6, 8)** **E (5, 4)**

1) You can use the coordinates that you've been given to work out which of the coordinates is within the square.

   The x-coordinates of the corners of the square are 3, 7, 3 and 7.
   So to be inside the square, the point must have an x-coordinate between 3 and 7.

   The y-coordinates of the corners of the square are 5, 5, 9 and 9.
   So to be inside the square, the point must have a y-coordinate between 5 and 9.

   In option D, the x-coordinate (6) is between 3 and 7, and the y-coordinate (8) is between 5 and 9. So the point **(6, 8)** is inside Yohan's square.

2) That gives you the answer — option D is the only option that's inside the square.

Practice Questions

1) Nadine is plotting a parallelogram on this coordinate grid. She plots two of the corners at (1, 3) and (2, 6). Which of the following could be the coordinates of the other two corners?

   A (4, 3) and (5, 4) **B** (5, 5) and (7, 7) **C** (6, 5) and (6, 4)
   D (7, 6) and (6, 3) **E** (3, 2) and (4, 7)

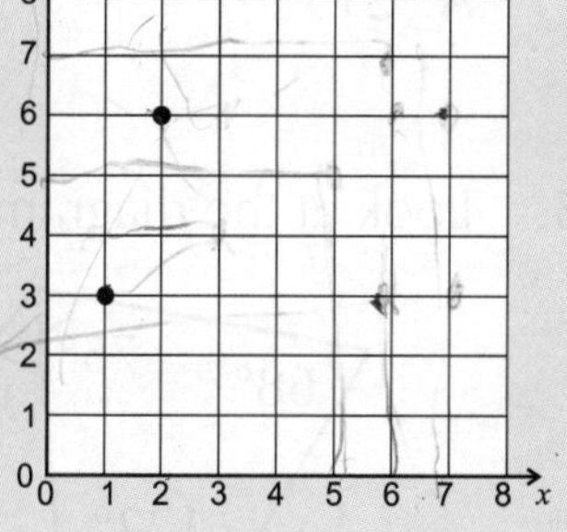

2) What will the coordinates of corner Y be after this triangle has been reflected in the mirror line?

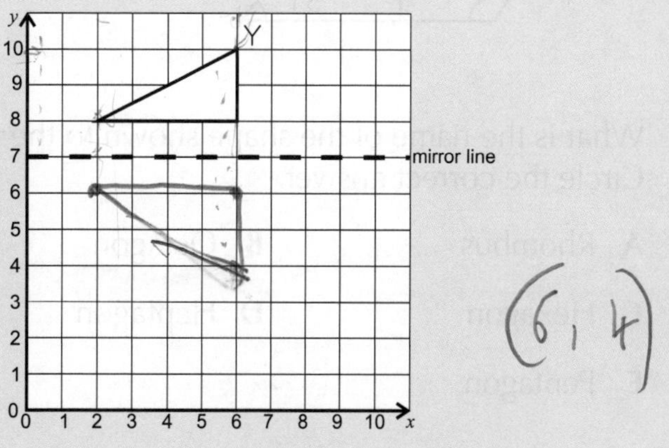

(6, 4)

Translate shapes one corner at a time...

When you're translating a shape, start by translating each point. Then join up all of the points with straight lines. You can check your work by making sure that the two shapes are identical.

Practice Questions

You've finished the whole Shape and Space section, so now it's time to test your skills with these Practice Questions. Have another look at any of the topics you're struggling with.

1. Estimate the size of angle w. Circle the correct answer.

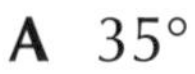

A 35° **B** 60° **C** 20° **D** 120° **E** 90°

2. Angles R and S lie on a straight line.
If angle R is 49°, what is angle S?

Answer: __________°

3. Look at the diagram below. What is the size of angle x?

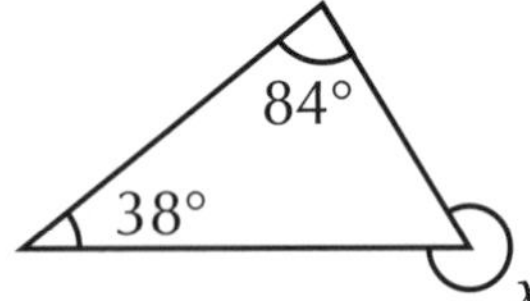

Answer: __________°

4. Angles g, h, j and k lie around a point. Angles g, h and j are obtuse.
Which of the following could be the size of angle k? Circle the correct answer.

A 215° **B** 90° **C** 150° **D** 73° **E** 98°

5. Look at the diagram below. What is the size of angle y?

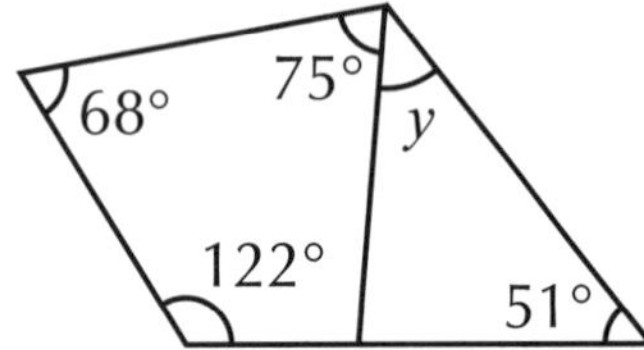

Answer: __________°

6. What is the name of the shape shown to the right?
Circle the correct answer.

A Rhombus **B** Octagon

C Hexagon **D** Heptagon

E Pentagon

7. Niamh has five identical straight sticks. She uses some or all of the sticks to make different shapes by laying them end to end. Which of the following shapes could she not have made? Circle the correct answer.

A Isosceles triangle **B** Trapezium **C** Regular pentagon **D** Rectangle

Practice Questions

8. Robbie is making a circular watch face. He paints the outside edge of the watch face silver. What part of the circle does he paint silver? Circle the correct answer.

   A Radius **B** Circumference **C** Diagonal **D** Vertex **E** Diameter

9. How many pairs of equal angles does a kite have?

   Answer: ________

10. A circular dinner plate has a diameter of 240 mm.
    What is the radius of the plate?

    Answer: ____________ mm

11. Jenny has drawn the isosceles triangle to the right.
    What is the size of angle *m*?

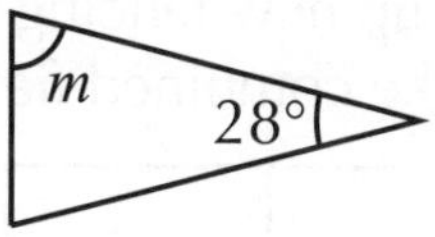

    m, 28°

    Answer: __________ °

12. Bassam used four different equilateral triangles to make the pattern shown below.
    What is the size of angle *b*?

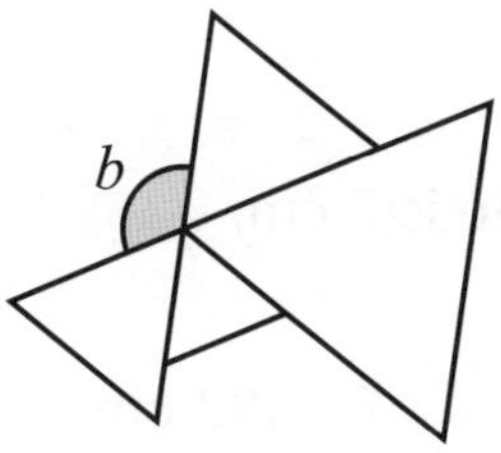

    b

    Answer: __________ °

13. Linh has been asked to draw an irregular quadrilateral.
    Which of the following shapes should she not draw? Circle the correct answer.

    A Rhombus **B** Kite **C** Square **D** Rectangle **E** Parallelogram

14. A regular heptagon has a perimeter of 84 cm.
    What is the length of each side?

    Answer: _________ cm

15. George is painting the lines on the outside of the rugby pitch shown below.
    One can of paint covers 100 m. How many cans of paint will he need?

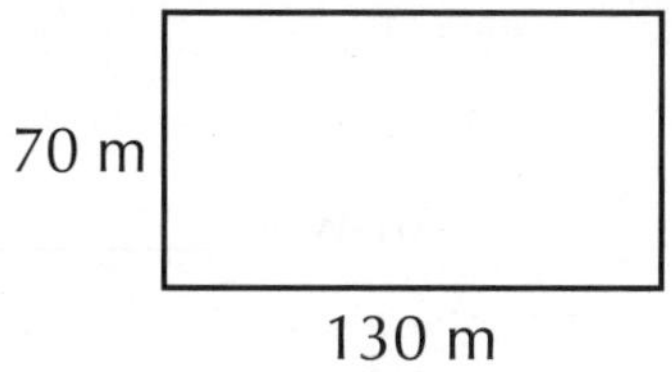

    70 m

    130 m

    Answer: __________

Practice Questions

16. Rhys uses three identical regular pentagons to make the pattern below.
Each pentagon has a perimeter of 35 cm.
What is the perimeter of the triangle in the centre of the pattern?

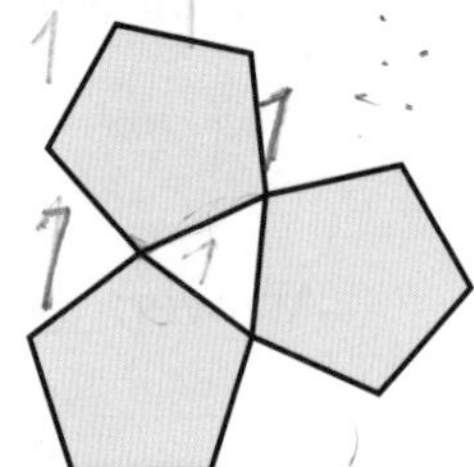

Answer: __________ cm

17. Irene owns field A, which has a fence all the way around the outside of it. She buys field B and wants to combine the two fields. She removes the section of fence between them and puts up new fencing around the rest of field B. How much longer is the new fence around the combined fields than the original fence around field A?

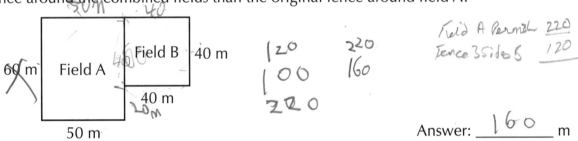

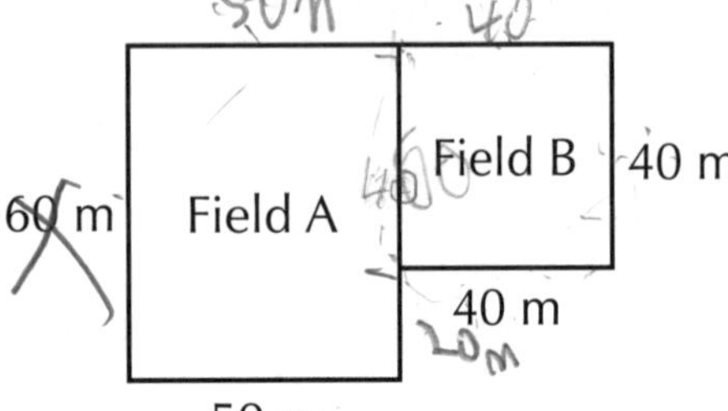

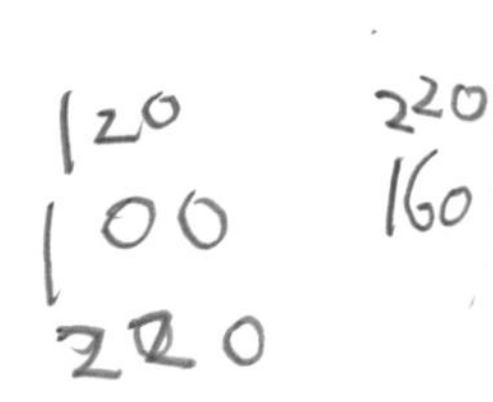

Answer: __________ m

18. A rectangle has an area of 56 cm². If the width of the rectangle is 7 cm, what is its length? Circle the correct answer.

A 5 cm **B** 6 cm **C** 7 cm **D** 8 cm **E** 392 cm

19. A ship is flying the flag shown below. What is the area of the flag?

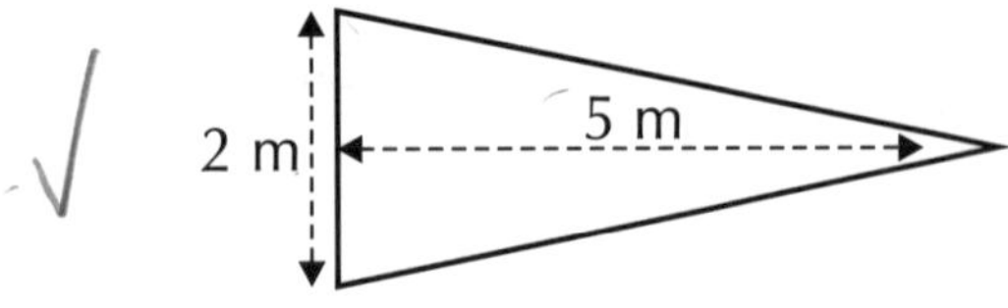

Answer: __________ m²

20. What is the area of the shape shown below?

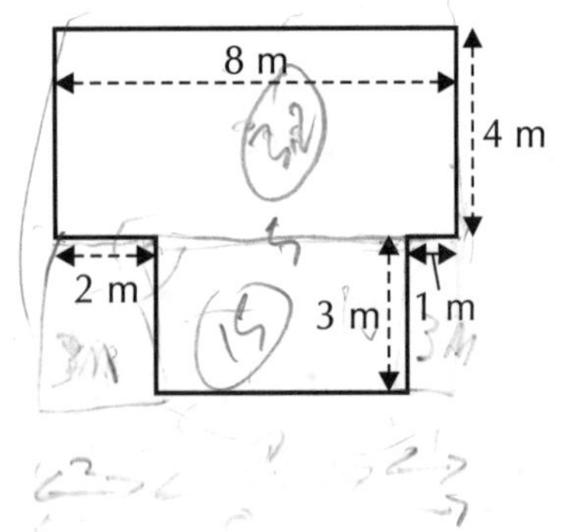

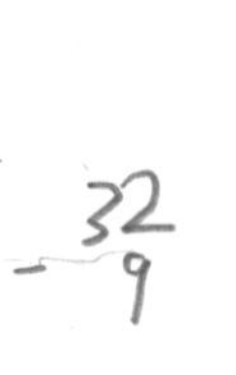

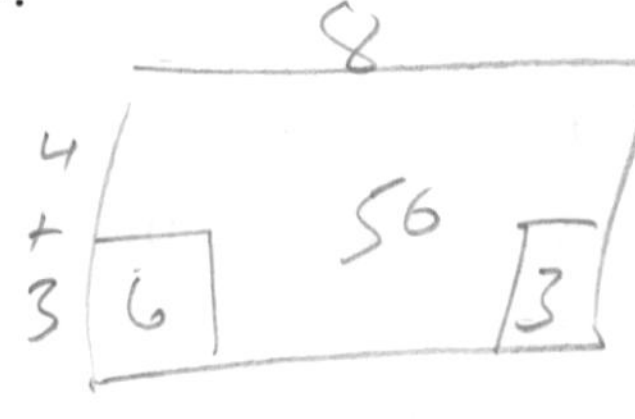

Answer: __________ m²

Practice Questions

21. Which of these shapes has the most lines of symmetry? Circle the correct answer.

    A Regular pentagon **B** Equilateral triangle **C** Square **D** Rhombus

22. How many lines of symmetry does the shape below have?

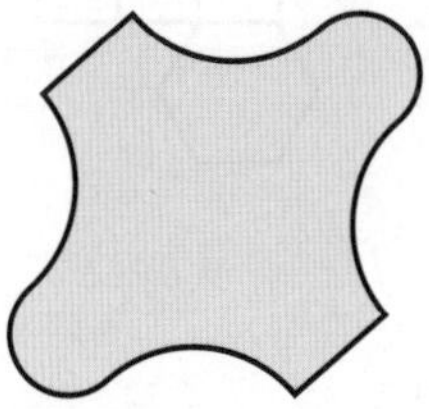

    Answer: ___________

23. What shape is made when this half shape is reflected in the mirror line? Circle the correct answer.

    mirror line

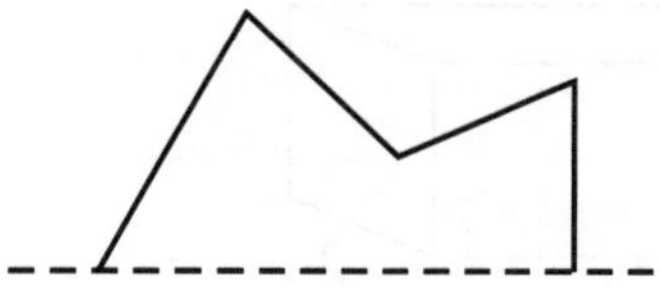

    A Octagon **B** Hexagon **C** Pentagon **D** Heptagon **E** Quadrilateral

24. Tessa has made a prism with 7 faces. What shape are the end faces? Circle the correct answer.

    A Square **B** Triangle **C** Hexagon **D** Heptagon **E** Pentagon

25. How many vertices does a triangle-based pyramid have?

    Answer: ___________

26. Jay has made the net shown below. What shape will be made when the net is folded?

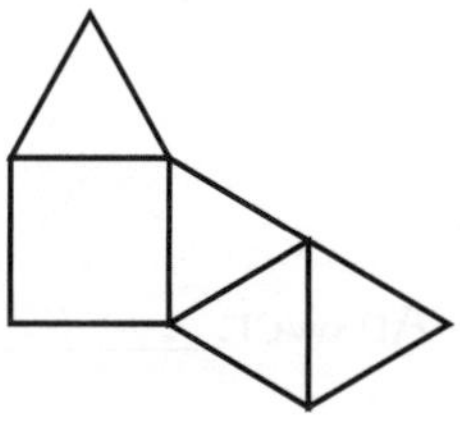

    Answer: ___________________________________

27. Marlon is putting sugar cubes into the container shown below. If the side length of each sugar cube is 2 cm, how many sugar cubes can he fit in the container?

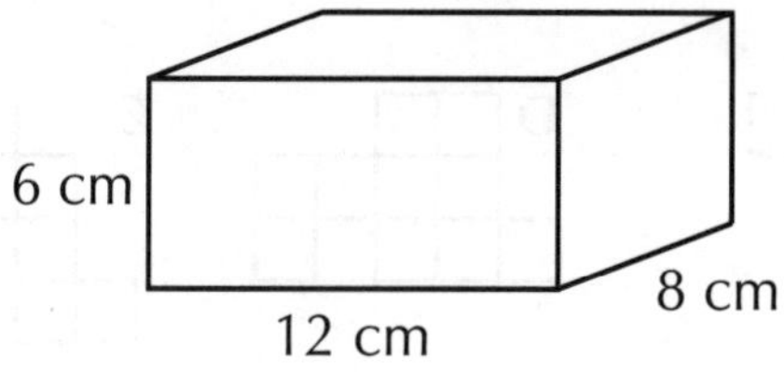

    6 cm

    12 cm

    8 cm

    Answer: ___________

Practice Questions

28. Which of these nets will not fold to make a prism? Circle the correct answer.

A 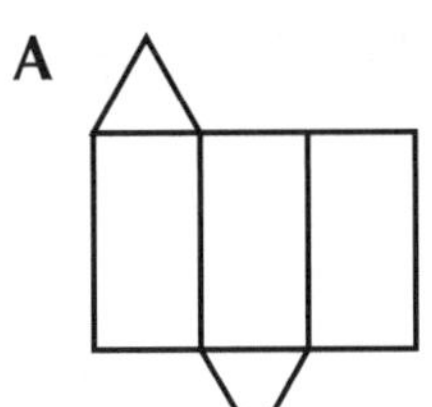

B 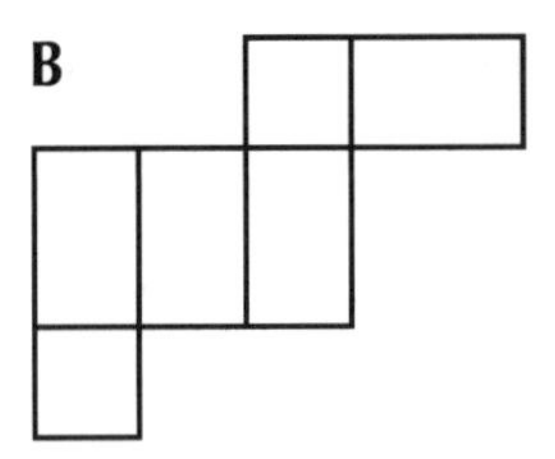

C 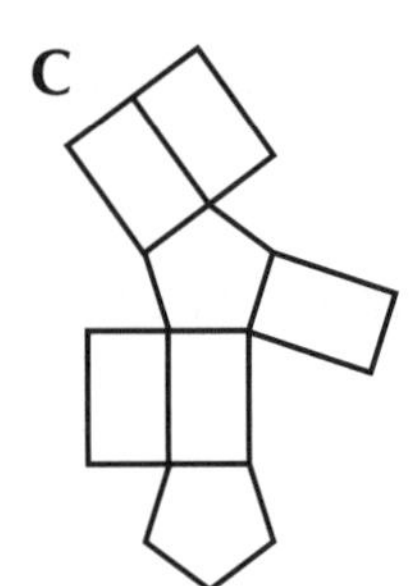

D 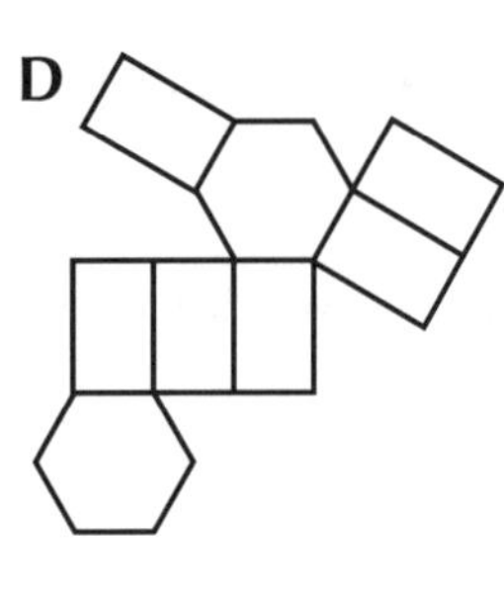

29. Meera's planter is shown below. The planter can hold 5 m^3 of soil.
What is the length of the planter?

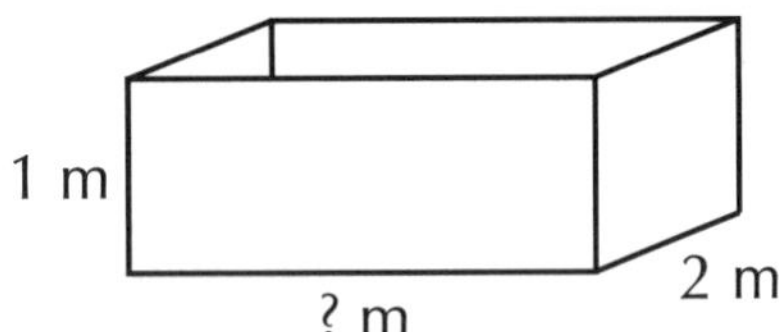

Answer: ____________ m

30. Olly has 400 cm^3 of water in a jug. He pours all of the water into the empty container shown below. How much more water does he need to add to fill the container?

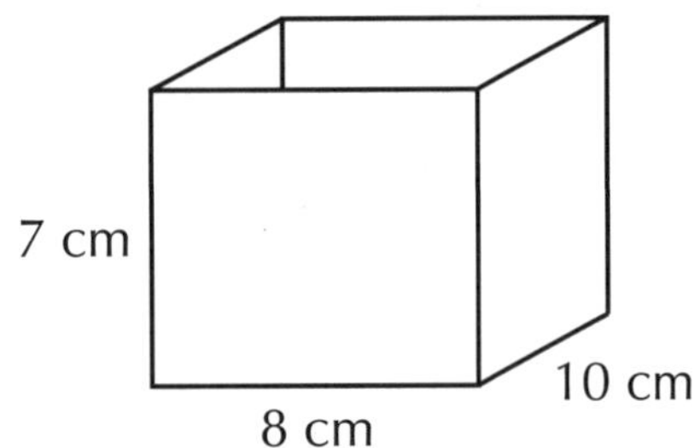

Answer: ________________ cm^3

31. Marianne used six wooden cubes to make the shape below.
She then painted the outside of the shape. How many cube faces did she paint?

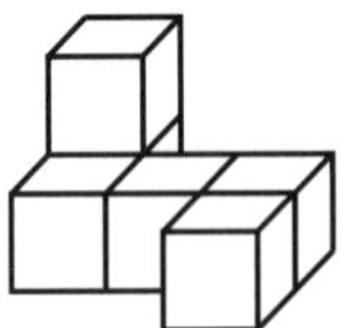

Answer: ____________

32. Robert has cut these two shapes out of squared paper.
He arranges them to make a new shape without overlapping the original shapes. Which of the following shapes could he have made? Circle the correct answer.

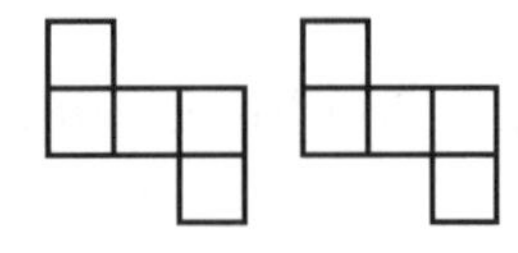

A 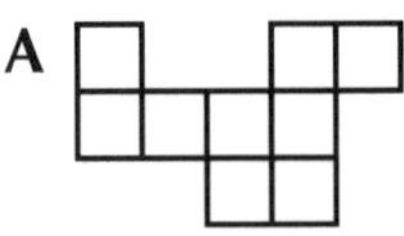

B 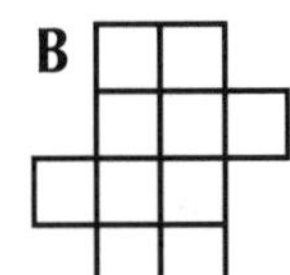

C 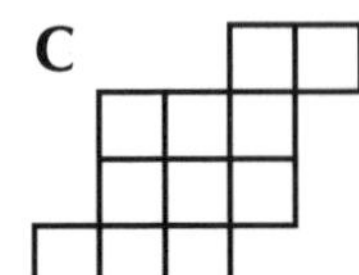

D 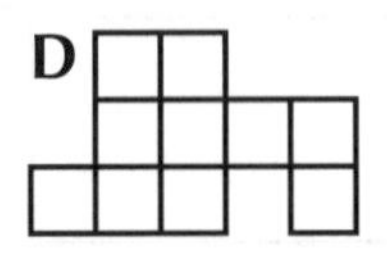

E 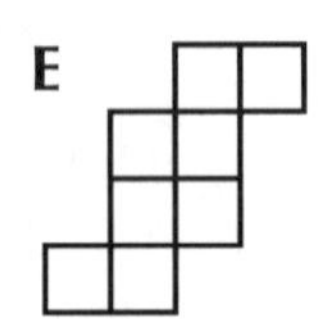

Practice Questions

33. Nneka starts at point X. She moves 3 squares east and then 6 squares north. In which direction would she then need to move to go straight to point Y? Circle the correct answer.

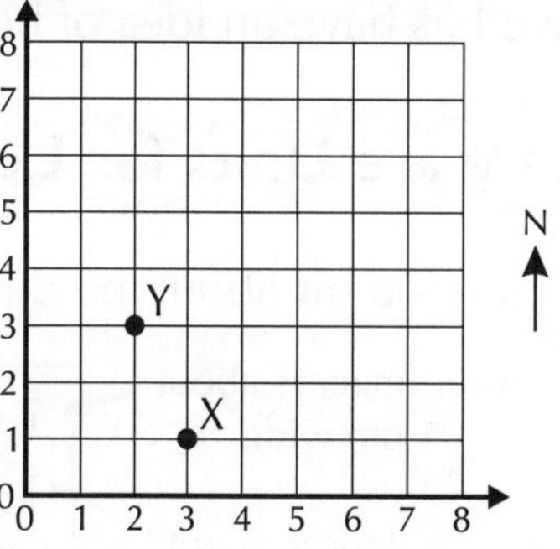

 **A** West  **B** South-east **C** North-west

 **D** North  **E** South-west

34. The shape shown below is a square. What are the coordinates of corner H?

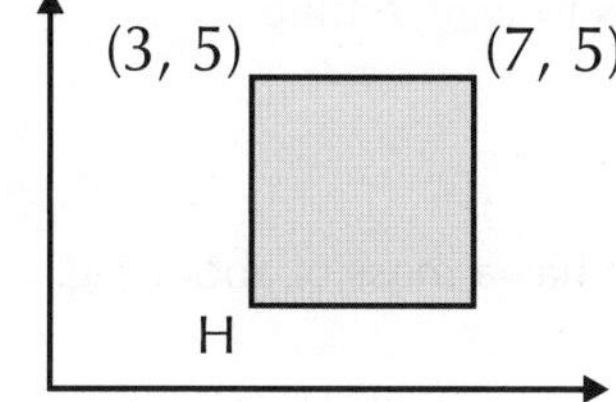

Answer: ______________

Alec has drawn the shape shown to the right.

35. What are the coordinates of point A when Alec reflects the shape in the mirror line?

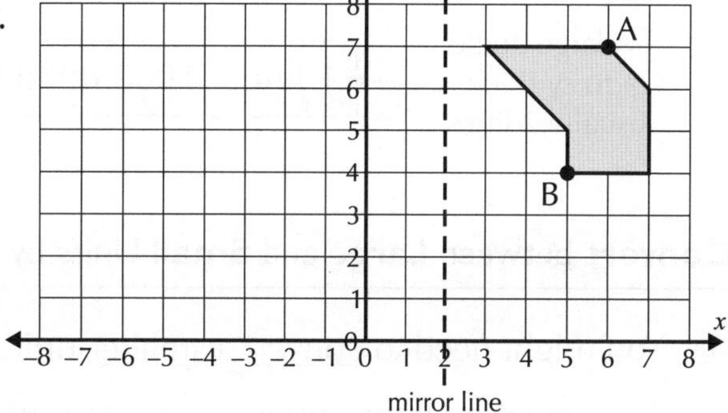

Answer: ______________

36. Alec translates the original shape 2 squares down and 8 squares to the left. What are the coordinates of point B on the translated shape?

Answer: ______________

37. Ruby translates a shape as shown below. What are the coordinates of point T?

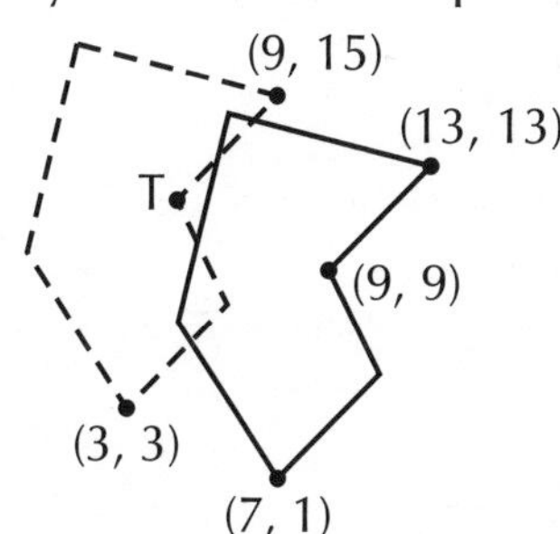

Answer: ______________

38. A map of a city square has been drawn on a coordinate grid. The four corners of the square are located at (4, 6), (8, 6), (8, 10) and (4, 10). Which of the following could be the coordinates of a statue located in the square? Circle the correct answer.

A (3, 7) **B** (5, 9) **C** (12, 11) **D** (9, 7) **E** (7, 5)

Units

For the exam, you'll need to be able to convert between different size units of measurement, as well as have an idea of how big each one is.

There are Units for **Length, Mass** and **Volume**

1) Here's a bit about the different units of length:

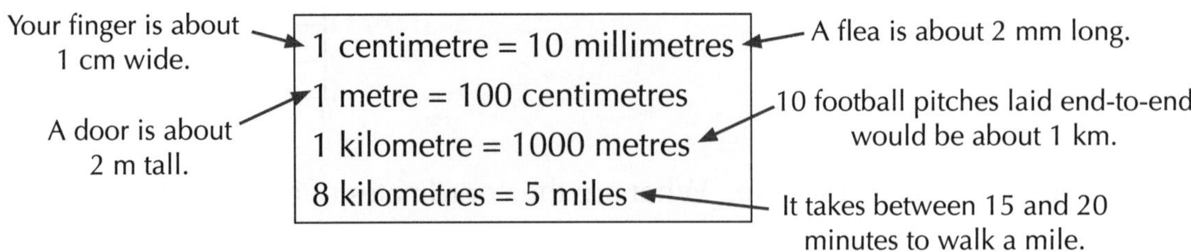

Your finger is about 1 cm wide.
1 centimetre = 10 millimetres
A flea is about 2 mm long.
A door is about 2 m tall.
1 metre = 100 centimetres
1 kilometre = 1000 metres
10 football pitches laid end-to-end would be about 1 km.
8 kilometres = 5 miles
It takes between 15 and 20 minutes to walk a mile.

2) Here's a bit about the different units of mass:

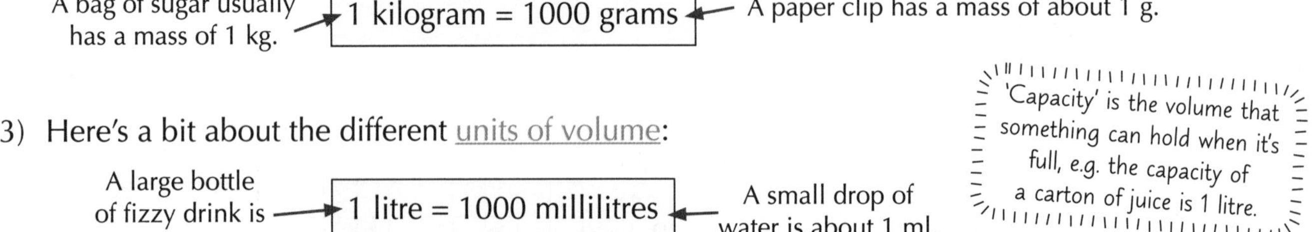

A bag of sugar usually has a mass of 1 kg.
1 kilogram = 1000 grams
A paper clip has a mass of about 1 g.
'Capacity' is the volume that something can hold when it's full, e.g. the capacity of a carton of juice is 1 litre.
A large bottle of fizzy drink is usually 2 litres.
1 litre = 1000 millilitres
A small drop of water is about 1 ml.

3) Here's a bit about the different units of volume:

Convert between **Large** and **Small** Units by **Multiplying** or **Dividing**

1) You might need to convert a smaller unit into a larger unit or a larger unit into a smaller one.
2) To convert a larger unit to a smaller unit you need to multiply. For example:

> To convert a mass that's in kg to a mass that's in g, multiply by 1000 (because there are 1000 g in a kg).
> 3.6 kg ⟶ 3.6 × 1000 = 3600 g

3) To convert a smaller unit to a larger unit you need to divide. For example:

> To convert a length that's in cm to a length that's in m, divide by 100 (because there are 100 cm in a m).
> 40 cm ⟶ 40 ÷ 100 = 0.4 m

Learn how to **Convert** between **Miles** and **Kilometres**

1) To convert km to miles, divide by 8 then times by 5. For example:

> 72 km ⟶ 72 ÷ 8 = 9, then 9 × 5 = 45 miles

2) To convert miles to km, divide by 5 then times by 8. For example:

> 55 miles ⟶ 55 ÷ 5 = 11, then 11 × 8 = 88 km

Units

11+ Example Questions

EXAMPLE:

Which of the following statements is true?

A There are 100 000 millilitres in 10 litres
B There are 100 000 grams in 10 kilograms
C There are 100 000 millimetres in 1 kilometre
D There are 100 000 centimetres in 1 kilometre
E There are 100 000 millimetres in 0.1 metres

1) Take each statement in turn and check whether it's true.

A 1 litre = 1000 ml, so 10 litres = 10 × 1000 ml = 10 000 ml — false.

B 1 kg = 1000 g, so 10 kg = 10 × 1000 g = 10 000 g — false.

C 1 km = 1000 m, 1 m = 100 cm and 1 cm = 10 mm,
so 1 km = 1000 × 100 × 10 mm = 1 000 000 mm — false.

D 1 km = 1000 m and 1 m = 100 cm,
so 1 km = 1000 × 100 cm = 100 000 cm — true. So the answer is D.

2) If you have time, check your answer by making sure E is false.

E 0.1 m = 10 cm and 1 cm = 10 mm, so 0.1 m = 10 × 10 mm = 100 mm,
so statement E is also false.

This glass holds 0.5 litres when it is full.
Which of the following is most likely to be the volume of water in it?

A 15 ml **B 165 ml** **C 330 ml**
D 33 ml **E 500 ml**

1) Work out how many millilitres of water there would be in a full glass.

1 litre = 1000 ml, so in 0.5 litres
there will be 1000 ml ÷ 2 = 500 ml.

2) Estimate the fraction of the glass that is filled.

It's about one third full. So the volume of water in the glass
will be about one third of 500 ml.
500 ml ÷ 3 is a hard calculation, so estimate using an easier calculation
— 600 ml ÷ 3 = 200 ml.

600 ml is larger than 500 ml, so you'd expect the answer
to be a bit smaller than 200 ml.

3) Check which of the choices match your estimate.

There's only one that's close — 165 ml, so the answer must be B.

Units

Jo has 1.6 kg of hot chocolate powder. She puts 30 g of powder in each of 5 mugs of hot water. How much hot chocolate powder does Jo have left?

A 1.57 kg B 1.3 kg C 1.45 kg D 0.1 kg E 1.585 kg

1) First work out how many grams of hot chocolate powder have been used.
   30 g in each of 5 mugs is a total of 30 × 5 = 150 g.

2) To find out how much hot chocolate powder is left you need to subtract 150 g from 1.6 kg, so make the units the same.
   The answers are in kg, so make the units both kg. ⟶ 150 g ÷ 1000 = 0.15 kg

3) Now subtract to find the mass of hot chocolate powder left.
   1.6 kg – 0.15 kg = 1.45 kg. So the answer is C.

A stalactite is hanging from a cave ceiling. It is currently 22 cm long. If it grows at a rate of 0.2 mm per year, how long, in centimetres, will it be in 200 years' time?

1) First, find out how much the stalactite will grow in 200 years by multiplying 0.2 mm by 200.
   The quick way to do 0.2 × 200 is to work out 0.2 × 100, and multiply the result by 2:
   0.2 × 100 = 20, 20 × 2 = 40 mm

2) You need to add the new growth to the stalactite's current length — but first make sure the units are the same.
   As you want the final answer in cm, convert the new growth to cm.
   1 cm = 10 mm, so divide 40 mm by 10 to get the number of cm: 40 ÷ 10 = 4 cm

3) Now add the current length and the new growth to find the length in 200 years' time.
   Length of stalactite = 22 cm + 4 cm = 26 cm

Practice Questions

1) Which of the following is most likely to be the mass of Tim's schoolbag with all of his books in?
   A 0.3 g **B** 3 g **C** 30 g **D** 3 kg **E** 30 kg

2) There are 28.75 litres of soup. 350 ml is spilt, and the rest is divided into 400 ml servings. How many servings are there?

3) Ashanti's stride is 50 cm. How many strides must she take to walk 10 km?
   A 20 000 **B** 2000 **C** 200 000 **D** 500 **E** 5000

Learn the conversions for length, mass and volume...

The question might not specifically ask you to convert units, but if it uses a mixture, you'll need to convert at least one of the measurements so they all use the same unit.

Time

There's a lot to remember for this topic. Time to get prepared...

There are lots of **Different Units** for **Measuring Time**

1) Here's how some of the different units of time are related to each other.

   1 minute = 60 seconds
   1 hour = 60 minutes
   1 day = 24 hours
   1 year = 365 days (366 in a leap year)

   Leap years occur every 4 years. The extra day is added to February.

2) There are 7 days in a week and 52 weeks in a year.
3) Months are a bit more tricky — there are 12 months in a year, but the number of days in each month is different.
4) You can memorise the number of days in each month using this poem.

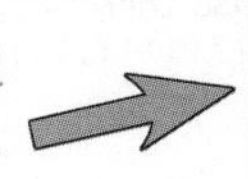

"30 days has September, April, June and November.
All the rest have 31, except February alone,
Which has 28 days clear, and 29 in each leap year."

Don't Get Confused between **Morning** and **Evening**

1) The hours on a 12-hour clock are shown by the numbers 1-12. The numbers then have either "am" or "pm" after them to show you whether it's morning or evening.
2) "am" runs from 12 midnight to 11:59 in the morning.
3) "pm" runs from 12 noon to 11:59 at night.
4) 24-hour time is the same as 12-hour time if it's morning, e.g. 9:00 am is the same as 09:00 on a 24-hour clock.
5) But you have to add on 12 hours if it's afternoon or evening, e.g. 1:00 pm is the same as 13:00 on a 24-hour clock.
6) When it gets to midnight, the 24-hour clock goes from 23:59 to 00:00.

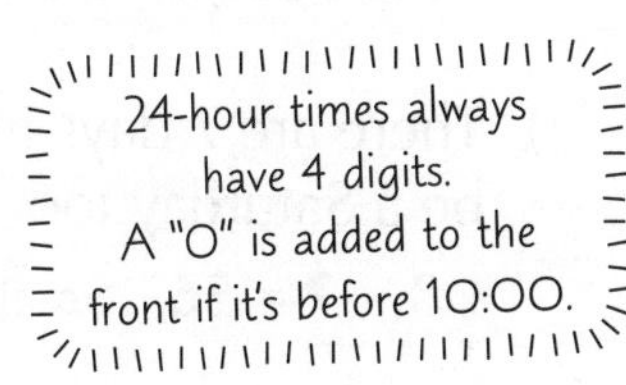

24-hour times always
have 4 digits.
A "0" is added to the
front if it's before 10:00.

11+ Example Questions

Which of the following 24-hour times is the same as ten to three in the afternoon?

A 15:10 B 02:50 C 15:50 D 14:50 E 03:50

1) "Ten to three" in the afternoon in 12-hour time is 2:50 pm.
2) Because it's in the afternoon, you add 12 hours to convert it to the 24-hour clock.

   2:50 + 12 hours = 14:50. So the answer is D.

Time

More **11+ Example** Questions

Jevan spent 45 minutes weeding and then 52 minutes mowing the grass. How long did he spend gardening?

A 1.37 hours **B 1 hour 37 minutes** **C 137 hours**
D 9.7 hours **E 97 hours**

1) Add the numbers of minutes together to get the total. ⟶ 45 + 52 = 97 minutes
2) Convert this to hours and minutes.
   There are 60 minutes in one hour. If you subtract 60 from 97 you're left with 37 minutes (97 – 60 = 37). So 97 minutes = **1 hour and 37 minutes** — **the answer is B.**

1.37 hours is not the same as 1 hour 37 minutes because there are 60 minutes in 1 hour and not 100.

Lorna was born on Saturday 8th March. What day of the week was Chizoba born on if she was born on 4th May the same year?

1) First, find how many days there are between the two dates. You can do this in short, easy stages — write down the numbers of days in each month between the dates.

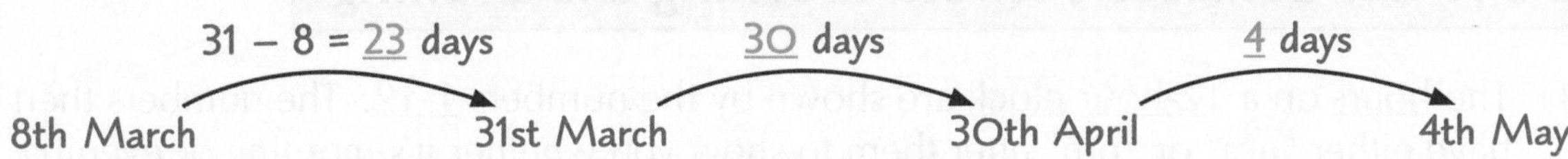

   Now add up the number of days: 23 + 30 + 4 = 57 days

2) There are 7 days in a week, so every 7th day after 8th March will be a Saturday too. Find the multiple of 7 which is closest to 57.
   8 × 7 = 56. So the 56th day after 8th March is a Saturday.

3) Now work out the day that 4th May falls on.
   There are 57 days between 8th March and 4th May, and the 56th day is a Saturday. So 4th May must be a **Sunday**.

To get to work one day, Elise walks for 12 minutes to get to the bus stop, then waits 6 minutes for her bus. The bus journey takes 18 minutes, then she walks for another 3 minutes to get to her office. She arrives at the office at 8:24 am. What time did she set off?

1) Add up the time Elise spends on each stage of her journey.
   12 + 6 + 18 + 3 = 39 minutes
2) Now find the time that is 39 minutes before 8:24 am.
   There are 24 minutes between 8 am and 8:24 am. This leaves 39 – 24 = 15 minutes of journey time before 8 am, so Elise set off at **7:45 am**.

You could work this out by counting back — i.e. count back 3 minutes from 8:24 am, then count back another 18 minutes, then 6, then 12.

Time

Hannah needs to get to Millham by 2 pm. What is the latest that she can get a bus from Dale Street?

Ulverstown	1254	1314	1334	1404
Dale Street	1259	1319	1339	1409
Railway Station	1308	1327	1348	1417
Canal Foot		1340		1430
Millham	1324	1347	1404	1437
Daltown	1345	1411	1425	1511

Times in timetables are often written without a colon, so 1254 is the same as 12:54.

1) Hannah needs to get to Millham by 2 pm, but the timetable is in 24-hour clock time. Convert 2 pm to the 24-hour clock.
   It's in the afternoon, so add 12 hours: 2 pm = 2 + 12 = 14:00

2) Now find the row for Millham. This lists the times that buses arrive there.

3) Find the latest time before 14:00 that Hannah can arrive at Millham.
   The bus that arrives at 14:04 is too late. The one before gets in at 13:47.

Ulverstown	1254	1314	1334	1404
Dale Street	1259	1319	1339	1409
Railway Station	1308	1327	1348	1417
Canal Foot		1340		1430
Millham	1324	1347	1404	1437
Daltown	1345	1411	1425	1511

4) Look up the column to find when this bus leaves Dale Street.
   It leaves Dale Street at 13:19.

Practice Questions

1) Some children's birthdays are given below. Which child is youngest?
   Meg — 14th May 2009 Fred — 16th March 2009 Geeta — 1st February 2008
   Jim — 28th December 2008 Max — 13th October 2009

2) Kerry completes one page of her Maths book each day, starting on 1st September. If there are 154 pages, in which month will she finish her book?

3) Jamie starts his homework at 4:53 pm. If he finishes it at 7:15 pm, how long did it take?
   A 2.22 hours **B** 202 minutes **C** 22 hours 2 minutes
   D 2 hours 22 minutes **E** 3 hours 38 minutes

Make sure you're happy with both 12-hour and 24-hour times...

The method used to find the difference between two dates can be used to find the difference between two times. E.g. to find the number of minutes between 9:46 am and 11:31 am:

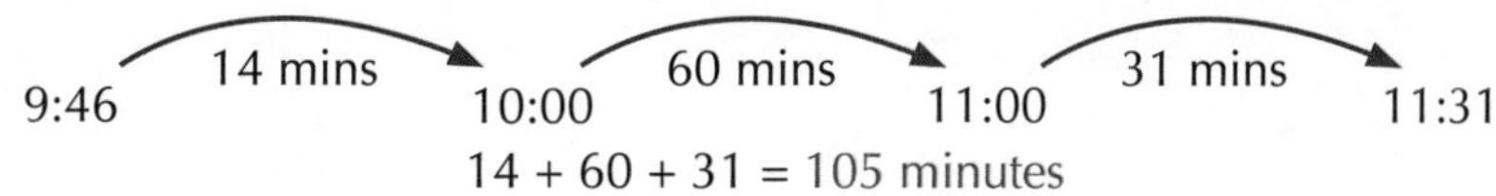

14 + 60 + 31 = 105 minutes

Practice Questions

Now you've finished the Units and Measures section,
check how much has sunk in with these Practice Questions.

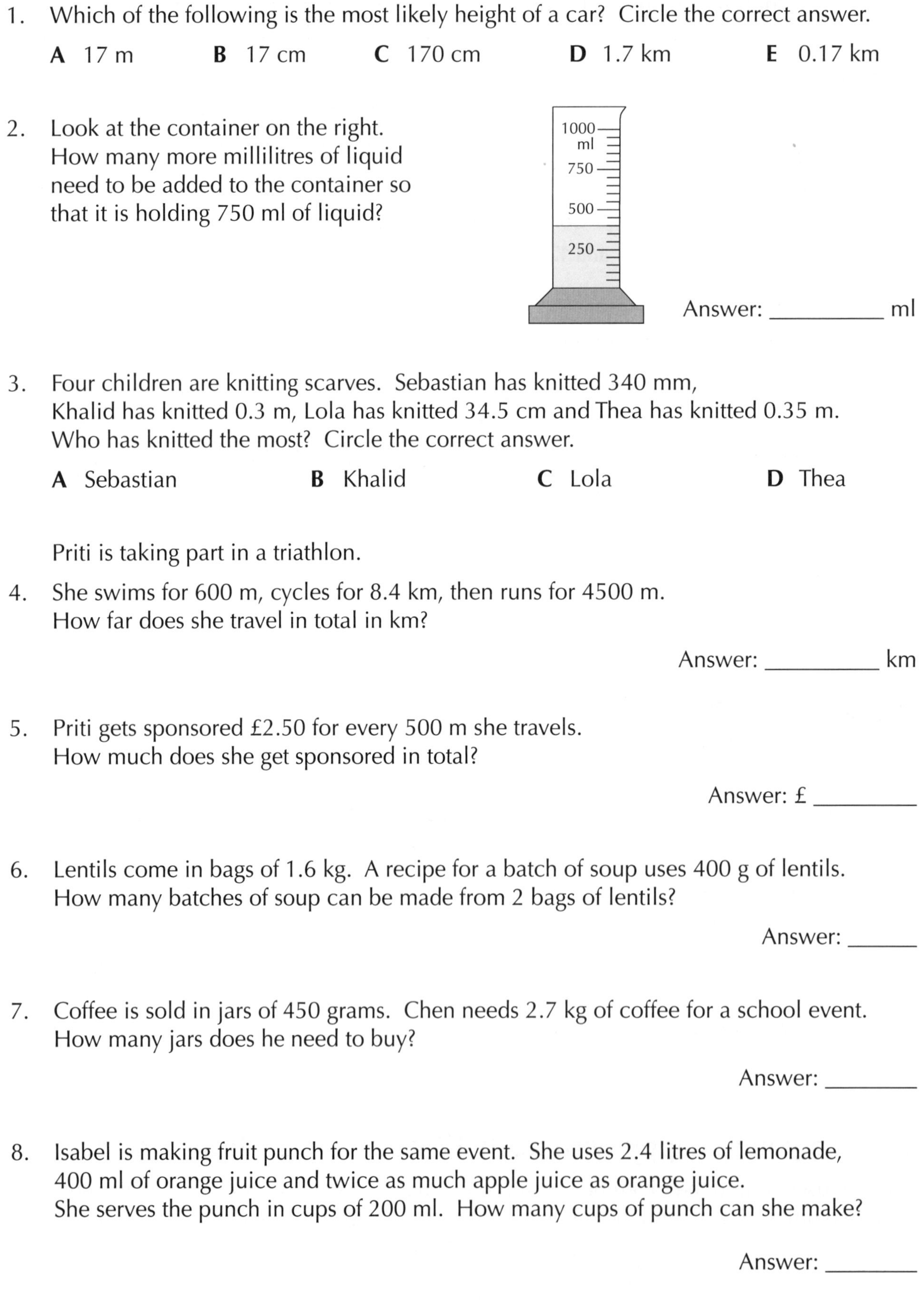

1. Which of the following is the most likely height of a car? Circle the correct answer.

   A 17 m **B** 17 cm **C** 170 cm **D** 1.7 km **E** 0.17 km

2. Look at the container on the right. How many more millilitres of liquid need to be added to the container so that it is holding 750 ml of liquid?

   Answer: ________ ml

3. Four children are knitting scarves. Sebastian has knitted 340 mm, Khalid has knitted 0.3 m, Lola has knitted 34.5 cm and Thea has knitted 0.35 m. Who has knitted the most? Circle the correct answer.

   A Sebastian **B** Khalid **C** Lola **D** Thea

Priti is taking part in a triathlon.

4. She swims for 600 m, cycles for 8.4 km, then runs for 4500 m. How far does she travel in total in km?

   Answer: ________ km

5. Priti gets sponsored £2.50 for every 500 m she travels. How much does she get sponsored in total?

   Answer: £ ________

6. Lentils come in bags of 1.6 kg. A recipe for a batch of soup uses 400 g of lentils. How many batches of soup can be made from 2 bags of lentils?

   Answer: ______

7. Coffee is sold in jars of 450 grams. Chen needs 2.7 kg of coffee for a school event. How many jars does he need to buy?

   Answer: ________

8. Isabel is making fruit punch for the same event. She uses 2.4 litres of lemonade, 400 ml of orange juice and twice as much apple juice as orange juice. She serves the punch in cups of 200 ml. How many cups of punch can she make?

   Answer: ________

Practice Questions

9. A digital watch shows the time 16:04. The watch is running 12 minutes fast.
   What is the correct time in the 12-hour clock? Circle the correct answer.

   A 16:16 **B** 15:52 **C** 4:52 pm **D** 3:52 pm **E** 4:16 pm

10. A netball tournament starts at 9:45 am and finishes at 1:20 pm.
    How long does it last for in hours and minutes?

    Answer: ______ hours ______ mins

11. Isla's birthday is on 14th July. Rory's birthday is 20 days before Isla's.
    What date is Rory's birthday?

    Answer: ____________________

12. Esme takes 5 minutes and 24 seconds to complete a puzzle.
    How long is this in seconds? Circle the correct answer.

    A 524 seconds **B** 324 seconds **C** 264 seconds **D** 384 seconds

Look at this train timetable.

North River	1118	1147	1203	1225	1241	1308
South Path	1136	1205	1221	1243	1259	1326
East Water	1202	1231	1247	1309		1352
West Mile	1219		1304		1342	1409

13. How long is the train journey from North River to East Water?

    Answer: _______ mins

14. Jiya needs to be in West Mile by 1:30 pm.
    What is the latest that she can catch a train from South Path?

    Answer: __________

15. Kofi has a piano lesson in North River. The lesson starts at 11:15 am and lasts for 35 minutes. The train station is 15 minutes away from his piano teacher's house.
    What is the earliest time Kofi can arrive at East Water?

    Answer: __________

16. Mr Adams lives 8 minutes away from the East Water train station.
    If he leaves his house at 11:55 am, how long will he have to wait for the next train?

    Answer: _______ mins

Mixed Problems

Some questions test your knowledge of more than one topic, so you might have to read a pie chart and work out some angles. The questions on these pages are examples, but you could be tested on any combination of topics.

11+ Example Questions

A cruise ship travels 30 $^1/_2$ kilometres every hour.
It left port at 7 pm on Monday and arrived at its destination at 1 am on Tuesday.

How far did it travel?

1) Work out how many hours the cruise ship was travelling for.

   On Monday the ship travelled for 5 hours between 7 pm and 12 am.
   On Tuesday the ship travelled for 1 hour between 12 am and 1 am.
   5 + 1 = 6 hours.

2) Now multiply 6 hours by 30$^1/_2$ kilometres.

   Use partitioning to find 6 × 30$^1/_2$. Partition 30$^1/_2$ into 30 and $^1/_2$.
   6 × 30 = 180, and 6 × $^1/_2$ = 3 (it's the same as half of 6).
   Add together your results: 180 + 3 = **183 km**.

3) The ship travelled 183 kilometres.

Penny packs 10 identical candles into a cuboid box. Each candle has a volume of 240 cm^3. The box is 30 cm long, 20 cm wide and 5 cm high.

What fraction of the volume of the box is taken up by the candles?

A $^1/_4$ **B** $^4/_5$ **C** $^3/_4$ **D** $^2/_5$ **E** $^3/_8$

1) First, multiply to find the total volume of 10 candles.

   The volume of one candle is 240 cm^3,
   so the volume of 10 candles is 10 × 240 = 2400 cm^3.

2) Then, calculate the volume of the box.

   Volume of a cuboid = length × width × height,
   so the volume of the box = 30 × 20 × 5 = 3000 cm^3.

3) Finally, write the volume of the candles as a fraction of the volume of the box.

   You need to simplify the fraction so it matches one of the options. → $^{2400}/_{3000}$ = $^{24}/_{30}$ = $^4/_5$ — the answer is B.

Mixed Problems

EXAMPLE: **Dylan has some shapes which have areas q and r.**

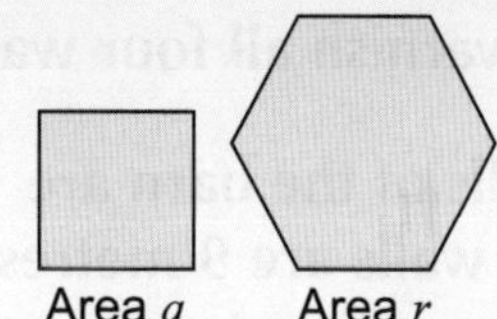
Area q
Area r

He cuts some of his shapes in half and makes a pattern.

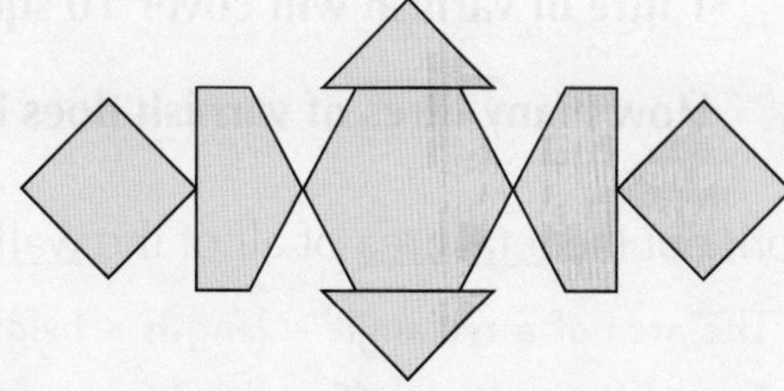

What is the area of the pattern?

A $2q + 3r$ **B** $3q + r$ **C** $3q + 2r$
D $3q + 4r$ **E** $4q + 4r$

Have a look back at pages 38-41 for more on algebra.

1) Work out what shapes make up the pattern.

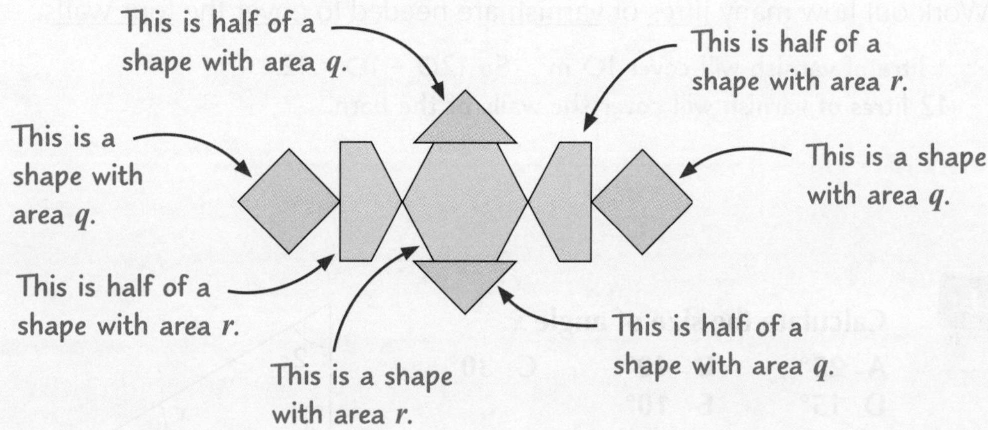
This is half of a shape with area q.
This is half of a shape with area r.
This is a shape with area q.
This is a shape with area q.
This is half of a shape with area r.
This is half of a shape with area q.
This is a shape with area r.

2) Now add together all of the areas.

There are two whole shapes and two half shapes with area q: $2 + ^1/_2 + ^1/_2 = 3$.
The pattern has a total of 3 shapes with area q, so these shapes have an area of $3q$.

There is one whole shape and two half shapes with area r: $1 + ^1/_2 + ^1/_2 = 2$.
The pattern has a total of 2 shapes with area r, so these shapes have an area of $2r$.

The total area of the pattern is the areas of the shapes added together, $3q + 2r$.

3) So the answer is C.

Always read mixed problem questions really carefully...

These questions can look quite difficult, but you just need to take your time with them. Work out what steps you need to follow to get to the answer before you start answering the question.

Mixed Problems

Cliff wants to varnish all four walls of his barn.

Two of the walls of the barn are 15 metres long and 2.5 metres high. The other two walls are 9 metres long and 2.5 metres high.

1 litre of varnish will cover 10 square metres.

How many litres of varnish does he need?

1) Work out the total area of all of the walls.

The area of a rectangle = length × height

Two of the walls are 15 m by 2.5 m, so the area of each wall is:
$15 \times 2.5 = (15 \times 2) + (15 \times 0.5) = 30 + 7.5 = 37.5 \text{ m}^2$

The other two walls are 9 m by 2.5 m, so the area of each wall is:
$9 \times 2.5 = (9 \times 2) + (9 \times 0.5) = 18 + 4.5 = 22.5 \text{ m}^2$

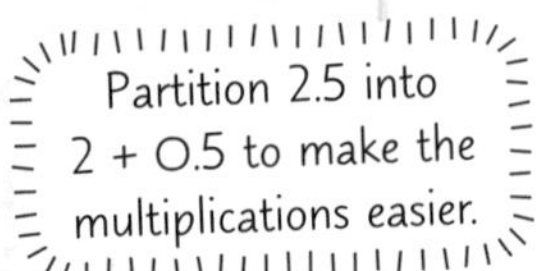

Partition 2.5 into
2 + 0.5 to make the
multiplications easier.

Add up the area of each wall:
$37.5 + 37.5 + 22.5 + 22.5 = 75 + 45 = 120 \text{ m}^2$

2) Work out how many litres of varnish are needed to cover the four walls.

1 litre of varnish will cover 10 m². So $120 \div 10 = 12$.
12 litres of varnish will cover the walls of the barn.

Calculate the size of angle *x*.

A 25°	**B 40°**	**C 30°**
D 15°	**E 10°**	

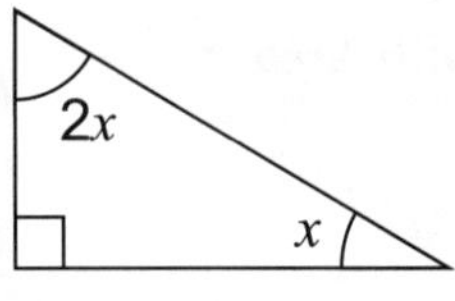

1) Use the information you have to make an equation.

Angles in a triangle add up to 180°.
One of the angles is a right angle (90°) so the other two angles must add up to 180° − 90° = 90°.

$2x + x = 90°$
So $3x = 90°$.

2) Use your equation to find the size of angle x.

Find x when $3x = 90°$.

$3x = 90°$
÷ 3 ÷ 3
$x = 30°$

The opposite of × 3 is ÷ 3, so divide both sides by 3.

That gives you the answer — x is 30°. C is correct.

Mixed Problems

EXAMPLE: **Jason's class conducted a survey. They asked the teachers who drove to school how many passengers they took with them.**

They collected their results in a bar chart.

What percentage of the teachers travelled with 3 passengers?

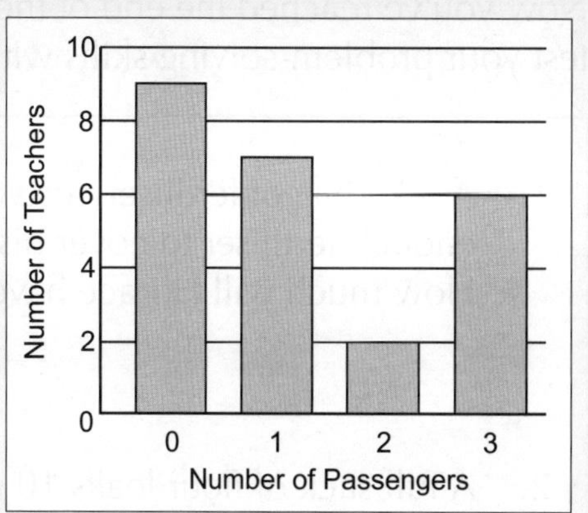

1) First work out how many teachers took part in the survey.

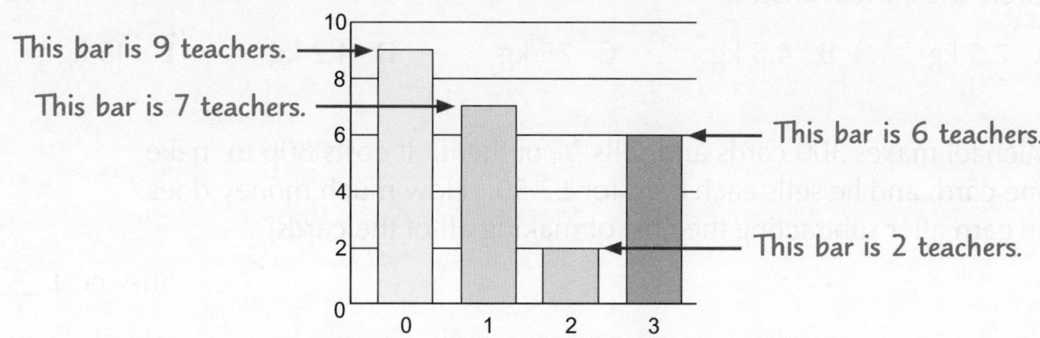

This bar is 9 teachers.
This bar is 7 teachers.
This bar is 6 teachers.
This bar is 2 teachers.

The total number of teachers is 9 + 7 + 2 + 6 = 24.

2) Now you can work out the percentage of teachers who travelled with 3 passengers.

6 teachers out of a total of 24 travelled with 3 passengers. This gives you the fraction $^6/_{24}$. This fraction can be simplified to $^1/_4$.

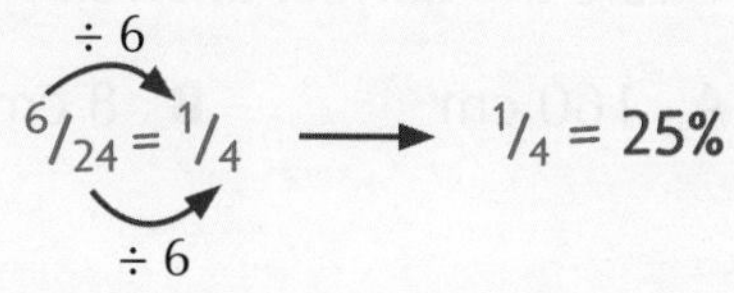

3) The percentage of teachers who travelled with 3 passengers is 25%.

Practice Questions

1) A swimming pool is 10 metres long, 10 metres wide and 1.6 metres deep. It costs 25p to fill 1 m³ of the pool with water. What is the cost of filling the pool to the top?

2) Mr O'Brian recorded the colour of the flowers in his garden in the pie chart shown. What percentage of his flowers were red?
A 5% **B** 12.5% **C** 25% **D** 42% **E** 54%

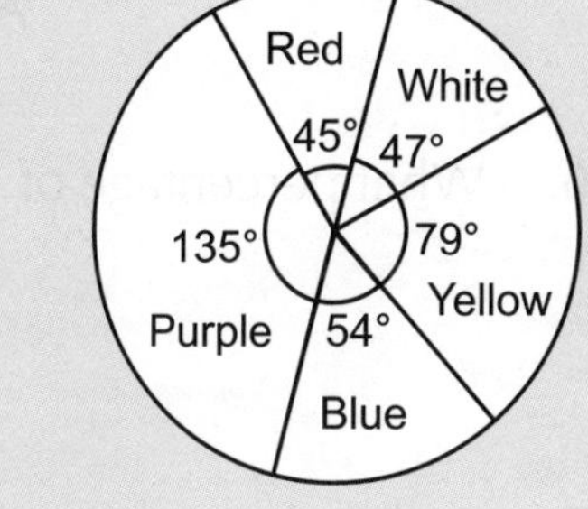

Revise any bits you find tricky...

Mixed question problems are a good way of seeing which topics you know really well. If there are any bits you're getting stuck on, go back and practise those topics a bit more.

Practice Questions

Now you've reached the end of the Mixed Problems section, test your problem-solving skills with these Practice Questions.

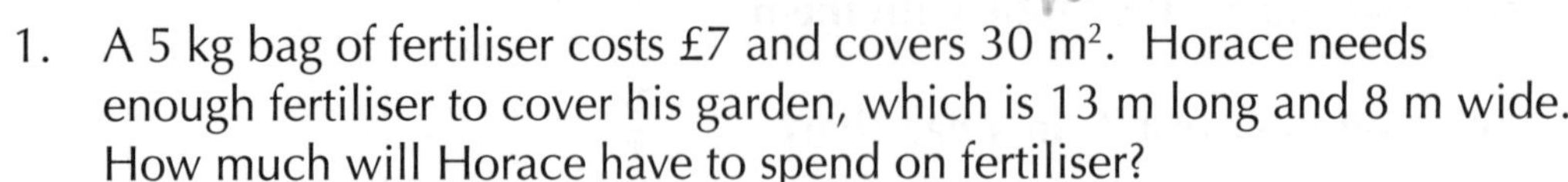

1. A 5 kg bag of fertiliser costs £7 and covers 30 m^2. Horace needs enough fertiliser to cover his garden, which is 13 m long and 8 m wide. How much will Horace have to spend on fertiliser?

   Answer: £ ________

2. A full sack of flour leaks 10 g of flour every second. After $7\frac{1}{2}$ minutes, all of the flour has leaked out of the sack. How much flour was in the sack originally, in kilograms? Circle the correct answer.

   A 7.5 kg **B** 4.5 kg **C** 75 kg **D** 4.2 kg **E** 45 kg

3. Michael makes 300 cards and sells $\frac{3}{5}$ of them. It costs 80p to make one card, and he sells each card for £2.50. How much money does he earn after subtracting the cost of making all of the cards?

   Answer: £ ________

4. A regular pentagon and a regular octagon have the same perimeter. Each side of the pentagon is 16 cm long. How long is each side of the octagon? Circle the correct answer.

   A 160 cm **B** 8 cm **C** 80 cm **D** 10 cm **E** 12 cm

Lei records how far she walks on five days and puts the distances on a line graph.

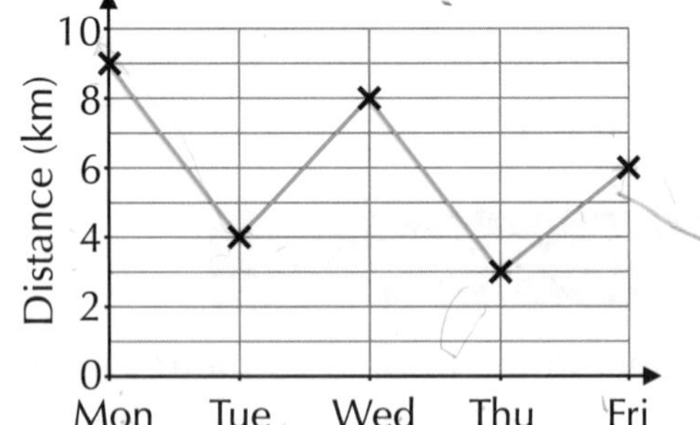

5. What is the mean distance she walks each day?

   Answer: ________ km

6. What percentage of the total distance does she walk on Monday?

   Answer: ________ %

7. A cleaning solution is made from bleach and water in the ratio 1 : 8. Kevin has a 750 ml bottle of bleach. He makes 2.7 litres of cleaning solution. How much bleach is left in the bottle?

   Answer: ________ ml

Practice Questions

8. Imogen buys a bag of sweets and eats 5% of the bag each day. How many days will it take her to eat $^3/_4$ of the bag? Circle the correct answer.

   A 20 **B** 12 **C** 5 **D** 18 **E** 15

9. Chinelo draws a shape on a coordinate grid. The corners of the shape have coordinates (x, y), $(x + 2, y)$, $(x, y - 6)$ and $(x + 2, y - 6)$. What type of shape has she drawn?

   Answer: ____________

10. Caroline runs 15 km to raise money for charity. She is sponsored £5 per kilometre for the first 10 km, then £8 for each kilometre after that. What is the mean amount she is sponsored per kilometre for her run? Circle the correct answer.

    A £6.50 **B** £6 **C** £9 **D** £5 **E** £7

Some items for sale at a cafe are shown on the right.

Menu	
Coffee	£1.80
Tea	£1.50
Brownie	£2.30
Cookie	£1.60

11. Linda has a £20 note. She buys a coffee, a tea and a brownie. What percentage of £20 does she have left?

    Answer: ________ %

12. Annabel and Tamal buy two coffees, a brownie and a cookie. They share the cost in the ratio 2 : 1. How much does Annabel pay?

    Answer: £ ________

13. What fraction of the whole numbers from 1 to 20 are prime? Circle the correct answer.

    A $^1/_8$ **B** $^1/_4$ **C** $^2/_5$ **D** $^8/_{10}$ **E** $^9/_{20}$

14. Look at the diagram below. What is the value of p?

    $3p$ $2p$ 65° 85°

    Answer: ________ °

15. Tafsir planted a flower on 5th May. It was 5 cm tall when it was planted, and it grew 4 mm each day. How tall was the flower on 16th June? Circle the correct answer.

    A 21.4 cm **B** 16.8 cm **C** 24.4 cm **D** 21.8 cm **E** 19.2 cm

Mixed Practice Tests

If you want to attempt each mixed practice test more than once, you will need to print **multiple-choice answer sheets** for these questions from our website — go to www.cgpbooks.co.uk/11plusanswersheets. If you'd prefer to answer them in standard write-in format, either write your answers in the spaces provided or circle the **correct answer** from the options **A** to **E**.

Give yourself **10 minutes** to complete this test. Write down your score in the box at the end.

Test 1

1. How many lines of symmetry does a regular octagon have?

Answer: ______

2. What fraction of the shape on the right is shaded?

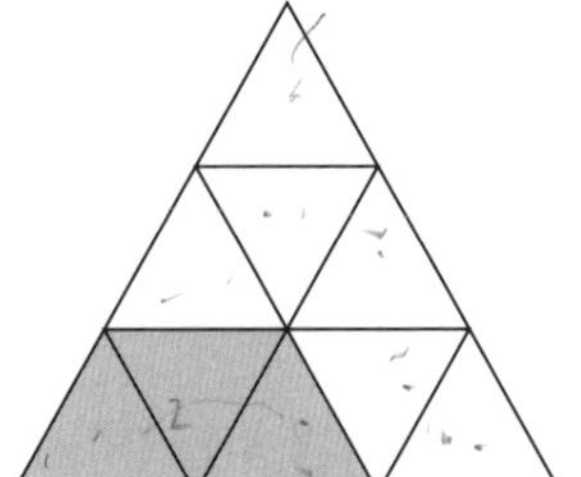

A $^1/_4$ **B** $^1/_2$ **C** $^3/_8$ **D** $^2/_5$ **E** $^1/_3$

3. Charlotte calls her friend at 4:55 pm. The phone call lasts for 37 minutes. At what time does the call end?

A 17:37 **B** 05:32 **C** 17:43 **D** 17:32 **E** 15:37

4. 393, 404, 415, ☐, 437, ...

What number should go in the box in the sequence above?

Answer: ______

5. The table on the right shows the different types of cake sold at a bakery in one day. How many lemon cupcakes did they sell?

	Large cakes	Cupcakes	Total
Lemon	4		
Chocolate		7	
Vanilla	3		12
Total	10		30

A 4 **B** 3 **C** 7 **D** 10 **E** 8

Mixed Practice Tests

6. Elsie has £271.42 in her savings. She gets £34.50 for her birthday, and then she spends £214.95 on a bicycle. How much money does she have left?

Answer: £ ________

7. A cafe served 39 meals at lunch time. All of the meals were served with either chips or salad. Which statement below could be true?

A Half of the meals were served with chips.

B Twice as many meals were served with salad than with chips.

C Four more meals were served with chips than with salad.

D Three quarters of the meals were served with chips.

E Twelve more meals were served with salad than with chips.

8. The square on the coordinate grid is translated so that the new coordinates of P are (–1, 2). What are the new coordinates of point S?

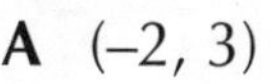

A (–2, 3) **B** (2, 1) **C** (1, 2)

D (3, –2) **E** (4, –2)

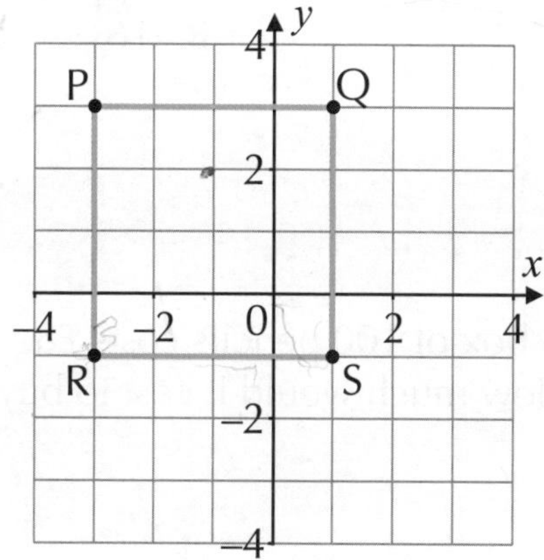

9. 1872 ÷ 12 = 156. What is 1872 ÷ 4?

Answer: ________

10. Amir asks 60 people if they prefer milk, white or dark chocolate. He puts the information in a pie chart. $^2/_5$ of the people he asked said they prefer milk chocolate and 35% said white chocolate. What angle will represent 'dark chocolate' on the pie chart?

Answer: ________ °

Total (out of 10): ☐

Mixed Practice Tests

Give yourself **10 minutes** to complete this test. Write down your score in the box at the end.

Test 2

1. Anna's hamster is 15 cm long, rounded to the nearest centimetre.
   What is the shortest possible length of her hamster?

   A 14.4 cm **B** 14.45 cm **C** 15.5 cm **D** 14.5 cm **E** 14 cm

2. What is 4030 ml in litres?

   Answer: ________ litres

3. Tony and Julian share 36 sweets in the ratio 5 : 4. How many sweets does Julian get?

   A 15 **B** 16 **C** 24 **D** 12 **E** 20

4. A box of 100 pencils costs £8.
   How much would it cost to buy 2400 pencils?

   Answer: £ ________

5. Hasif buys 8 postcards from a shop. Each postcard costs 60p.
   How much change will he get if he pays with a £5 note?

   A £0.60 **B** 40p **C** £1.20 **D** 80p **E** 20p

6. What is the area of the shape on the right?

   Answer: ________ cm²

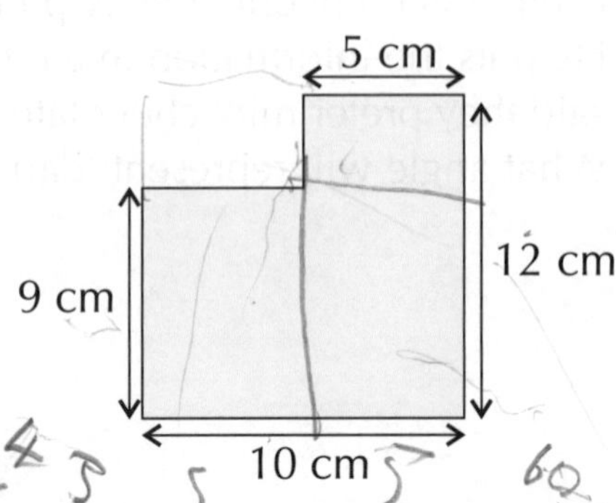

Mixed Practice Tests

7. Winston was born in MMIX. The church in his village was built 352 years before he was born. In what year, in digits, was the church built?

Answer: ________

8. Milly measures the lengths of some keys.
The lengths are 6 cm, 8 cm, 9.5 cm, 5 cm and 6.5 cm.
What is the mean length of the keys?

A 7.5 cm **B** 8.5 cm **C** 7 cm **D** 6.5 cm **E** 9 cm

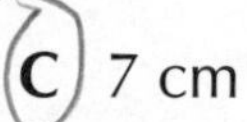

9. Lucy makes 729 hair clips. She sells them in packs of 12.
She fills as many packs as she can. How many hair clips does she have left over?

Answer: ________

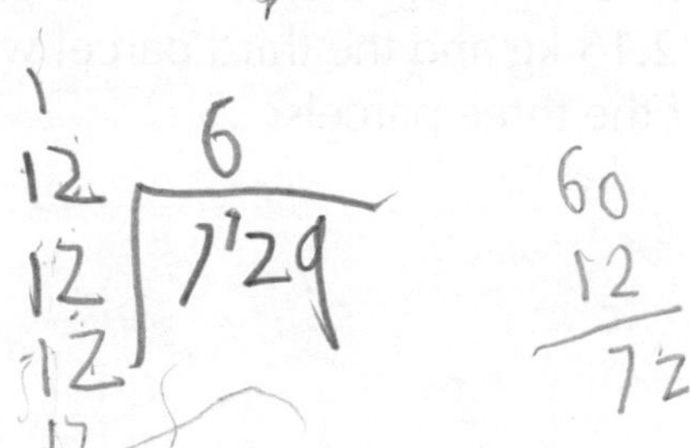

10. This pictogram shows where Year 6 pupils went on their last holiday.
What fraction of the pupils went to the USA on holiday?

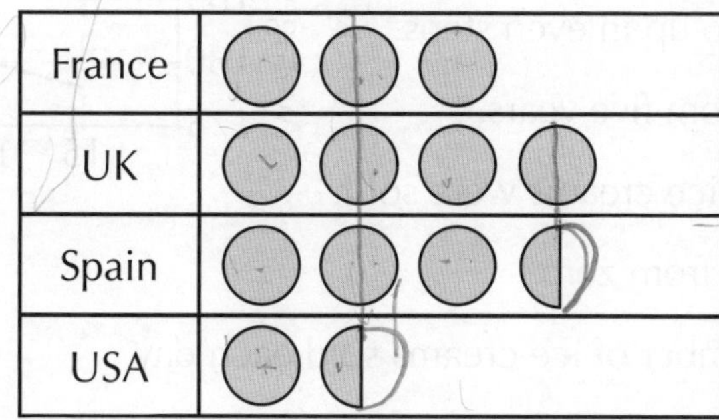

Key: ● = 2 pupils

A 1/5 **B** 3/12 **C** 1/3 **D** 1/2 **E** 1/8

Total (out of 10): ☐

Mixed Practice Tests

Give yourself **10 minutes** to complete this test. Write down your score in the box at the end.

Test 3

1. Bernie describes a shape. He says, "It has four sides that are all the same length, two pairs of parallel sides and two pairs of equal angles." What is Bernie's shape?

   A Square **B** Kite **C** Rectangle **D** Trapezium **E** Rhombus

2. One day in February, the temperature in Madrid is 12 °C. On the same day, the temperature in Oslo is –4 °C. How much warmer is it in Madrid?

   Answer: ______ °C

3. What is 25% of 48?

   A 12 **B** 6 **C** 16 **D** 18 **E** 24

4. Ramin has three parcels to deliver. The first parcel weighs 3.78 kg, the second parcel weighs 2.15 kg and the third parcel weighs 4.5 kg. What is the total weight of the three parcels?

   Answer: ______ kg

5. This line chart shows the average daily sales of ice cream at an ice cream van from 2015 to 2019. Why is this graph misleading?

   Average daily sales: 175, 180, 185, 190, 195, 200
   Year: 15, 16, 17, 18, 19

   A The horizontal axis doesn't go up in even steps.

   B The graph only shows data from five years.

   C We don't know what flavour ice creams were sold.

   D The vertical axis doesn't start from zero.

   E We don't know the exact number of ice creams sold each day.

6. What is 32 × 77 + 68 × 77?

   Answer: ______

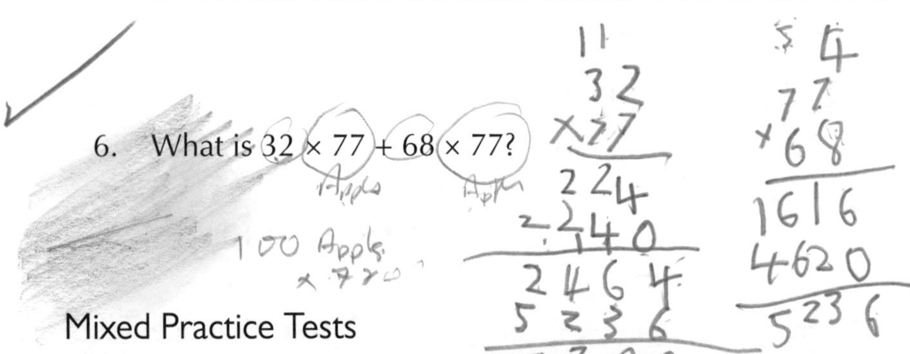

Mixed Practice Tests

7. Hiring a rowing boat costs £8, and then £5 for each hour.
What is the cost, in pounds, of hiring a rowing boat for H hours?

A $5 + 8H$ 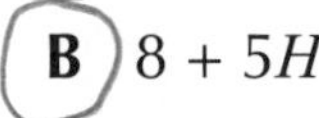 **B** $8 + 5H$ **C** $5 \times (8 + H)$ **D** $5 - 8H$ **E** $8 - 5H$

8. Greg wants to catch a train from Angelby to Castleton. The train timetable is shown below.

Angelby	1108	1234	1417
Bagthorpe	1125	1251	1434
Castleton	1147	1313	1456
Donford	1208	1334	1517

He needs to be in Castleton by 2:45 pm. It takes 12 minutes to get to Angelby station from his house. What is the latest time he can leave home to arrive in Castleton on time?

Answer: _____ : _____

9. Eleanor makes salad dressing by mixing olive oil and vinegar in the ratio 3 : 2.
She has 800 ml of vinegar. How many litres of salad dressing can she make?

Answer: _______ litres

10. Olive builds the shape on the right out of cubes.
Which shape below is the same as Olive's?

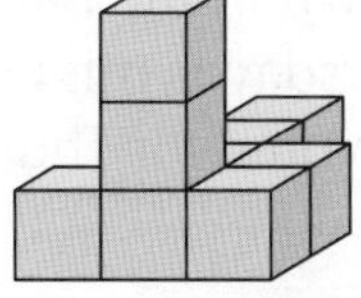

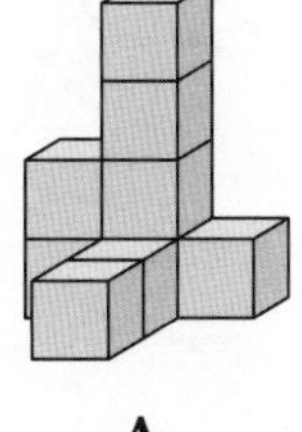

A

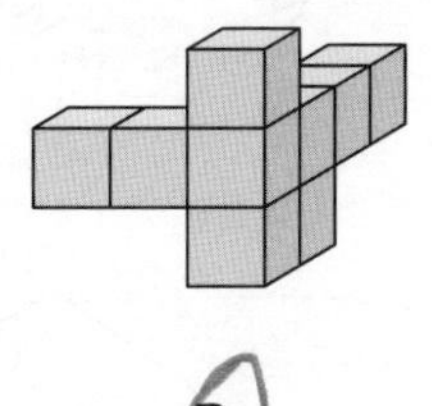

B

C

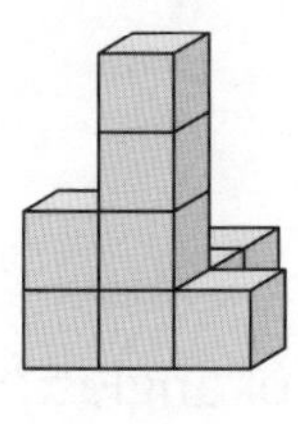

D

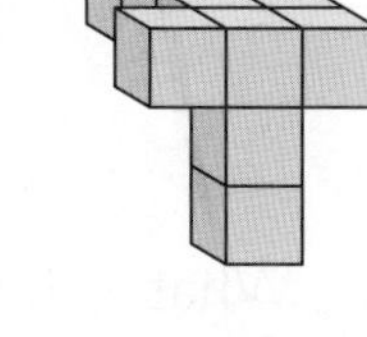

E

Total (out of 10): 

Mixed Practice Tests

Give yourself **10 minutes** to complete this test. Write down your score in the box at the end.

Test 4

1. Five people record their scores on a video game.

Name	Jemma	Luke	Halima	Suzy	Patrick
Score	1831	1673	1828	1839	1799

Who got the highest score?

A Jemma **B** Luke **C** Halima **D** Suzy **E** Patrick

2. What is 37.2 – 24.83?

Answer: __________

3. To get to school, Nick walks 660 m to the bus stop, and then travels 5.7 km on the bus.
How far is Nick's journey to school, in kilometres?

Answer: _________ km

4. 40 pupils vote for their favourite day of the week.
The results are shown in the bar chart,
but the bar for Thursday is missing.
How many pupils voted for Thursday?

Answer: ______

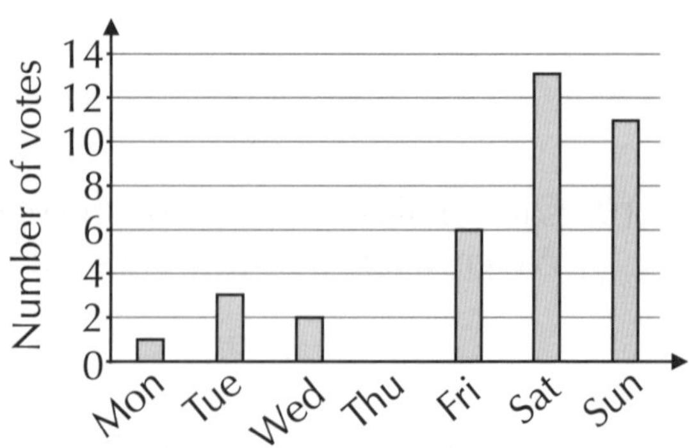

5. What is the size of angle x?

A 76° **B** 72° **C** 108°

D 104° **E** 88°

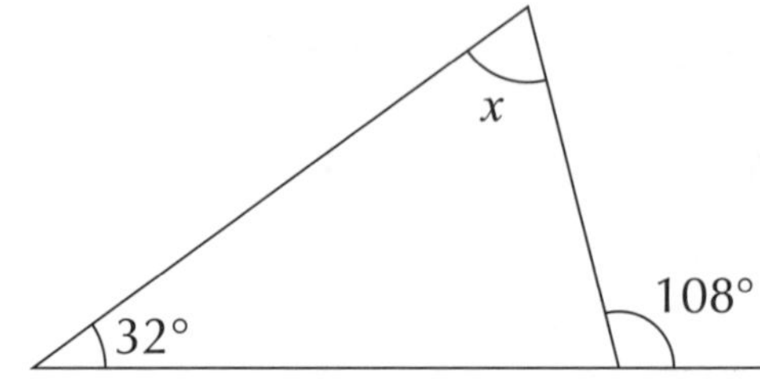

Mixed Practice Tests

6. A model train is made up of 8 identical carriages. Each carriage is 7.3 cm long. What is the total length of the model train?

Answer: ________ cm

7. A cuboid is 20 cm long and 15 cm wide. It has a volume of 7500 cm^3. What is the height of the cuboid?

A 40 cm **B** 25 cm **C** 20 cm **D** 30 cm **E** 10 cm

8. Look at the table on the right. Which number could go in the shaded section?

A 4 **B** 12 **C** 1

D 7 **E** 2

	Prime	Not prime
Factor of 12	?	6
Not a factor of 12	5	9

9. Rebecca uses the ingredients on the right to make biscuits. Each biscuit uses 30 g of dough. She gives 5 of the biscuits to her sister. How many biscuits does she have left?

A 21 **B** 14 **C** 25 **D** 16 **E** 12

Ingredients	
Flour	350 g
Butter	180 g
Sugar	120 g

10. Imani cuts four identical equilateral triangles and a square out of some card. She uses the shapes to make the star shown on the right. The star has a perimeter of 32 cm. What is the area of the square piece of card?

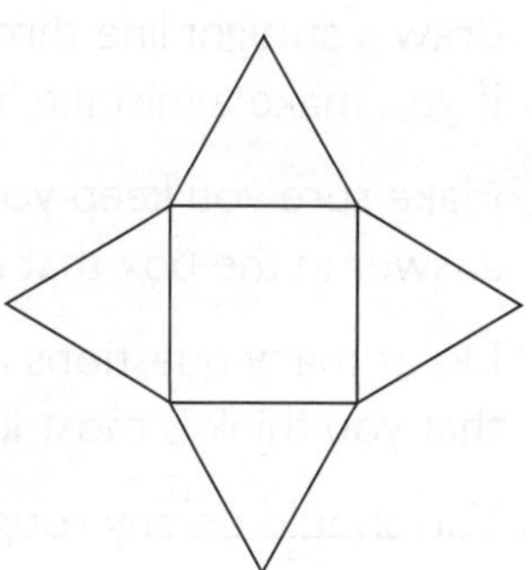

Answer: _________ cm^2

Total (out of 10): 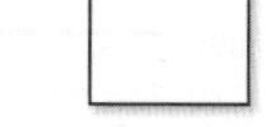

There are **multiple-choice answer sheets** for these questions on our website — go to www.cgpbooks.co.uk/11plusanswersheets. If you want to attempt each paper more than once, you will need to print a separate answer sheet for each attempt.

11+ Maths

For Ages 10-11
Practice Paper 1

For GL Assessment

Read the following:

Do not start the test until you are told to do so.

1. This is a multiple-choice test.
2. There are 50 questions and you will have 50 minutes to do the test.
3. You should mark your answer to each question in pencil on the answer sheet you've printed from www.cgpbooks.co.uk/11plusanswersheets.
4. You should only mark one answer for each question. To mark your answer, draw a straight line through the rectangle next to the option you have chosen. If you make a mistake, rub it out and mark your new answer clearly.
5. Make sure you keep your place on the answer sheet and mark your answer in the box that has the same number as the question.
6. Do as many questions as you can. If you get stuck on a question, choose the answer that you think is most likely to be correct, then move on to the next question.
7. You should do any rough working on a separate piece of paper.
8. You should not use a calculator on this test.

Work carefully, but go as quickly as you can.

1 Which of the following is a multiple of both 3 and 4?

A 8 **B** 15 **C** 18 **D** 16 **E** 12

2 The line graph shows the goals scored by four teams in a football league.

Goals scored

Match day

Village FC

Rivertown

Wood United

Park Rovers

On how many match days did two teams score the same number of goals?

A 1 **B** 2 **C** 3 **D** 4 **E** 5

3 The cost of a coach trip is split equally between 20 passengers.
What percentage of the total cost will each passenger pay?

A 5% **B** 19% **C** 26% **D** 20% **E** 9%

4 Arushi has a total of 30 shirts. 12 of her shirts have a collar.
What fraction of her shirts do not have a collar?

A $\frac{1}{4}$ **B** $\frac{3}{5}$ **C** $\frac{2}{5}$ **D** $\frac{5}{6}$ **E** $\frac{4}{5}$

5 Peter's train departs at 11:52 am. He arrives at his destination at 17:12.
How long was his train journey?

A 4 hours and 20 minutes **B** 5 hours and 12 minutes
C 5 hours and 14 minutes **D** 6 hours and 14 minutes
E 5 hours and 20 minutes

Turn over to the next page

6 Which of these is the most suitable unit to measure the length of a swimming pool?

A m **B** cm **C** ml **D** km **E** mm

7 What number is the arrow pointing to on this number line?

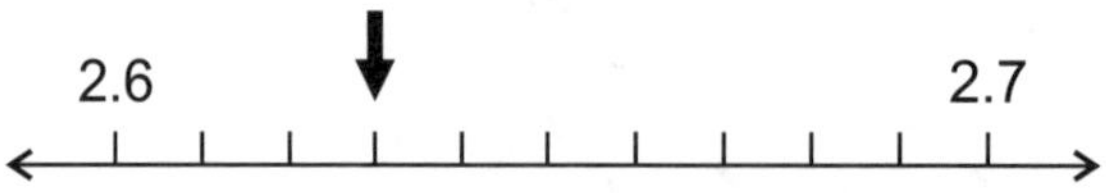

A 2.73 **B** 2.62 **C** 2.03 **D** 2.63 **E** 2.64

8 A number is 9.63 when rounded to the nearest hundredth.
Which of these could not be the original number?

A 9.630 **B** 9.625 **C** 9.624 **D** 9.634 **E** 9.632

9 Pupils were asked to vote for a new school tie design. The table shows the results.

	Regular	**Clip-on**	**Total**
Stripes	20	33	53
No stripes	3	16	19
Total	23	49	72

Which of the following statements is true?

A More pupils voted for a regular tie than a clip-on tie.
B A clip-on tie with no stripes was the least popular choice.
C Fewer pupils voted for a tie with stripes than a tie with no stripes.
D A regular tie with stripes was the most popular choice.
E A clip-on tie was more popular than a regular tie.

10 Umar uses his computer to do a complex calculation.
It starts at 6 pm on 29th March and finishes 72 hours later.
On what date does the computer finish the calculation?

A 3rd April **B** 31st March **C** 1st April **D** 30th March **E** 2nd April

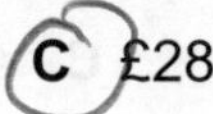

11 9 tickets to a cinema cost £63. How much will 4 tickets cost?

A £16 **B** £21 **C** £28 **D** £36 **E** £7

12 The pictogram shows the numbers of different types of film in Ellie's film collection.

Animation	● ● ●
Comedy	● ◖
Romance	● ● ◖
Action	◖

Key: ● = 4 films

What is the total number of Animation and Romance films in Ellie's collection?

A 12 **B** 22 **C** 20 **D** 24 **E** 26

13 Which of these expressions is the largest?

A $\frac{1}{2}$ of 30 **B** 25% of 40 **C** $\frac{4}{5}$ of 25 **D** 50% of 20 **E** $\frac{1}{4}$ of 60

14 Alex and Jin share the cost of a meal.
Alex paid £p and Jin paid £6 less than Alex.
Which of these expressions shows the cost of the meal in pounds?

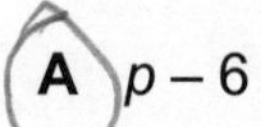

A $p - 6$ **B** $2p$ **C** $2p + 6$ **D** $2p - 6$ **E** $p + 6$

15 Which of these shapes has the most lines of symmetry?

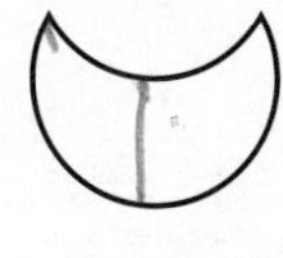

A

B

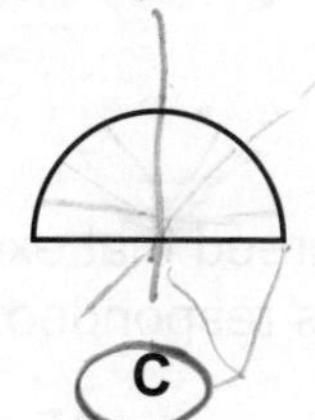

C

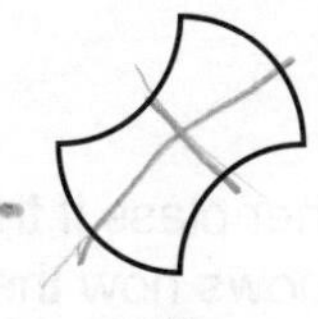

D

E

16 In Jeff's garden, the ratio of red roses to white roses is 3 : 7.
There are 45 red roses. How many white roses are there?

A 15 **B** 21 **C** 120 **D** 49 **E** 105

Turn over to the next page

17 What is the size of the shaded angle?

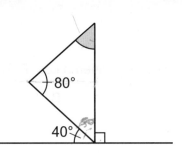

A 40° **B** 60° **C** 45°
D 50° **E** 35°

18 Deacon spent £3.45 on his dessert.

Dessert Menu	
Cheesecake	£3.20
Ice cream	£1.80
Apple pie	£2.75
Fresh cream	£1.10
Fudge sauce	95p
Custard	70p

Which of the following could he have bought?

A Ice cream and fudge sauce
B Apple pie and fresh cream
C Cheesecake and fudge sauce
D Apple pie and custard
E Cheesecake and fresh cream

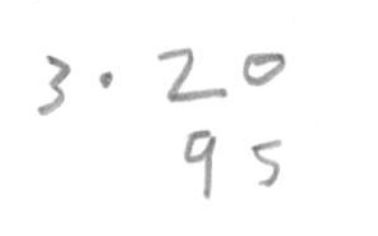

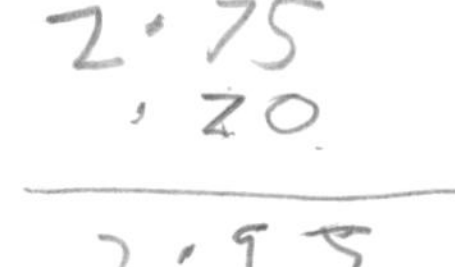

19 A game of laser tag costs £7.99. How much do 3 games cost?

A £21.67 **B** £23.97 **C** £21.89 **D** £22.97 **E** £24

20 Vicky draws a regular octagon. She divides it into triangles by drawing a straight line from its centre to each of its corners.

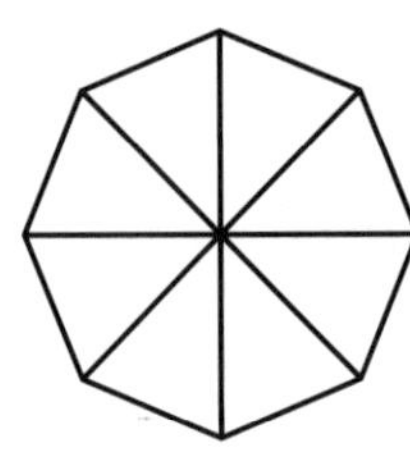

Which of these statements is true?

A The triangles are all right-angled.
B The triangles are all isosceles.
C The triangles are all equilateral.
D The triangles are all scalene.
E None of the above.

21 Sabeen asked her class if they agreed that exercise was fun.
The pie chart shows how the class responded.

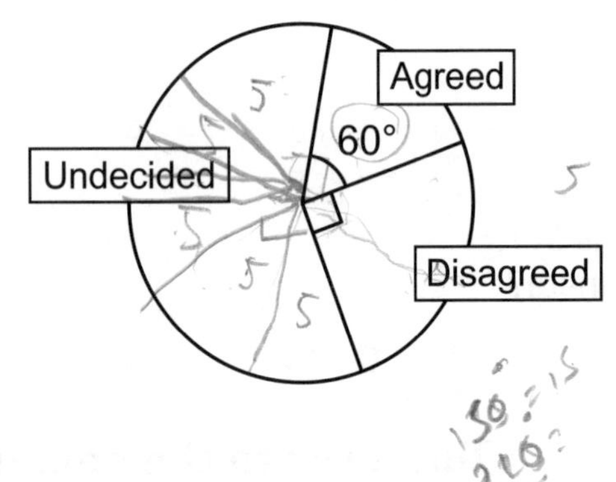

15 pupils either agreed or disagreed.
How many pupils were undecided?

A 29
B 20
C 46
D 21
E 32

22 Lesley glued three photos onto a rectangular piece of card.
Each photo is 6 cm by 8 cm in size, and has a 1 cm gap on all sides.

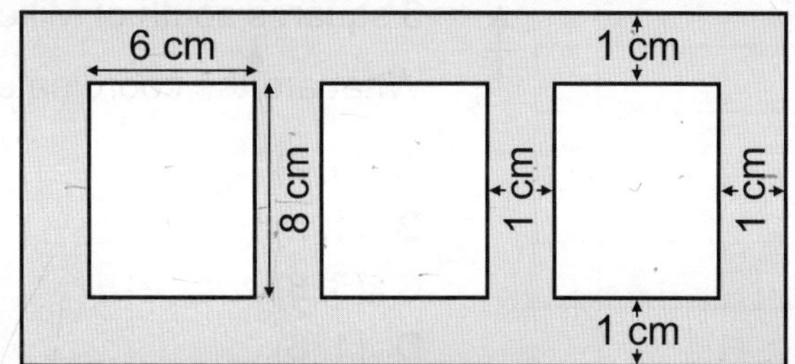

What is the area of the piece of card?

A 220 cm² **B** 144 cm² **C** 240 cm² **D** 200 cm² **E** 160 cm²

23 Joanna makes a bar chart showing the number of different coloured cars in a car park.

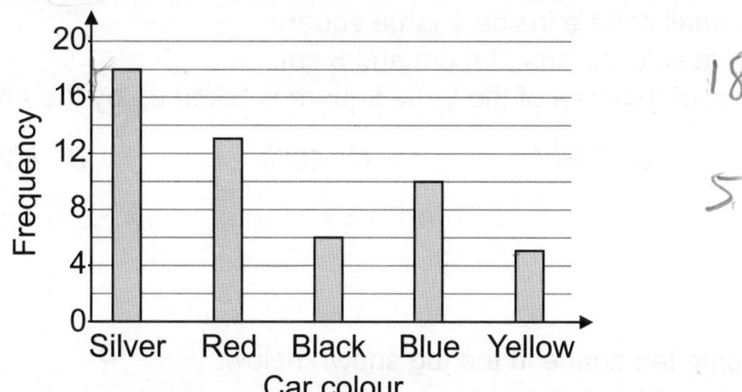

How many more silver cars than yellow cars were there in the car park?

A 11 **B** 13 **C** 9 **D** 14 **E** 12

24 Callum has written a rule for a number sequence:

Multiply the previous number by 3, then subtract 2.

The first number is 2. What is the third number in the sequence?

A 6 **B** 7 **C** 12 **D** 4 **E** 10

25 Steph uses this formula to calculate the time T (in minutes) it takes her to prepare n pizzas.

$$T = 5n + 4$$

How many seconds does it take her to prepare 3 pizzas?

A 1200 **B** 1140 **C** 2100 **D** 1500 **E** 1800

Turn over to the next page

26 Look at the grid below.

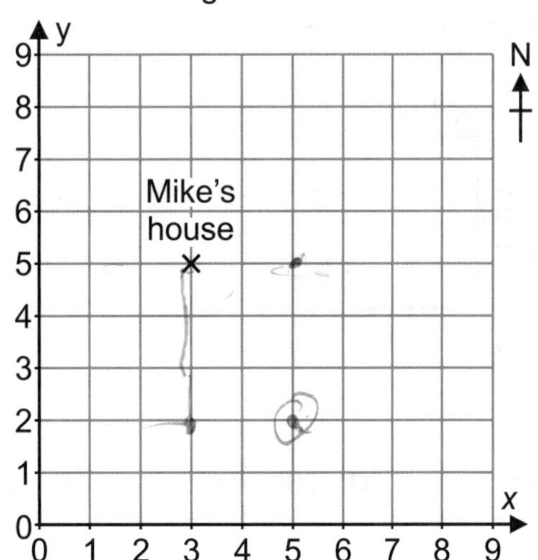

Lisa's house is 2 squares east and 3 squares south of Mike's house.

What are the coordinates of Lisa's house?

A (5, 2)
B (1, 2)
C (5, 8)
D (1, 8)
E (2, 5)

27 Gwen draws a small square inside a large square.
The squares have side lengths of 4 cm and 8 cm.
What percentage of the area of the large square is taken up by the area of the small square?

A 50% **B** 25% **C** 40% **D** 80% **E** 75%

28 Doug makes some lemonade in the jug shown below.

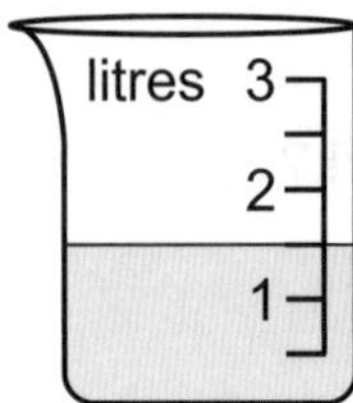

He pours 570 ml of the lemonade into a glass.
How much lemonade is left in the jug?

A 570 ml **B** 1430 ml **C** 430 ml
D 930 ml **E** 1070 ml

29 2.601 2.061 2.06 2.106 2.006

Which of the following shows the decimals above in order from smallest to largest?

A 2.06, 2.601, 2.061, 2.106, 2.006
B 2.006, 2.06, 2.061, 2.106, 2.601
C 2.006, 2.106, 2.06, 2.061, 2.601
D 2.106, 2.006, 2.06, 2.061, 2.601
E 2.006, 2.106, 2.061, 2.06, 2.601

30 The table shows the number of books read by five people last year.

Name	Number of books
Henry	6
Imran	7
Jolana	14
Keith	3
Lara	10

What was the mean number of books read?

A 7 **B** 7.5 **C** 8 **D** 8.5 **E** 9

31 Jonah's cafe sells cake in small 80 g pieces and large 150 g pieces. He has a single 1200 g cake left to sell. Which of these combinations would result in the smallest amount of cake left over?

A 5 small and 4 large pieces
B 1 small and 7 large pieces
C 3 small and 6 large pieces
D 5 small and 5 large pieces
E 10 small and 2 large pieces

32 3182 ÷ 43 = 74

What is 31.82 ÷ 43?

A 74 **B** 7.4 **C** 7.04 **D** 0.74 **E** 0.074

33 Betty has drawn a shape.

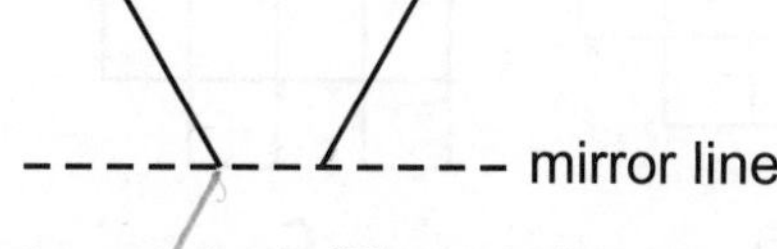

She reflects it in the mirror line to create a different shape.
What is the name of the new shape?

A Octagon **B** Triangle **C** Pentagon **D** Hexagon **E** Kite

Turn over to the next page

34 Which of these calculations is equal to 5 × 39 + 7 × 91?

A 5 × 40 + 7 × 90 – 2
B 5 × 40 + 7 × 90 + 2
C 5 × 40 + 7 × 90
D 5 × 40 + 7 × 90 – 12
E 5 × 40 + 7 × 90 + 12

35 Nate charges £32 for a manicure. Each manicure takes 25 minutes.
Yesterday he spent 300 minutes giving manicures.
How much money did he make?

A £320 **B** £362 **C** £375 **D** £384 **E** £400

36 Which of the following statements about the number 125 is true?

A It is odd and a prime number.
B It is even and not a prime number.
C It is even and a cube number.
D It is odd and a cube number.
E It is prime and a cube number.

37 Navid makes this shape using plastic cubes.

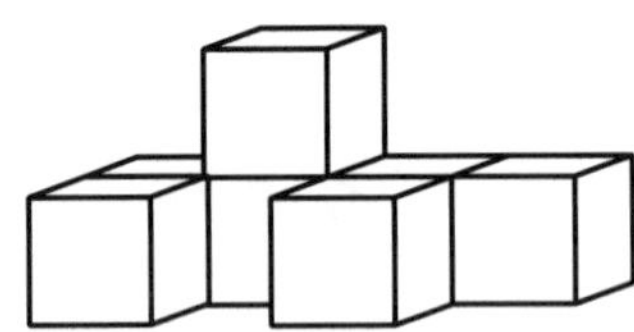

He looks down at the shape from directly above.
Which of the following layouts does he see?

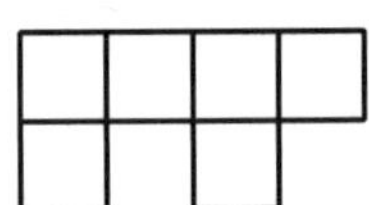
A

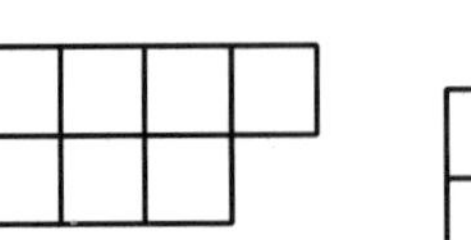
B

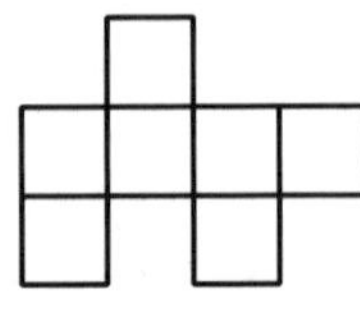
C

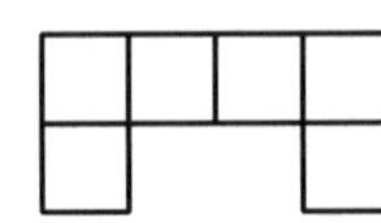
D

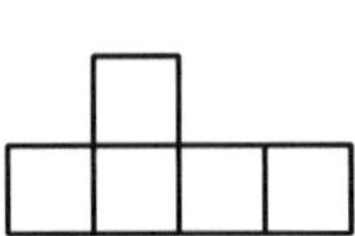
E

38 Noreen uses 3 identical isosceles triangles to create this shape.

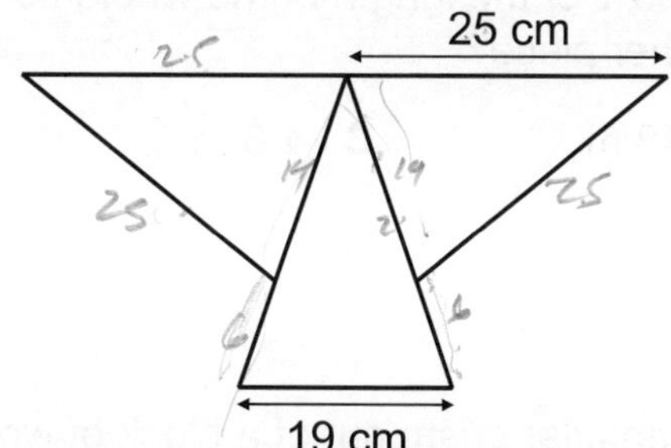

What is the perimeter of the shape?

A 125 cm **B** 131 cm **C** 112 cm **D** 207 cm **E** 119 cm

39 Two faces of a prism are right-angled triangles.
How many right angles are there on the faces of the prism in total?

A 18 **B** 16 **C** 12 **D** 10 **E** 14

40 Kelly has £25 to spend at a funfair.

Ticket Prices	
Roller Coaster	£4.75
Pirate Ship	£2.25
Haunted House	£2.00
Tilt 'n' Whirl	£1.75
Carousel	£1.20

She visits the haunted house once and rides the pirate ship twice.
How many times can she afford to ride the roller coaster?

A 1 **B** 2 **C** 3
D 4 **E** 5

41 What is $(9-4)^2 + 3 \times 7$?

A 14 **B** 28 **C** 57 **D** 46 **E** 25

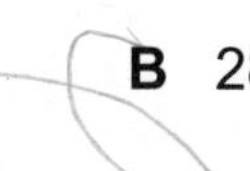

42 Josh places his mixing bowl on top of a scale. The bowl weighs 84 g.
He then pours flour into the bowl without resetting the scale.
He wants to weigh out 1.5 kg of flour. How much more does he need?

A 555 g **B** 629 g **C** 584 g
D 471 g **E** 639 g

Turn over to the next page

43 Diego has an 80 cm length of ribbon. He cuts it into two pieces. The length of one piece is 65% of the length of the whole ribbon. What is the length of the other piece?

A 5.2 m **B** 0.48 m **C** 4.8 m **D** 0.28 m **E** 0.52 m

44 Flora wants to carve this triangular prism out of a block of wood.

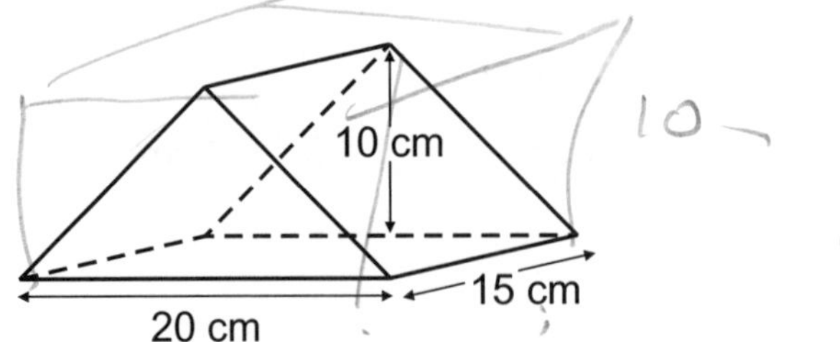

She can only buy blocks of wood in cuboid shapes.
What is the volume of the smallest cuboid that she could use?

A 3000 cm^3 **B** 1500 cm^3 **C** 300 cm^3 **D** 200 cm^3 **E** 2000 cm^3

45 Look at this set of numbers. One number is missing.

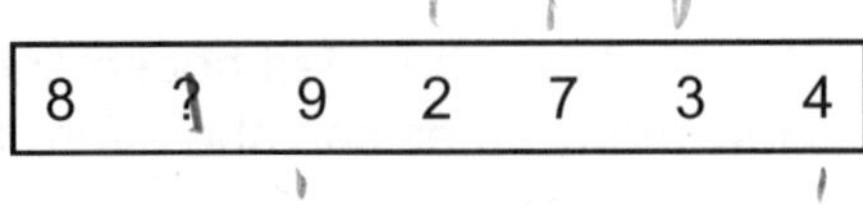

The ratio of prime to non-prime numbers is 3 : 4.
The ratio of square to non-square numbers is 2 : 5.
Which one of these could be the missing number?

A 5 **B** 25 **C** 11 **D** 12 **E** 16

46 A pentagon is translated to a new position, as shown.

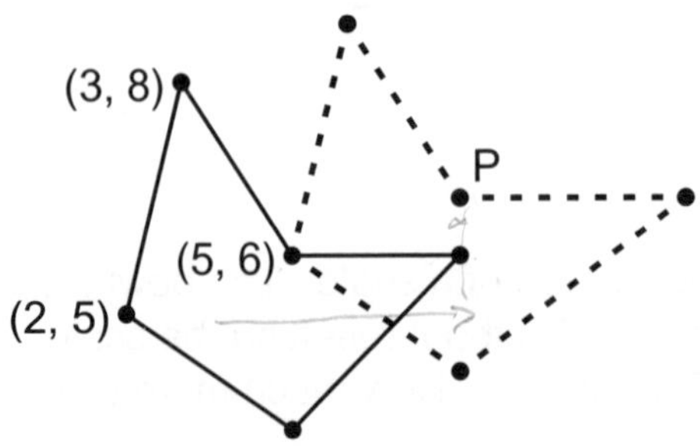

What are the coordinates of the point P?

A (7, 8) **B** (5, 7) **C** (6, 9) **D** (8, 7) **E** (2, 1)

47 Which of these expressions is the same as $4(x + 8)$?

A $4x + 8$ **B** $x + 32$ **C** $4x + 12$ **D** $4x + 32$ **E** $x + 12$

48 Carys sees the following chart in a newspaper.

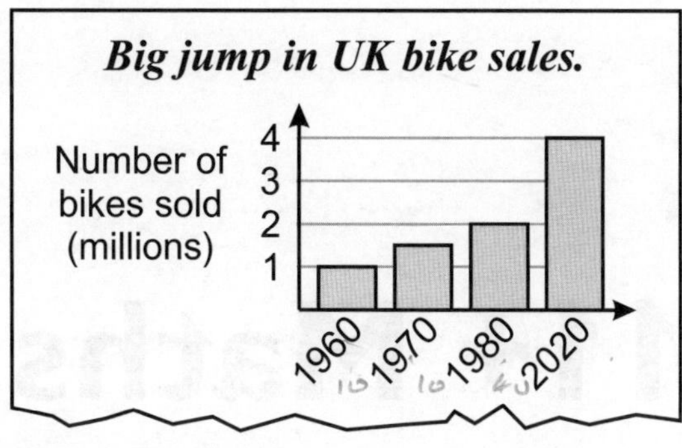

Why is the chart misleading?

A It doesn't show the number of bikes sold in other countries.

B The graph shows no data from before 1960.

C The scale on the horizontal axis is uneven.

D The number of bikes should be written in thousands.

E A line graph would be a better way to show the data.

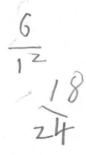

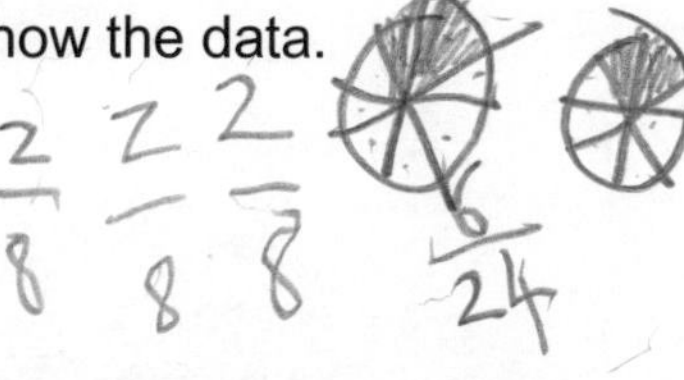

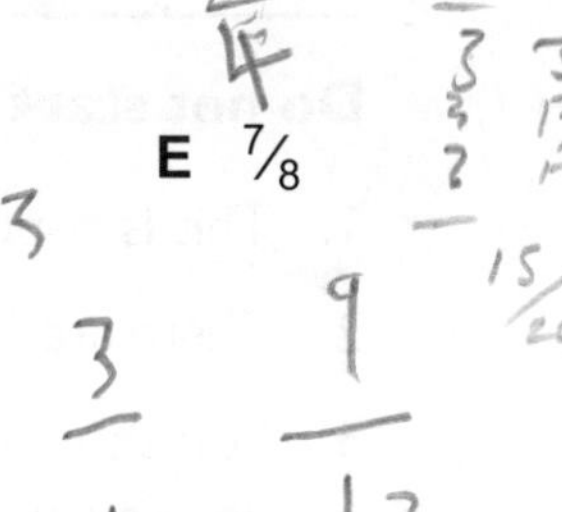

49 There are 3 pizzas at a party. Each pizza is cut into 8 equal slices.
Jodie takes one slice of each pizza and two of her friends do the same.
What fraction of the pizza slices remain?

A $^3/_{12}$ **B** $^5/_8$ **C** $^3/_8$ **D** $^1/_{15}$ **E** $^7/_8$

50 Which of the following nets would fold up to make a cube with the shaded faces on opposite sides?

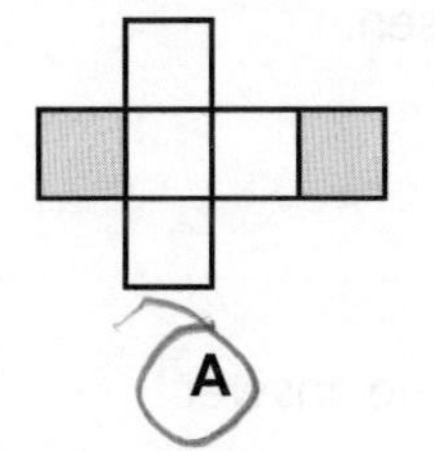

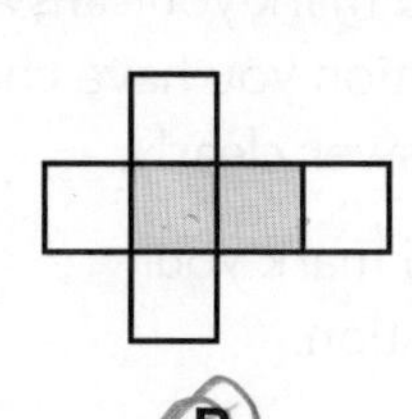

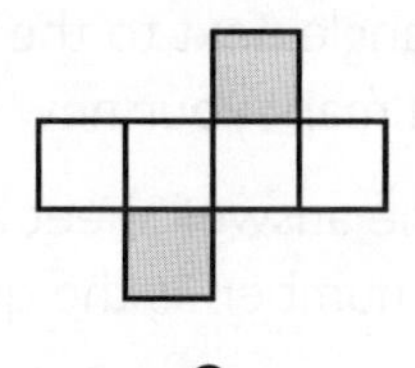

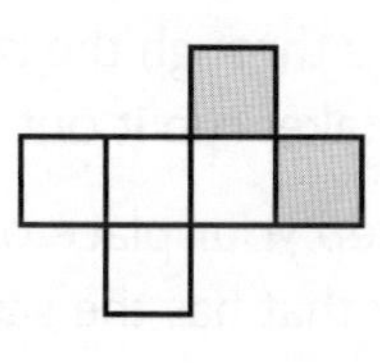

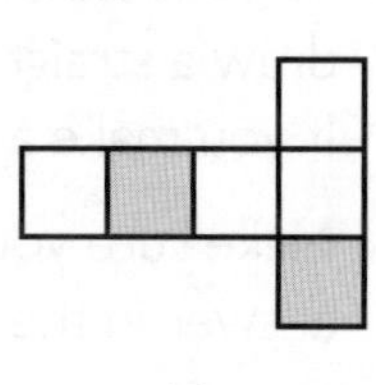

A **B** **C** **D** **E**

End of test

There are **multiple-choice answer sheets** for these questions on our website — go to www.cgpbooks.co.uk/11plusanswersheets. If you want to attempt each paper more than once, you will need to print a separate answer sheet for each attempt.

11+ Maths

For Ages 10-11
Practice Paper 2

For GL Assessment

Read the following:

Do not start the test until you are told to do so.

1. This is a multiple-choice test.
2. There are 50 questions and you will have 50 minutes to do the test.
3. You should mark your answer to each question in pencil on the answer sheet you've printed from www.cgpbooks.co.uk/11plusanswersheets.
4. You should only mark one answer for each question. To mark your answer, draw a straight line through the rectangle next to the option you have chosen. If you make a mistake, rub it out and mark your new answer clearly.
5. Make sure you keep your place on the answer sheet and mark your answer in the box that has the same number as the question.
6. Do as many questions as you can. If you get stuck on a question, choose the answer that you think is most likely to be correct, then move on to the next question.
7. You should do any rough working on a separate piece of paper.
8. You should not use a calculator on this test.

Work carefully, but go as quickly as you can.

1 A milk bottle contains 2.75 litres of milk.
How much is this in millilitres?

A 275 ml **B** 0.275 ml **C** 2750 ml **D** 27.5 ml **E** 27 500 ml

2 Wesley finds out how many Year 5 and Year 6 pupils go to different school clubs.

	Year 5	Year 6
Choir	7	24
Football	16	18
Chess	21	13
Orchestra	18	17

Which club is attended by the largest number of Year 5 and 6 pupils?

A Choir **B** Football **C** Chess **D** Orchestra **E** Impossible to tell

3 In the number 80 572, which digit is in the thousands place?

A 8 **B** 0 **C** 5 **D** 7 **E** 2

4 The bar chart shows the number of times that Amit missed his school bus in a year.

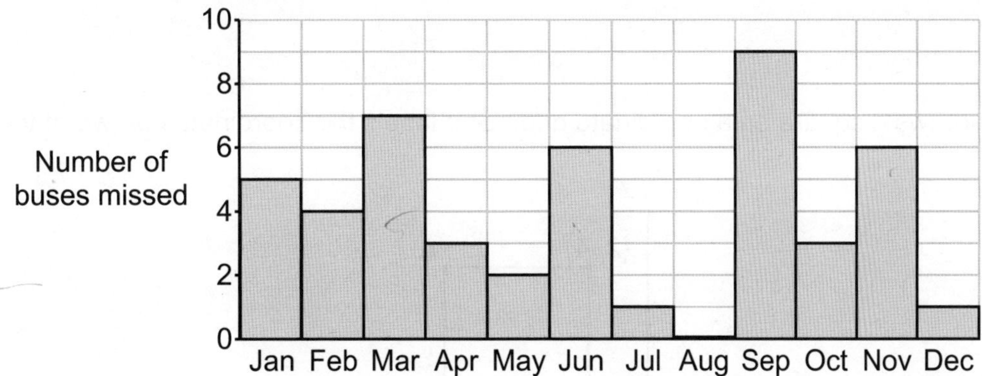

In how many months did Amit miss his bus more than 5 times?

A 2 **B** 5 **C** 3 **D** 4 **E** 6

Turn over to the next page

5 A watering can is filled with 1.756 litres of water.
How much water is in the watering can to the nearest 10 ml?

A 1.76 litres **B** 1.7 litres **C** 2 litres **D** 1.8 litres 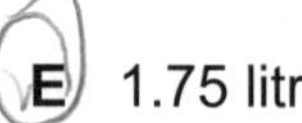 **E** 1.75 litres

6 How many lines of symmetry does the shape on the right have?

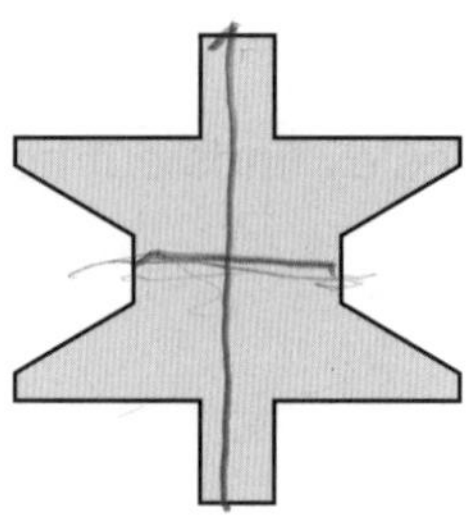

A 1 **B** 3 **C** 2
D 0 **E** 4

7 Mrs Singh writes one true statement and four untrue statements about the numbers 8, 27 and 64 on a whiteboard. Which statement is true?

A All of the numbers are square numbers.
B All of the numbers can be divided exactly by 2.
C All of the numbers have 4 as a factor.
D All of the numbers are cube numbers.
E All of the numbers are multiples of 3.

8 Megan's birthday is on 18th July and Kemal's birthday is on 4th August.
If Megan's birthday is on a Saturday, what day will Kemal's birthday be on?

A Monday **B** Thursday **C** Sunday **D** Friday **E** Tuesday

9 Sally draws a square on a coordinate grid. She labels the coordinates of two of the corners.

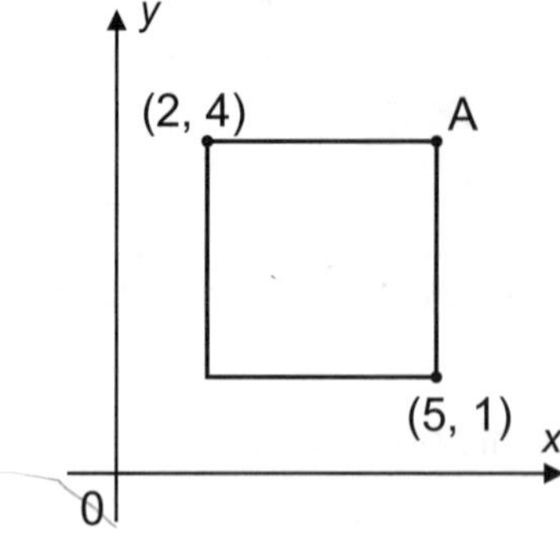

What are the coordinates of point A?

A (5, 4) **B** (5, 5) **C** (1, 5) **D** (2, 5) **E** (4, 5)

10 A plane has a wingspan of 58 m. A scale model of the plane is 1000 times smaller. What is the wingspan of the model plane?

A 5.8 cm **B** 58 000 cm **C** 58 cm **D** 5.8 m **E** 0.0058 m

11 Look at the diagram below. What is the value of *k*?

$2k$ k

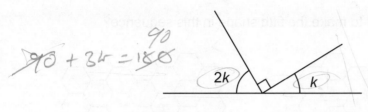

A 15° **B** 30° **C** 25° **D** 60° **E** 45°

12 What is the smallest common multiple of 9 and 12?

A 12 **B** 36 **C** 72 **D** 60 **E** 27

13 Which of the following shapes could go in the shaded section of the Venn diagram below?

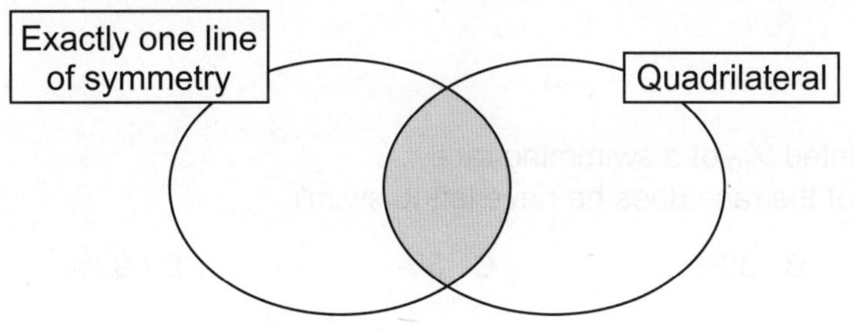

A Square **B** Isosceles triangle **C** Kite
D Rhombus **E** Parallelogram

14 A serving of cereal weighs 35 g. A cereal box contains 40 servings. How many kilograms of cereal are in the box?

A 75 kg **B** 1.4 kg **C** 4.4 kg **D** 0.75 kg **E** 14 kg

Turn over to the next page

15 The clock on the right shows the time that Ursula leaves her house one afternoon. She is out of the house for 2 hours and 25 minutes. At what time does she return home?

A 16:15 **B** 17:25 **C** 16:05

D 17:05 **E** 15:05

16 How many hexagons are needed to make the fifth shape in this sequence?

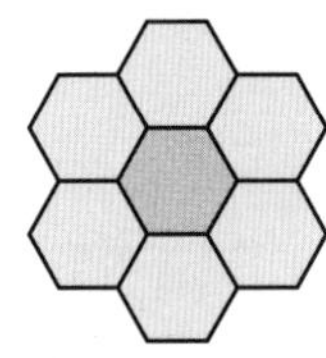
shape 1

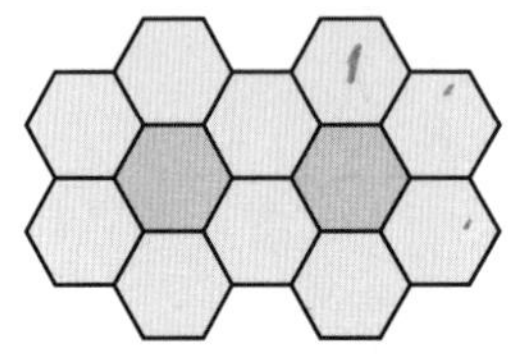
shape 2

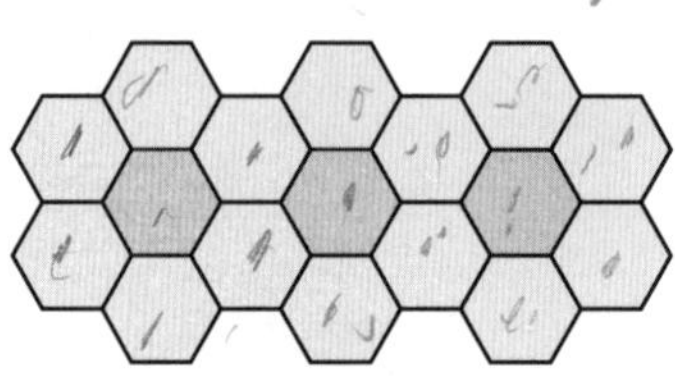
shape 3

A 12 **B** 25 **C** 17 **D** 22 **E** 27

17 A circular mirror has a radius of 12 cm.
What is the diameter of the mirror?

A 24 cm **B** 48 cm **C** 8 cm **D** 6 cm **E** 60 cm

18 Joshua has completed $^7/_{10}$ of a swimming race.
What percentage of the race does he have left to swim?

A 70% **B** 30% **C** 3% **D** 93% **E** 7%

19 Which of the nets below cannot be folded to make a triangular prism?

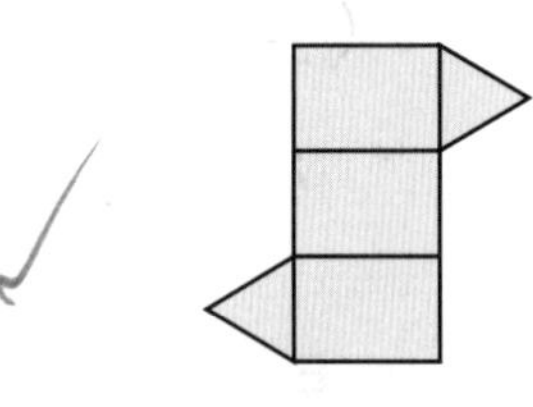
A

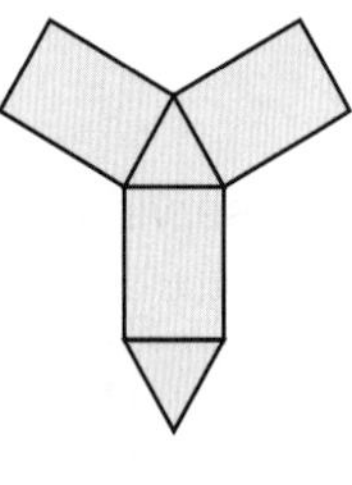
B

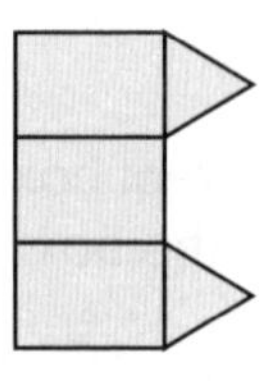
C

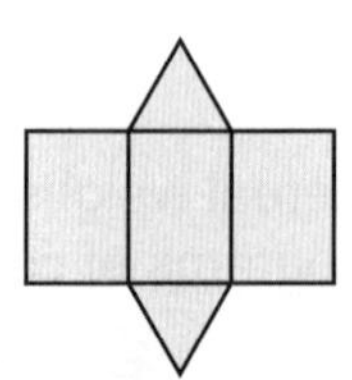
D

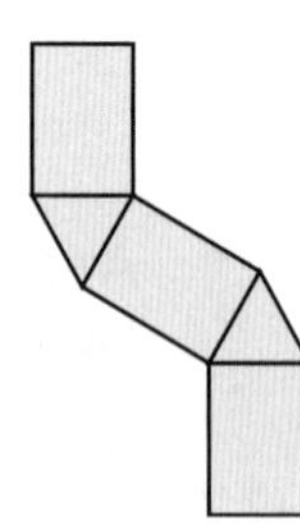
E

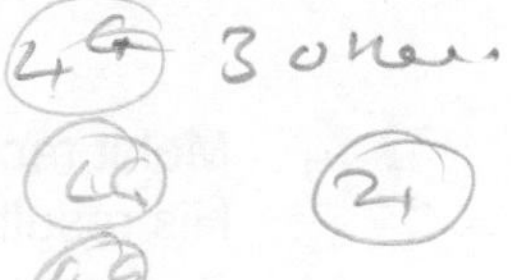

20 On a farm, 4 in every 7 animals are goats. The farm has 32 goats.
How many animals are there on the farm in total?

A 56 **B** 24 **C** 45 **D** 36 **E** 72

21 Sunil cycles 23.5 km on Wednesday, 36.8 km on Thursday and 16.4 km on Friday.
How far does he cycle in total?

A 56.3 km **B** 71.3 km **C** 67.4 km **D** 76.7 km **E** 83.8 km

22 A leisure centre releases a new timetable of classes.
The next class starts as soon as the previous one finishes.
How many minutes longer is the karate class than the yoga class?

Class	Time
Karate	11:35
Tennis	12:55
Yoga	14:15
Football	15:10

A 20 **B** 45 **C** 50
D 35 **E** 25

23 The diagram below shows a triangle inside a square.

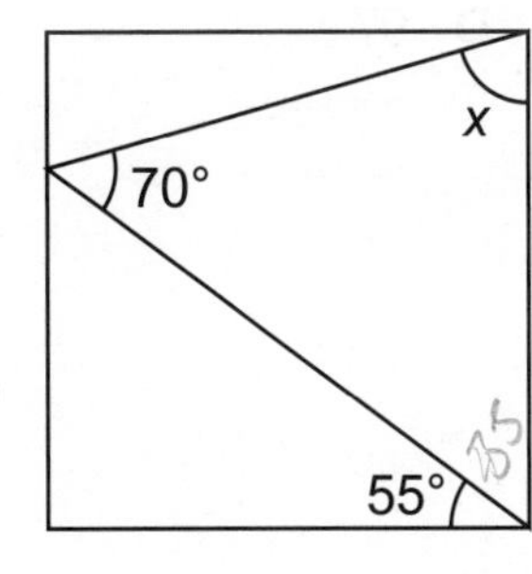

What is the size of angle x?

A 20°
B 35°
C 30°
D 105°
E 75°

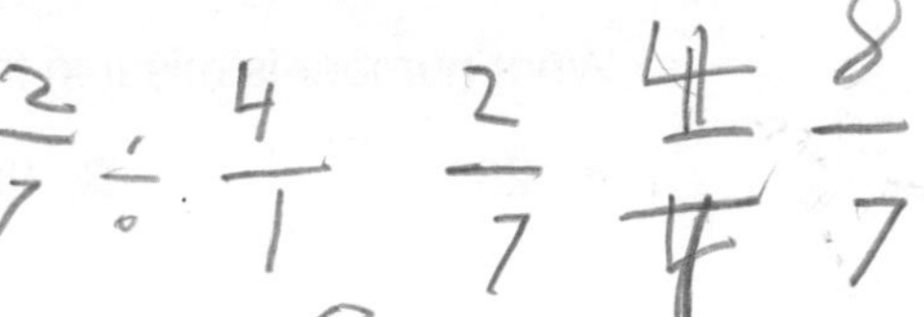

24 Karen shares $\frac{2}{7}$ of a bag of cat food equally between 4 cat bowls.
What fraction of the bag is in each bowl?

A $\frac{8}{7}$ **B** $\frac{2}{14}$ **C** $\frac{1}{7}$ **D** $\frac{1}{14}$ **E** $\frac{1}{28}$

25 Buttons come in small packs and large packs. There are 8 buttons in a small pack and 24 buttons in a large pack. Krish buys four small packs and two large packs.
How many buttons does he buy?

A 80 **B** 32 **C** 40 **D** 74 **E** 48

Turn over to the next page

26 Mohit records the temperature in his garden each day for a week.
His results are shown on this line graph.

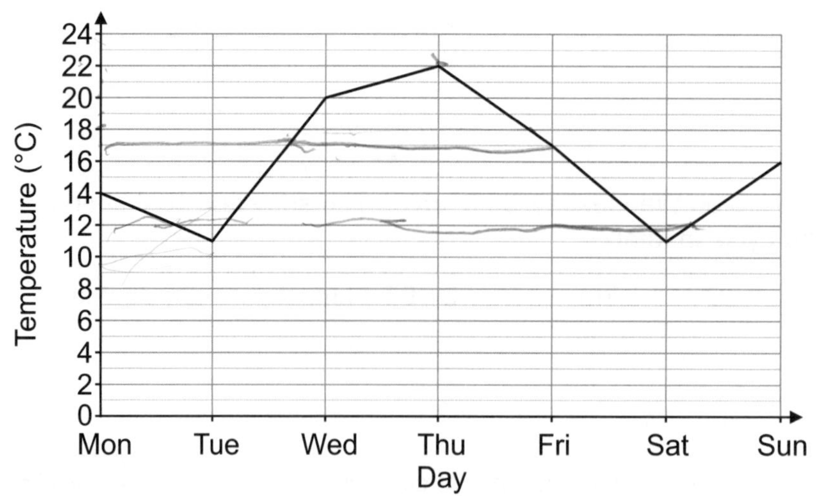

On which day was it 5 °C colder than it was on the hottest day?

A Monday **B** Tuesday **C** Friday **D** Saturday **E** Sunday

27 Helena is thinking of a prime number. It is bigger than 90 but smaller than 100.
What number is Helena thinking of?

A 91 **B** 93 **C** 95 **D** 97 **E** 99

28 218 × 99 = 21 800 – ☐

What number is missing from the calculation above?

A 28 **B** 99 **C** 2180 **D** 218 **E** 299

29 Kayla makes 3660 g of marmalade. She shares it equally between 12 jars.
How much marmalade is in each jar?

A 350 g **B** 312 g **C** 300 g **D** 120 g **E** 305 g

30 Which number in this table is in the wrong place?

A 16 **B** 81 **C** 56
D 9 **E** 17

	Even	Odd
Square	16, 64	9, 49
Not square	8, 56	17, 81

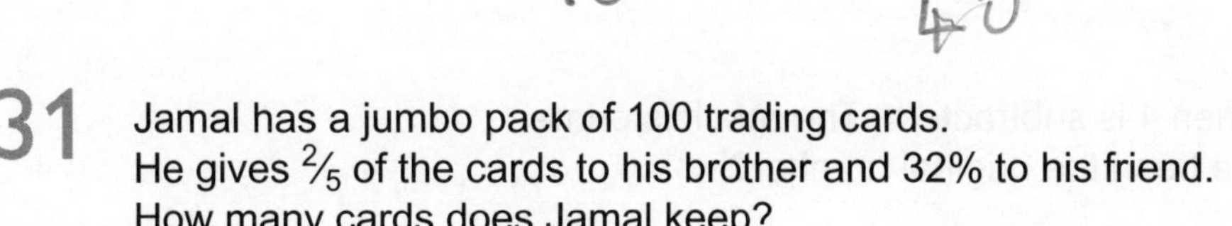

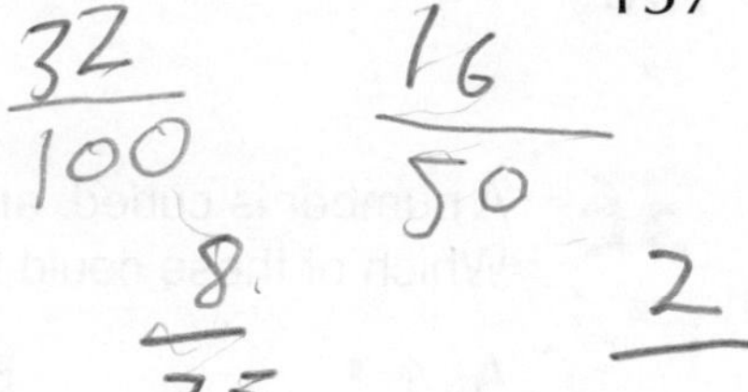

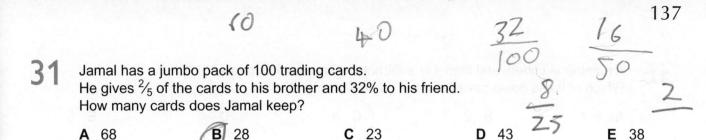

31 Jamal has a jumbo pack of 100 trading cards.
He gives $\frac{2}{5}$ of the cards to his brother and 32% to his friend.
How many cards does Jamal keep?

A 68 B 28 C 23 D 43 E 38

32 The design below is made out of four identical regular hexagons.
The perimeter of the shape is 32 cm.

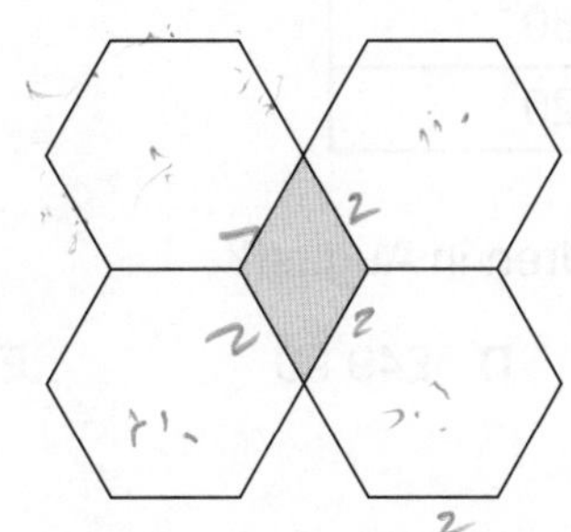

What is the perimeter of the shaded region?

A 16 cm
B 2 cm
C 12 cm
D 6 cm
E 8 cm

33 What is $160 \div 4^2 + 4$?

A 14 B 44 C 12 D 20 E 8

34 A gardener has 1 kg of compost. He fills three pots with x grams of compost each.
Which expression gives the amount of compost he has left in grams?

A $1 - 3x$ B $3x - 1$ C $1000 - 3x$ D $3x - 1000$ E $1000x - 3$

35 Four members of a running club record how long it takes them to run 5 km to the nearest minute.

Name	Marie	Kazuo	Lyla	Jon
Time (minutes)	26	24	22	32

What is the mean time taken to complete 5 km?

A 21 mins B 24 mins C 28 mins D 26 mins E 25 mins

Turn over to the next page

36 A number is cubed, and then 4 is subtracted. The result is prime.
Which of these could have been the original number?

A 1 **B** 2 **C** 3 **D** 4 **E** 5

37 The table below shows the price of tickets at a water park in different months of the year.

	April-September	October-March
Adult	£12.20	£7.80
Child	£8.50	£5.20

How much would it cost to buy tickets for 3 adults and 2 children in August?

A £53.60 **B** £46.40 **C** £33.60 **D** £49.90 **E** £31.20

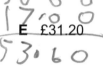

38 Georgia wants to build an open-topped box to store her action figures. She makes the base and walls of the box out of five square pieces of cardboard with 12 cm long sides.

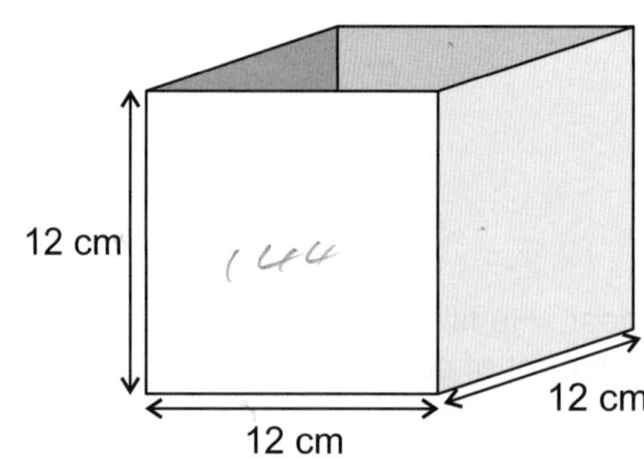

What is the total area of card she uses to build the box?

A 72 cm² **B** 300 cm² **C** 144 cm² **D** 720 cm² **E** 600 cm²

39 Tanya builds the shape below out of identical wooden cubes.

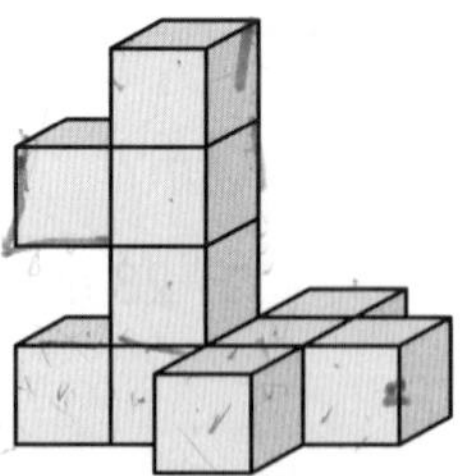

The edge of each cube is 2 cm long. What is the volume of the shape?

A 10 cm³ **B** 120 cm³ **C** 72 cm³ **D** 80 cm³ **E** 64 cm³

40 Oliver is going bowling with five friends. He pays for everyone in the group with two £20 notes and gets £2.50 back in change. How much does it cost for one person to go bowling?

A £6.25 **B** £7.25 **C** £8 **D** £7. 50 **E** £6.75

41 The pictogram below shows the height, to the nearest cm, of members of a drama club.

Less than 130 cm	■ ■ ▪
130-139 cm	■ ■ ■ ■
140-149 cm	■ ■ ■ ▮
150-159 cm	■ ■ ▮
More than 160 cm	▪

Key: ■ = 4 members

What percentage of club members are at least 150 cm tall?

A 25% **B** 11% **C** 30% **D** 50% **E** 22%

42 Yan has a cuboid fish tank that is 30 cm wide, 50 cm high and 40 cm long. She fills it with water at a rate of 3000 cm^3 every minute. If she starts filling the tank at 09:45, at what time will the tank be full?

A 09:47 **B** 10:05 **C** 10:15 **D** 10:00 **E** 10:45

43 One of the numbers in the data set below is missing.

16	23	15	?	14

The mean of all five numbers is 18. What is the missing number?

A 12 **B** 32 **C** 18 **D** 22 **E** 15

Turn over to the next page

44 Look at the article below.

> **<u>APPLES ARE THE MOST POPULAR FRUIT</u>**
>
> In a recent survey, 50 people were asked, 'What is your favourite fruit?'.
> 40% of the people said that apples are their favourite fruit,
> while 25 people said their favourite fruit is pears.

Why is this article misleading?

A It doesn't say which other fruits were chosen.
B The article doesn't tell you the ages of the people asked.
C The figures in the article show that fewer people chose pears.
D The headline doesn't match the data given in the article.
E It doesn't say where the survey was carried out.

45 Rachel has 60 coins in her piggy bank. All of the coins are either 20p coins or 50p coins. The ratio of 20p coins to 50p coins is 2 : 3. How much money is in Rachel's piggy bank?

A £22.80 **B** £24.80 **C** £20.40 **D** £19.20 **E** £28.40

46 Harry asks some pupils at his school how they usually travel to school. He records their answers in this pie chart.

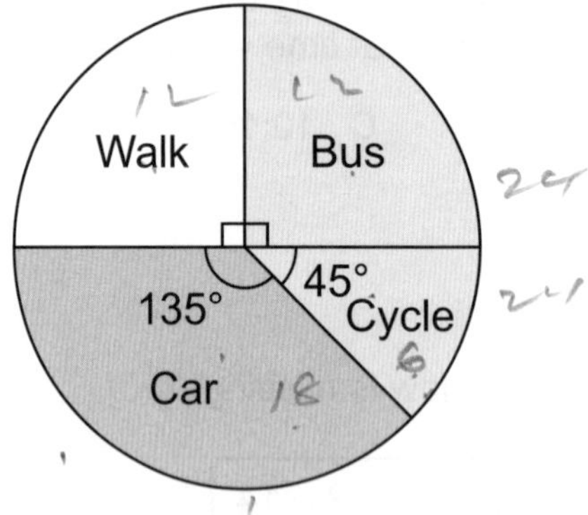

18 people travel to school by car. How many pupils did Harry ask in total?

A 36 **B** 60 **C** 30 **D** 24 **E** 48

47 The nth term rule of a sequence is $5n + 1$.
What is the smallest square number that appears in this sequence?

A 5 **B** 49 **C** 16 **D** 36 **E** 81

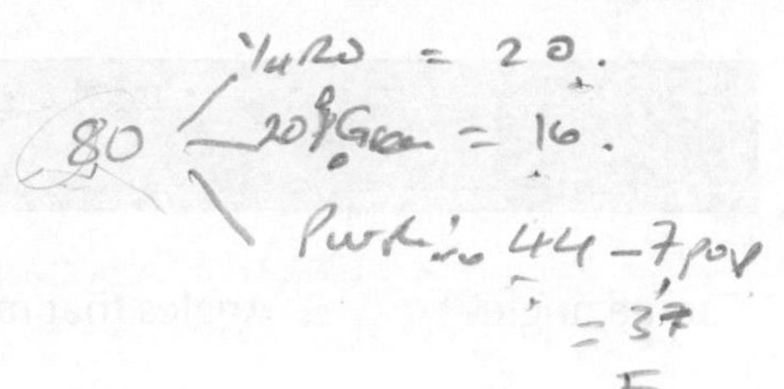

48 Reggie buys 80 balloons for a birthday party.
$\frac{1}{4}$ of them are red, 20% are green and the rest are purple.
7 of the purple balloons pop when he blows them up.
How many purple balloons does Reggie have left?

A 27 **B** 37 **C** 34 **D** 44 **E** 29

49 The shape on the coordinate grid below is translated 4 units left and 5 units up.

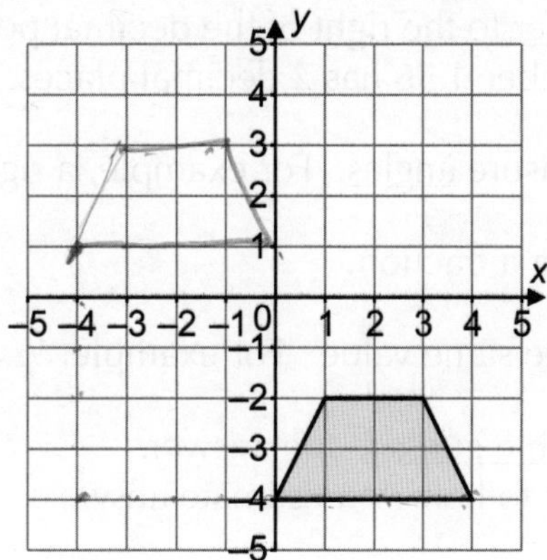

Which of the following coordinates is not a corner of the translated shape?

A (–2, 3) **B** (–1, 3) **C** (–4, 1) **D** (0, 1) **E** (–3, 3)

50 Micah makes the two shapes on the right out of square tiles.
He puts the two shapes together to make a new shape.
The two original shapes don't overlap and aren't reflected, but they can be rotated.

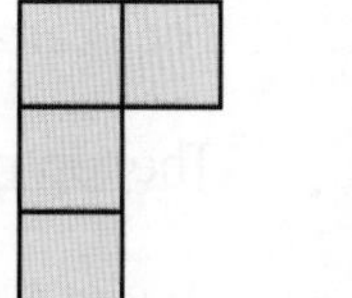
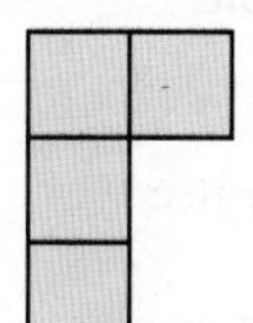

Which of these shapes can't he make?

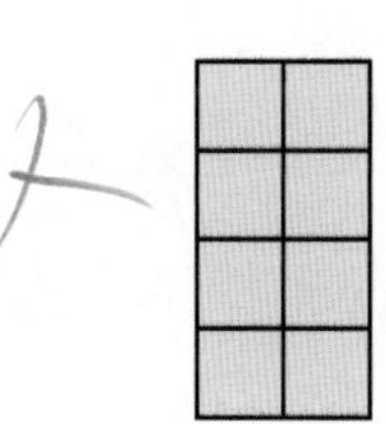
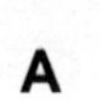
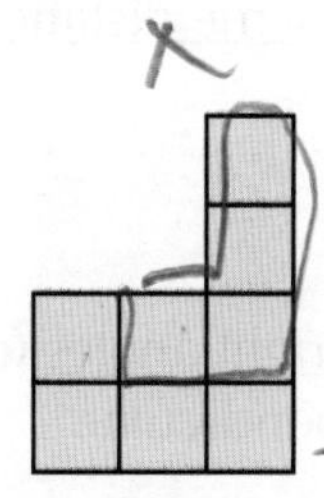
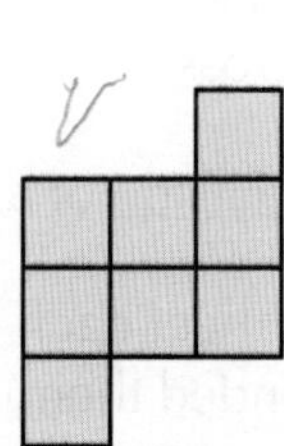
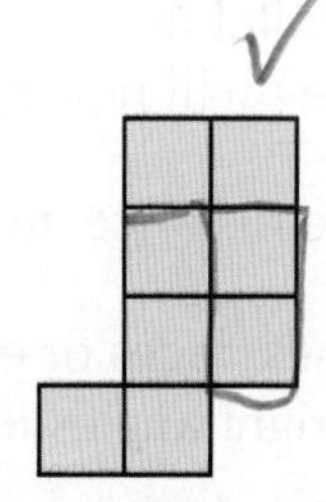
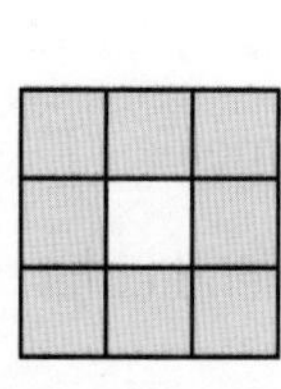

A **B** **C** **D** **E**

End of test

Glossary

acute angles	Angles that measure less than 90°. They are smaller than right angles.
area	The amount of space covered by a 2D (flat) shape. It is measured in square units (e.g. cm^2).
average	A typical (or 'normal' value). The mean is a type of average.
coordinates	They tell you the position of a point on a grid. For example, (3, 4) means 3 units along the horizontal x-axis and 4 units up the vertical y-axis.
decimal places	The places in a number to the right of the decimal point. For example, the number 4.56 has 2 decimal places.
degrees, °	The units used to measure angles. For example, a right angle measures 90°.
denominator	The bottom number of a fraction.
equivalent	Something that has the same value. For example, $\frac{1}{2}$ and $\frac{2}{4}$ are equivalent fractions.
estimate	An estimate is a sensible guess at the answer. You can use rounding to help you estimate answers.
factor	A whole number that divides exactly into another whole number. For example, the factors of 6 are 1, 2, 3 and 6.
frequency	How many times something appears in a set of data.
mass	Mass is what most people mean when they say 'weight'. A brick has a greater mass than a loaf of bread. Mass is measured in grams or kilograms.
multiple	Multiples are the numbers in a times table that goes on forever. For example, the multiples of 4 are 4, 8, 12, 16...
numerator	The top number of a fraction.
obtuse angles	Angles that measure more than 90° but less than 180°. They're bigger than right angles.
parallel	Parallel lines, faces and edges are always the same distance apart. They will never meet or cross.
perimeter	The distance around the outside of a shape.
perpendicular	Lines, faces or edges that meet each other at right angles (or would meet at right angles if you extended them) are perpendicular.
polygon	A 2D (flat) shape with straight sides.
prime	A prime number is a number that has exactly two factors: 1 and itself. For example, 2, 3, 5 and 7 are all prime numbers.
ratio	A comparison between one part and another part. For example, if there were 4 girls and 1 boy on a bus, the ratio of boys to girls would be 1 : 4.
volume	The amount of space taken up by a 3D shape. It is measured in cubed units (e.g. cm^3).

Answers

Section One — Number Knowledge

Page 5 — Place Value

1 **E** — All the numbers have the same units, so you need to look at the tenths. Four of the numbers have 4 in the tenths (Option B has 5, so it's not the answer), which means you need to look at the hundredths. E has the smallest number of hundredths, 3, so E is the answer.

2 **B** — A — incorrect, the numbers are 0.03 and 0.3 away from 7.
B — correct, both numbers are 0.11 away from 7.
C — incorrect, the numbers are 0.2 and 0.02 away from 7.
D — incorrect, the numbers are 0.06 and 0.1 away from 7.
E — incorrect, the numbers are 0.1 and 0.19 away from 7.

Page 7 — Rounding Up and Down

1 **D** — The 7 (in the ten thousands column) is being rounded. The 4 (in the thousands column) is less than 5 so 174 782 rounds down to 170 000.

Page 11 — Number Knowledge

1 **C** — A — false, 3 is a factor of 24 and is not a multiple of 2.
B — false, 13 is a common factor of 13 and 52.
C — true, 3 is a prime number and a multiple of 3.
D — false, no prime number is a square number.
A prime number only has 2 factors, one and itself.
E — false, not all numbers ending in 3 are multiples of 3, e.g. 13.

2 **C** — 72 can be divided exactly by 4, 6, 8 and 9. $72 \div 4 = 18$, $72 \div 6 = 12$, $72 \div 8 = 9$, $72 \div 9 = 8$. But 72 doesn't divide exactly by 7.

Page 13 — Number Sequences

1 **39** — The sequence is 4, 9, 15. The difference between the numbers is increased by one each time. The difference between 4 and 9 is 5, and 9 and 15 is 6. To find the fourth number you'd add 7, to find the fifth you'd add 8, and to find the sixth you'd add 9. $15 + 7 = 22$. $22 + 8 = 30$. $30 + 9 = 39$.

Page 16 — Fractions

1 **D** — Lydia gave Gemma $^2/_5$ of her pie, so Lydia is left with $^3/_5$ of her pie. Rose gave Gemma $^1/_5$ of her pie, so Rose is left with $^4/_5$ and Gemma has $^2/_5 + {}^1/_5 = {}^3/_5$ of a pie. So Lydia and Gemma have the same amount of pie.

2 **C** — Alex's fraction of the apples is divided into 3 groups. So divide $^2/_3$ by 3: $^2/_3 \div 3 = {}^2/_{(3 \times 3)} = {}^2/_9$

Page 19 — Percentages, Fractions and Decimals

1 **C** — There are 8 triangles in this shape and 2 are shaded in, so $^2/_8$ of the shape is shaded. You can simplify $^2/_8$ to $^1/_4$. $^1/_4$ is equal to 25%.

2 **B** — Reading off the chart, 20% of children chose pink as their favourite colour. 20% of 90 is the same as $^2/_{10}$ of 90. $90 \div 10 = 9$. $9 \times 2 = 18$.

3 **A** — A — 25% of 4 is the same as $^1/_4$ of 4. $4 \div 4 = 1$, $1 \times 1 = 1$
B — $^3/_4$ of 8. $8 \div 4 = 2$. $2 \times 3 = 6$.
C — $^2/_5$ of 10. $10 \div 5 = 2$. $2 \times 2 = 4$.
D — 10% of 25 is the same as $^1/_{10}$ of 25:
$25 \div 10 = 2.5$, $2.5 \times 1 = 2.5$
E — $^2/_6$ of 18. $18 \div 6 = 3$. $3 \times 2 = 6$.

Page 21 — Ratio and Proportion

1 **1 : 2 orange cows to black and white cows** — Write the ratio out using the numbers in the question: 48 : 96. Simplify the ratio by dividing both sides by the same number, e.g. divide both 48 and 96 by 12 to give a ratio of 4 : 8, then divide 4 and 8 by 4 to give a ratio of 1 : 2. 1 : 2 is in its simplest form because it can't be divided.

2 **60** — Turn the proportion into a fraction: $^5/_7$ of the blocks are green. $^1/_7$ of $84 = 84 \div 7 = 12$, so $^5/_7$ of $84 = 12 \times 5 = 60$ green blocks.

Pages 22-25 — Practice Questions

1 **D** — 9 is in the second column to the left of the decimal point. This is the tens column, so the value is 9 tens.

2 **C** — All the numbers have the same ten thousands, so look at the thousands. B has 3 thousands and the rest have 4, so it can't be B. Look at the hundreds — D has 2 hundreds and the others have 3, so D isn't the answer. Then look at the tens — C has 5 tens and A has 2 tens, so the answer is C.

3 **130** — There are ten divisions between 100 and 150. The difference between 100 and 150 is 50, so each division is worth $50 \div 10 = 5$. The arrow is pointing to the 6th division to the right of 100, so it is pointing at $100 + (6 \times 5) = 130$.

4 **C** — 4.7 is 0.3 away from 5. 5.35 is 0.35 away from 5. 5.15 is 0.15 away from 5. 4.8 and 5.2 are both 0.2 away from 5. 0.15 is the smallest, so the answer is C.

5 **20** — The 1 (in the tens column) is being rounded. The 9 (in the ones column) is more than 5, so 19.21 rounds up to 20.

6 **19** — The 9 (in the ones column) is being rounded. The 2 (in the tenths column) is less than 5, so 19.21 rounds down to 19.

7 **60 000** — The 5 (in the ten thousands column) is being rounded. The number in the thousands column is 5, so 55 300 rounds up to 60 000.

8 **B** — 7.12 rounds down to 7.1 because 2 (in the hundredths column) is less than 5. 7.05, 7.08 and 7.09 all round up to 7.1 because the digits in the hundredths columns are all 5 or more. 7.15 rounds up to 7.2 because there is a 5 in the hundredths column, so the answer is B.

9 **550 000** — The number will be smaller than 600 000, so the answer will have 5 hundred thousands. The digit in the ten thousands column has to be the smallest digit that rounds up, which is 5, so the answer is 550 000.

10 **37** — 39 isn't a prime number because it is a multiple of 3 ($39 = 3 \times 13$). 38 isn't prime because it is a multiple of 2 ($38 = 2 \times 19$). 37 is prime because its only factors are 1 and itself.

11 **D** — −14 °C would be furthest to the left if you wrote the numbers on a number line, so it has the lowest value.

12 **45** — The first few multiples of 9 are 9, 18, 27, 36, 45, 54...
The first few multiples of 15 are 15, 30, 45, 60...
The smallest number that appears in both of the lists is 45.

13 **B** — Work out each calculation to see which one isn't true. $4^3 = 4 \times 4 \times 4 = 64 < 75$, so A is correct. $9^2 = 9 \times 9 = 81$, so B is not correct. $3^3 = 3 \times 3 \times 3 = 27 > 20$, so C is correct. $7^2 = 7 \times 7 = 49 < 50$, so D is correct. So the answer is B.

14 **E** — She shares the doughnuts between 6 people (herself and five others). They are shared equally, so everyone gets the same number of doughnuts. This means the number in the box must be a multiple of 6 — the only option that is a multiple of 6 is 18.

15 **8** — The number of gold coins must be either 1, 8 or 27 because these are the only cube numbers smaller than 44. If he had one gold coin, there would be $44 - 1 = 43$ silver coins, but this isn't a square number. If he had 8 gold coins, he would have $44 - 8 = 36$ silver coins. $36 = 6^2$, so it's a square number, so he has 8 gold coins.

16 **7** — The factors of 35 are 1, 5, 7 and 35.
The factors of 84 are 1, 2, 3, 4, 6, 7, 12, 14, 21, 28, 42 and 84.
The only prime number that appears in both lists is 7.

17 **B** — A — MXVI = 1000 + 10 + 5 + 1 = 1016.
B — MCIX = 1000 + 100 + 9 = 1109.
C — CMXC = 900 + 90 = 990.
D — DCCX = 500 + 100 + 100 + 10 = 710.
E — MLXI = 1000 + 50 + 10 + 1 = 1061.
So MCIX has the highest value.

18 **8** — The factors of 40 are 1, 2, 4, 5, 8, 10, 20 and 40. The factors of 72 are 1, 2, 3, 4, 6, 8, 9, 12, 18, 24, 36 and 72. The greatest number that appears in both lists is 8.

19 **15** — To get from the third number to the fourth number, you add 8, and to get from the fourth number to the fifth, you add 8, so the rule for the sequence is 'add 8'. So the missing number is $7 + 8 = 15$.

20 **13** — The first shape has 4 dots, the second shape has 7 dots and the third shape has 10 dots. The number of dots increases by 3 each time, so the next shape will have $10 + 3 = 13$ dots.

21 **5** — Make a sequence by subtracting 7 each time: 79, 72, 65, 58, 51, 44... The sequence goes below 50 after 5 subtractions, so it takes 5 hours.

22 **23** — After 8 hours, he will have eaten $8 \times 7 = 56$ grapes. So there will be $79 - 56 = 23$ grapes left.

23 **E** — $\frac{10}{25}$ is the same as $\frac{2}{5}$. $\frac{12}{30}$, $\frac{4}{10}$ and $\frac{6}{15}$ are also the same as $\frac{2}{5}$ when the fractions are simplified. $\frac{30}{50}$ is the same as $\frac{3}{5}$, so E is not equivalent to $\frac{10}{25}$.

24 **B** — $\frac{2}{5}$, $\frac{1}{3}$ and $\frac{4}{9}$ are all less than $\frac{1}{2}$. $\frac{5}{6}$ is more than $\frac{1}{2}$, so this fraction is the biggest. So Beth has completed the most.

25 $\mathbf{\frac{7}{9}}$ — Add the two fractions together: $\frac{1}{3} + \frac{4}{9} = \frac{3}{9} + \frac{4}{9} = \frac{7}{9}$

26 $\mathbf{\frac{13}{30}}$ — Find equivalent fractions that have the same denominator, then subtract: $\frac{5}{6} - \frac{2}{5} = \frac{25}{30} - \frac{12}{30} = \frac{13}{30}$

27 **D** — $1 - \frac{7}{9} = \frac{9}{9} - \frac{7}{9} = \frac{2}{9}$, so 12 pages is $\frac{2}{9}$ of the book. $\frac{1}{9}$ of the book is $12 \div 2 = 6$ pages, so the whole book has $6 \times 9 = 54$ pages.

28 **C** — $\frac{3}{50}$ is equivalent to $\frac{6}{100}$, and $\frac{6}{100} = 6\%$.

29 **30%** — There are 20 triangles in the rectangle. 6 of the triangles are shaded, so $\frac{6}{20} = \frac{3}{10} = 30\%$ of the rectangle is shaded.

30 **220** — They have $100\% - 45\% = 55\%$ left. 50% of $400 = 400 \div 2 = 200$. 5% of $400 = 200 \div 10 = 20$. So 55% of $400 = 200 + 20 = 220$.

31 **48%** — $\frac{7}{25} = \frac{28}{100} = 28\%$. Add up the percentages he has used: $28\% + 24\% = 52\%$. So there's $100\% - 52\% = 48\%$ of the flour left.

32 **D** — $0.25 = 25\% < 30\%$, so A is true. $\frac{1}{5} = 20\% > 15\%$, so B is true. $0.9 = 90\%$, so C is true. $\frac{4}{5} = 0.8$, so D is not true. $\frac{3}{10} = 0.3 > 0.25$, so E is true.

33 **60 : 300** — There are $1 + 5 = 6$ parts in total. 1 part is $360 \div 6 = 60$ and 5 parts is $5 \times 60 = 300$, so the answer is 60 : 300.

34 **7 : 3** — Count the squares in the diagram. Side a is 7 squares long and side b is 3 squares long, so the ratio is 7 : 3.

35 **A** — The ratio of people to inflatables in the pool is 4 : 3. There are $3 \times 4 = 12$ inflatables, so there will be $4 \times 4 = 16$ people.

36 **60** — There are $4 \times 20 = 80$ people, so there will be $3 \times 20 = 60$ inflatables.

37 **144 g** — Find out the mass of each screw: $180\text{ g} \div 20 = 9\text{ g}$. He has used 4 screws, so the mass of the screws he has used is $4 \times 9\text{ g} = 36\text{ g}$. So the mass of the remaining screws is $180\text{ g} - 36\text{ g} = 144\text{ g}$.

Section Two — Working with Numbers

Page 27 — Addition

1 **B** — Round each value to the nearest pound: £13.89 rounds up to £14.00. £3.35 rounds down to £3.00. £12.30 rounds down to £12.00. Add the rounded values together to estimate the answer: £14.00 + £3.00 + 12.00 = £29.00. The answer is either B or D. As you rounded down by 65p and up by 11p, the estimate is lower than the actual answer. So the actual answer must be B — £29.54. (You could also use a written method.)

2 **48.43 seconds** — Add the four numbers together using the column method:

$$\begin{array}{r} 12.37 \\ 11.88 \\ 13.24 \\ +\ 10.94 \\ \hline 48.43 \\ {\scriptstyle 2} \end{array}$$

Their total time for the race was 48.43 seconds.

Page 29 — Subtraction

1 **E** — You need to subtract 48.28 from 75.63. Partition 48.28 into 40.00, 8.00, 0.20 and 0.08. $75.63 - 40.00 = 35.63$, then $35.63 - 8.00 = 27.63$ $27.63 - 0.20 = 27.43$, and $27.43 - 0.08 = 27.35$

2 **Anita** — Use the rounding method to estimate the difference in scores for each person. Round each score to the nearest whole number:

Joe: 62 – 58 = 4% Holly: 64 – 60 = 4%
Lucille: 63 – 63 = 0% Anita: 65 – 60 = 5%

(Dave's score decreased between test 1 and test 2, so Dave is not included.) As no one else's score increased by around 5%, Anita is the correct answer.

Page 31 — Multiplying and Dividing by 10, 100 and 1000

1 **B** — Start by working out how many books of tickets were sold. Divide the number of tickets sold by the number of tickets in a book: $1000 \div 10 = 100$ books. Then divide the amount of money made by the number of books sold to find the cost of each book: $375 \div 100 = £3.75$.

2 **0.0042** — $4.2 \div 10 = 0.42$. The number that fills in the blank should equal 0.42 when it's multiplied by 100. So, divide 0.42 by 100 to find the missing number. $0.42 \div 100 = 0.0042$.

Page 34 — Multiplication

1 **27 650** — 350 is 100 times larger than 3.5. 79 is 10 times larger than 7.9. So, the answer to 350×79 will be 1000 (100×10) times larger than 27.65. $27.65 \times 1000 = 27\,650$.

2 **D** — Estimate the answer by rounding each value to the nearest whole number and then multiplying the rounded values together. 6.9 rounds up to 7, 8.2 rounds down to 8. $8 \times 7 = 56$, so the answer is around 56. The only realistic option is option D, 56.58.

3 **954** — Use written multiplication to find the answer:

$$\begin{array}{r} 53 \\ \times\ 18 \\ \hline 4\,2_{2}4 \\ +\ 530 \\ \hline 954 \end{array}$$

Page 37 — Division

1 **2.2** — First, convert the decimal into a whole number: $8.8 \times 10 = 88$. Then do the division: $88 \div 4 = 22$. You multiplied 8.8 by 10 at the beginning, so divide your answer by 10 now: $22 \div 10 = 2.2$.

2 **11** — Divide 14.50 by 1.30 to see how many lots of 1.30 there are in 14.50. Partition 14.50 into numbers that are easier to work with. Find a number that's close to 14.50 and is a multiple of 1.30 — there are 10 lots of 1.30 in 13.00, which leaves you with 1.50 left over. This is enough to buy 1 more soft toy ($1.50 - 1.30 = 0.20$). The total number of toys you can buy is $10 + 1 = 11$.

3 **C** — The answer to $19\,200 \div 4$ will be four times larger than the answer to $19\,200 \div 16$ (because 4 is four times smaller than 16). So, multiply 1200 by 4 to find the answer to $19\,200 \div 4$. $1200 \times 4 = 4800$.

4 **33** — You need to divide 264 by 8. Split 264 into two smaller numbers that are easier to divide — e.g. 64 and 200. $64 \div 8 = 8$ and $200 \div 8 = 25$. Add the answers together to find the final answer: $8 + 25 = 33$ levels

5 **£112** — Divide £1680 by 15 using long division.

$$\begin{array}{r} 0112 \\ 15\overline{)1680} \\ -15 \\ \hline 18 \\ -15 \\ \hline 30 \\ -30 \\ \hline 0 \end{array}$$

Page 41 — Algebra

1 **£75** — The number of hours is 3 and the cost of the parts is £20. Put these values into the formula.
$C = 25 + 10h + p = 25 + 10 \times 3 + 20 = 25 + 30 + 20 = 75$
The cost of the electrician is £75.

2 **E** — The numbers in the sequence increase by 5 between each term, so the rule for the sequence will begin $5n$. When you multiply any of the terms by 5, you always need to add 1 to get the next number in the sequence. So, the expression for the nth term is $5n + 1$.

3 **D** — Work out each part of the algebraic expression:
The width of the room is 3 metres. The length of the room is $4 \times 3 = 12$ metres (4 times the width). The height of the room is y metres. To calculate the volume, multiply the width, length and height together: Volume $= 3 \times 12 \times y = 36y$

Pages 42-45 — Practice Questions

1 **5622** — 999 is 1 less than 1000. 4623 + 1000 = 5623, so subtract 1 to find 4623 + 999 = 5623 – 1 = 5622.

2 **C** — 8.9 is 0.1 less than 9 and 7.9 is 0.1 less than 8. So 8.9 + 7.9 is 0.1 + 0.1 = 0.2 less than 9 + 8. 9 + 8 = 17, so 8.9 + 7.9 = 17 – 0.2 = 16.8 cm — option C.

3 **28.2** — Add up the four numbers using the column method. Write 7 as 7.0.

$$\begin{array}{r} 8.4 \\ 9.1 \\ 7.0 \\ +\ 3.7 \\ \hline 28.2 \\ {\scriptstyle 1} \end{array}$$

So her total score was 28.2.

4 **B** — Partition 6.78 into 6.00, 0.70 and 0.08. 90 – 6.00 = 84.00, then 84.00 – 0.70 = 83.30 and 83.30 – 0.08 = 83.22.

5 **5330** — Subtract using the column method.

$$\begin{array}{r} 7450 \\ -\ 2120 \\ \hline 5330 \end{array}$$

So the answer is 5330.

6 **A** — Add up the three numbers using the column method.

$$\begin{array}{r} 2.18 \\ 4.65 \\ +\ 3.22 \\ \hline 10.05 \\ {\scriptstyle 1\ \ 1} \end{array}$$

So they have £10.05 in total.

7 **£1.43** — You need to subtract £3.22 from £4.65. Partition £3.22 into £3.00, £0.20 and £0.02.
£4.65 – £3.00 = £1.65, then £1.65 – £0.20 = £1.45 and £1.45 – £0.02 = £1.43. So Josh has £1.43 more than Tammy.

8 **£6.51** — First, subtract £22.99 from £50. £22.99 is £0.01 less than £23, so £50 – £22.99 = £50 – £23 + £0.01 = £27 + £0.01 = £27.01. Now partition £20.50 into £20.00 and £0.50 and subtract from £27.01. £27.01 – £20.00 = £7.01, then £7.01 – £0.50 = £6.51. So Monib has £6.51 left.

9 **8022** — 4578 tickets were sold for show 1 and 3444 tickets were sold for show 3. Add these numbers with the column method.

$$\begin{array}{r} 4578 \\ +\ 3444 \\ \hline 8022 \\ {\scriptstyle 111} \end{array}$$

10 **1013** — First, find the number of tickets sold for shows 2 and 3 combined. Partition 2018 (the tickets sold for show 2) into 2000, 10 and 8 then add to 3444 (the tickets sold for show 3).
3444 + 2000 = 5444, then 5444 + 10 = 5454 and 5454 + 8 = 5462.
Then subtract this from 6475 (the tickets sold for show 4) using the column method.

$$\begin{array}{r} 6475 \\ -\ 5462 \\ \hline 1013 \end{array}$$

So 1013 more tickets were sold for show 4.

11 **233 g** — First, add up the masses you know. 290 is 10 less than 300, so 290 + 262 = 300 + 262 – 10 = 562 – 10 = 552 g. Then subtract this from the total mass of the three oranges. Partition 552 into 500, 50 and 2.
785 – 500 = 285, then 285 – 50 = 235 and 235 – 2 = 233.
So the third orange has a mass of 233 g.

12 **14.68** — To divide by 100, move the digits two places to the right.

13 **C** — The opposite of multiplication is division, so divide 57 840 by 1000 to find the missing number. To divide by 1000, move the digits three places to the right. 57 840 ÷ 1000 = 57.84.

14 **£127** — Multiply the number of bars by the cost of each bar. To multiply by 100, move the digits two places to the left.
100 × £1.27 = £127.

15 **10** — You would need to divide the mass of the first pile by 100 to work out the mass of the second pile. You need to multiply the mass of the second pile by 10 to work out the mass of the third pile. Combining these statements tells you that you would have to divide the mass of the first pile by 100 then multiply by 10 to find the mass of the third pile. Dividing by 100 then multiplying by 10 is the same as dividing by 10, so the third pile is 10 times lighter than the first pile.

16 **120** — First, work out the total number of marbles he buys: 12 × 100 = 1200. Then divide by the number of boxes to work out how many marbles are in each box: 1200 ÷ 10 = 120 marbles.

17 **168** — First, work out the number of fish they eat in total in a day. 6 × 4 = 24 fish. There are 7 days in a week, so multiply by 7 to find the total number of fish they eat in a week.

$$\begin{array}{r} 24 \\ \times\ \ 7 \\ \hline 168 \\ {\scriptstyle 2} \end{array}$$

18 **C** — All of the options are multiplications, so compare the numbers in each option. Smaller numbers in the calculation will give a smaller answer. The smallest numbers in the options are 5.43 and 7.9, which are both in option C, so it gives the smallest answer.

19 **150 000** — Start with a simpler calculation: 5 × 3 = 15. 500 is 100 times larger than 5 and 300 is 100 times larger than 3, so 500 × 300 is 100 × 100 = 10 000 times larger than 5 × 3. 15 × 10 000 = 150 000.

20 **300 m** — Multiply the number of metres it rises each second by the number of seconds:
1.5 × 200 = 1.5 × 2 × 100 = 3 × 100 = 300 m

21 **D** — 3 is 3 times smaller than 9, so the missing number needs to be 3 times larger than 120 for the two multiplications to be equal. 120 × 3 = 360, so the missing number is 360 — option D.

22 **C** — There are 12 months in a year, so multiply the distance she runs each month by 12. Partition 12 into 10 and 2.
140 × 10 = 1400, then 140 × 2 = 280.
So she runs 1400 + 280 = 1680 km in a year.

23 **560** — You need to multiply the number of pencils Padma has by 5 and then by 4 to find the number of pencils Una has. Multiplying by 5 and then by 4 is the same as multiplying by 5 × 4 = 20, so multiply 28 by 20. 20 = 2 × 10, so 28 × 20 = 28 × 2 × 10 = 56 × 10 = 560 pencils.

24 **C** — You could find the missing number by dividing 182 by 26, but it is easier to use the fact that multiplication is the opposite of division to work out which number multiplies with 26 to give 182. Try the answer choice in the middle first so that you can narrow down the other options if that one is wrong.

$$\begin{array}{r} 26 \\ \times\ \ 7 \\ \hline 182 \\ {\scriptstyle 4} \end{array}$$

Since 26 × 7 = 182, the missing number is 7 — option C.

25 **6.95** — 48.65 is 100 times smaller than 4865, so 48.65 ÷ 7 will be 100 times smaller than 4865 ÷ 7. So 48.65 ÷ 7 = 695 ÷ 100 = 6.95.

26 **120 cm** — You need to work out 480 ÷ 4. Since 480 is 10 times larger than 48, 480 ÷ 4 is 10 times larger than 48 ÷ 4 = 12. 12 × 10 = 120, so each piece is 120 cm long.

27 **865** — Use short division to work out 4325 ÷ 5:

$$\begin{array}{r} 0\;8\;6\;5 \\ 5\overline{)4\;{}^{4}3\;{}^{3}2\;{}^{2}5} \end{array}$$

4325 ÷ 5 = 865, so there are 865 ants in each farm.

28 **£0.64** — Partition £3.20 into £3 and £0.20 = 20p before dividing by 5. £3 ÷ 5 = $^3/_5$ = $^6/_{10}$ = £0.60, and 20p ÷ 5 = 4p = £0.04. So each pastry was £0.60 + £0.04 = £0.64.

29 **D** — You need to be able to divide the total number of chairs by 11 or 12 without a remainder. One number that would work is 11 × 12 = 132 (since 132 ÷ 11 = 12 and 132 ÷ 12 = 11). All of the options are larger than this, so try doubling it. 132 × 2 = 264 — option D. Since 264 is twice as large as 132, 264 ÷ 11 and 264 ÷ 12 will be twice as large as 132 ÷ 11 and 132 ÷ 12. So 264 ÷ 11 = 24 and 264 ÷ 12 = 22. Both of these are whole numbers, so 264 could be the total number of chairs.

30 **205** — You need to be able to divide the number of comic books by 9 and get a remainder of 7. Find a number divisible by 9 close to 200. 9 × 11 = 99, so 9 × 22 = 9 × 11 × 2 = 99 × 2 = 198. Add 7 to get a number that gives a remainder of 7 when divided by 9. 198 + 7 = 205, which is between 200 and 210. So Leon has 205 comic books.

31 **77** — Change n in the expression to 12, then follow BODMAS to work out the answer: 6 × 12 + 5 = 72 + 5 = 77.

32 **C** — Multiply both terms in the brackets by 3. $(3 \times t) + (3 \times 4) = 3t + 12$.

33 **D** — The mugs can hold $7 \times x = 7x$ ml and the glasses can hold $3 \times y = 3y$ ml. So they can hold $7x + 3y$ ml in total — option D.

34 **B** — The numbers in the sequence increase by 5 between each term, so the rule for the sequence will begin $5n$. For the first term, $n = 1$. So $5n = 5 \times 1 = 5$. The first term is 4, so you need to subtract 1 to get the expression to give the correct value. So, the expression for the nth term is $5n - 1$.

35 **6** — First, add 6 to both sides. This gives $5x = 30$, so divide by 5 on both sides to find $x = 30 \div 5 = 6$.

36 **54** — For the 100th term, $n = 100$. Change n in the expression to 100: 100 ÷ 2 + 4 = 50 + 4 = 54, so the 100th term is 54.

37 **£25** — Change g in the formula to 4 and p to 3. $B = 5 \times 4 + 3 + 2 = 20 + 3 + 2 = 25$, so it would cost £25.

38 **2** — Change p in the formula to 5 and B to 17, then work out the value of g. $17 = 5g + 5 + 2$, so $17 = 5g + 7$. Subtract 7 from both sides to get $10 = 5g$, then divide both sides by 5 to get $g = 10 \div 5 = 2$.

39 **£105** — The electrician charges £20 per hour, so they charge 3 × £20 = £60 for their time. Subtract this and the call-out fee from the total amount they charge to find the cost of the parts. £195 – £60 – £30 = £105.

Section Three — Number Problems

Page 47 — Mixed Calculations

1 **D** — The calculations show the prices of all the items rounded up to the nearest 10p. The only part that's different about all of the options is the number of pence added or subtracted from the end. Work out how many pence have been added to each of the prices to round them up.
Orange = 39p, which is rounded to 40p by adding 1p.
3 oranges are bought, so 3p is added to the total.
Carrot cake = £1.99, which is rounded to £2 by adding 1p.
2 carrot cakes are bought, so 2p is added to the total.
Tuna roll = 99p, which has been rounded to £1 by adding 1p.
1 tuna roll is bought, so 1p is added to the total.
Work out how many pence have been added in total.
3p + 2p + 1p = 6p. So D is the answer because you'd need to take 6p away from the total to get the right amount.

2 **B** — Don't forget BODMAS — for all the calculations, you will need to do the multiplication before the additions and subtractions. The numbers in the different additions and subtractions range from 12 to 15. The total number added to or subtracted from each calculation differs by about 5 (e.g. 15 − 13 = 2 and 12 − 15 = –3). The numbers in the different multiplications also range from 12 to 15, but when multiplied together the results will differ by a greater amount than the additions and subtractions (e.g. 15 × 13 = 195 and 14 × 13 = 182). So the calculation with the greatest numbers in the multiplication will give the largest answer. The largest multiplication is 13 × 15, and two options include this multiplication. The result of the multiplication will be the same for both, so just work out which of the two has the greatest number added to the multiplication:
B: Total added = 14 − 12 = 2 C: Total added = 12 − 13 = –1
B is the answer.

Page 51 — Word Problems

1 **E** — To get 42 tulips, Lena needs to buy 6 bunches of tulips (42 ÷ 7 = 6). To get 42 roses, Lena needs to buy 7 bunches of roses (42 ÷ 6 = 7). So 6 × £4.50 = £27 and 7 × £3.50 = £24.50. £27 + £24.50 = £51.50.

2 **£1.70** — You need to work out how much Benni spent: £10 − £1.50 = £8.50.
5 sandwiches cost £8.50, so 1 sandwich costs £8.50 ÷ 5 = £1.70.

3 **£17.10** — Work out the profit that Simone makes on each bracelet. 50p − 20p = 30p. Then multiply this by the number she sells. The easiest thing to do here is to round the number she sells (57) up to an easier number (60), then do the multiplication. 30 × 60 can be worked out by finding 3 × 6 = 18, then add on the two zeros to give 1800p, or £18.00. Because you rounded the number sold up by three, you just need to subtract the cost of 3 bracelets (3 × 30p = 90p) from £18.00 to get the answer.
£18.00 – 90p = £17.10.

Pages 52-53 — Practice Questions

1 **9** — The rules of BODMAS tell you to work out brackets, then division, and finally subtraction:
42 ÷ 3 – (1 + 4) = 42 ÷ 3 – 5 = 14 – 5 = 9.

2 **C** — Follow the rules of BODMAS to calculate each expression.
A: 14 ÷ 2 + 3 – 1 = 7 + 3 – 1 = 10 – 1 = 9
B: 9 – 3 + 5 ÷ 2 = 9 – 3 + 2.5 = 6 + 2.5 = 8.5
C: 3 ÷ 2 + 3 × 2 = 1.5 + 3 × 2 = 1.5 + 6 = 7.5
D: (8 – 6) ÷ 2 + 5 = 2 ÷ 2 + 5 = 1 + 5 = 6
E: 3 × 1 + 12 – 9 = 3 + 12 – 9 = 15 – 9 = 6

3 **3800** — Since 28 and 72 are both multiplied by 38, you can add them together first. 28 + 72 = 100, then 100 × 38 = 3800.

4 **C** — Follow the rules of BODMAS to calculate each expression.
A: 90 + 30 ÷ 15 – 5 = 90 + 2 – 5 = 92 – 5 = 87
B: 90 – 30 ÷ 15 + 5 = 90 – 2 + 5 = 88 + 5 = 93
C: 90 ÷ 30 + 15 – 5 = 3 + 15 – 5 = 18 – 5 = 13
D: 90 + 30 – 15 ÷ 5 = 90 + 30 – 3 = 120 – 3 = 117
E: 90 – 30 + 15 ÷ 5 = 90 – 30 + 3 = 60 + 3 = 63

5 **30** — BODMAS tells you to start with the brackets. Use partitioning to find 80 × 2.5. Partition 2.5 into 2 and 0.5. 80 × 2 = 160 and 80 × 0.5 = 40. So 80 × 2.5 = 160 + 40 = 200. Now work out 6000 ÷ 200. You can simplify by dividing both numbers by 100 first. 6000 ÷ 200 = 60 ÷ 2 = 30.

6 **C** — £5 per hour for 3 hours comes to £5 × 3, then add on the fixed fee of £10 to get £5 × 3 + £10. The BODMAS rule says that multiplication comes before addition, so no brackets are needed.

7 **E** — First Sharla subtracts 5, so you need n – 5. She then divides by 2, but as division comes before subtraction in BODMAS, you need brackets to make sure the subtraction is done first: $(n – 5) \div 2$. Then, add 7 to get $(n – 5) \div 2 + 7$.

8 **100 minutes** — £10 = 10 × 100 = 1000p. Half of this is 1000p ÷ 2 = 500p. So Chris needs to use 500p worth of call time to reduce his credit by half. At 5p per minute, that's 500 ÷ 5 = 100 minutes.

9 **8** — Do the operations in reverse. 70 – 6 = 64.
Louise squares her number to get 64, and $8^2 = 8 \times 8 = 64$.

10 **20 weeks** — Alfie swims twice a week (Tuesdays and Thursdays) and 3.5 km each time he swims. So every week he swims 3.5 km × 2 = 7 km in total. Now divide 140 km by 7 km to find the answer: 140 ÷ 7 = 20 weeks.

11 **B** — The pineapple and watermelon cost £0.95 + £2.75 = £3.70. So Mac has £5 – £3.70 = £1.30 left over to spend on kiwi fruit.
Convert to pence:
1.30 × 100 = 130p. At 15p each, 10 kiwi fruit cost 150p — this is too much. 9 kiwi fruit cost 15p × 9 = 135p, which is still too much, but 8 kiwi fruit cost 15p × 8 = 120p. So Mac buys 8 kiwi fruit and has 130p – 120p = 10p left.

12 **E** — A could be true (e.g. Tiana could have donated 18 jumpers and 9 T-shirts). This means that C could be true.
The amounts of each item add up to an odd number (27).
So one amount must be odd and the other amount must be even.
The difference between an even and an odd number is always odd.
E says that the difference is even (8), so E cannot be true.
B could be true (e.g. Tiana could have donated 17 jumpers and 10 T-shirts) and D could be true (e.g. Tiana could have donated 16 T-shirts and 11 jumpers).

13 **14** — 17 easy questions are worth a total of 17 × 3 = 51 points. That leaves 149 – 51 = 98 points from hard questions. Each hard question is worth 7 points, so Sanjay answered 98 ÷ 7 = 14 of them.

14 **E** — Four mugs cost £2.25 × 8. Partition £2.25 into £2 and £0.25.
So £2.25 × 8 = (£2 × 8) + (£0.25 × 8) = £16 + £2 = £18.
Now divide by 4: one mug costs £18 ÷ 4 = £4.50.

15 **D** — You're looking for a number that is 4 more than a multiple of 7. The first few multiples of 7 are 7, 14, 21 and 28. Add 4 to each: 7 + 4 = 11, 14 + 4 = 18, 21 + 4 = 25 and 28 + 4 = 32.
So Aaron could have started with 25 carrots. You could also divide each option by 7. The number of carrots leaves a remainder of 4 when divided by 7. E.g. 25 ÷ 7 = 3 remainder 4.

Section Four — Data Handling

Page 55 — Data Tables

1 **B** — The number of children who own more than 15 DVDs is shown by the frequencies in the bottom two rows of the table. Find the total number of children by adding these frequencies together: 13 + 6 = 19.

2 **£6** — First find the total amount spent on senior citizen tickets by subtracting the cost of the adult tickets, child tickets and the booking fee from the "Amount to pay".
£212.50 – £2.50 – £32 – £160 = £18.
The table shows that three senior citizen tickets were bought, so divide £18 by 3 to find the cost of one ticket: £18 ÷ 3 = £6

Page 59 — Displaying Data

1 **36** — You know that 20° = 2 children, so 10° = 1 child.
The whole pie chart is 360° and 360° ÷ 10° = 36, so there are 36 children in the class.

Page 61 — Analysing Data

1 **21** — Mean = (22 + 23 + 17 + 17 + 26) ÷ 5 = 105 ÷ 5 = 21.

Page 63 — Misleading Data

1 **C** — The headline suggests that sales of pencils have fallen by a massive amount. If you read the graph, the sales have only actually fallen from 500 million to 498 million. The graph makes it look like the sales have fallen more sharply because the axis doesn't start at zero — the drop isn't very big compared to the overall number of pencils sold.

Pages 64-67 — Practice Questions

1 **9** — 21 pupils chose swimming in total, and 12 of them were in Class A, so 21 – 12 = 9 were in Class B.

2 **C** — Work out how many pupils chose gymnastics in Class A: 28 – 12 – 6 = 10. So 10 + 12 = 22 pupils chose gymnastics, which is more than chose swimming (21) or cricket (10).

3 **53** — Add up the totals for each row: 21 + 10 + 22 = 53.

4 **D** — There are fewest symbols in the Purple Emperor row, so this is the least common type of butterfly.

5 **6** — There are $1\frac{1}{2}$ more symbols in the Tortoiseshell row than in the Red Admiral row. Each symbol means 4 butterflies, so there are $4 \times 1\frac{1}{2} = 6$ more Tortoiseshell butterflies.

6 **44** — There are 10 whole symbols and 2 half symbols, so 11 whole symbols in total. So there are 11 × 4 = 44 butterflies.

7 **30** — 100 books were borrowed on Tuesday and 70 books were borrowed on Monday. So 100 – 70 = 30 more books were borrowed on Tuesday.

8 **C** — The bar for Wednesday is significantly smaller than the others, and a similar number of books were borrowed on the other four days, so it's most likely that the library was only open for half a day on Wednesday.

9 **74** — Find the total number of books borrowed:
70 + 100 + 30 + 80 + 90 = 370.
There are five days, so divide the total by 5: 370 ÷ 5 = 74.

10 **$75** — Go up from £60 on the horizontal axis until you get to the green line. Then go across to the vertical axis and read off the value in dollars.

11 **£320** — From the graph, $100 is £80.
So 4 × $100 = $400 = 4 × £80 = £320.

12 **C** — From the graph, $25 = £20, so $27 will be just over £20, but not as much as £27. So the scarf costing £19 is the only possible option.

13 **B** — The angles in a pie chart add up to 360°, so subtract the angles you know from 360°: 360° – 90° – 90° – 120° = 60°

14 **60** — 120° is $\frac{1}{3}$ of 360°, so 20 children is $\frac{1}{3}$ of the total number of children. So multiply by 3 to find the total number of children: 20 × 3 = 60.

15 **3:25 pm** — There are 5 divisions between 0 cm and 10 cm, so one division is worth 10 ÷ 5 = 2 cm. Go across from 28 on the vertical axis until you get to the green line. Then go down to the horizontal axis and read off the time.

16 **D** — When the water was turned off, the depth doesn't change, so the green line will be flat. This happens between 3:10 pm and 3:20 pm.

17 **36 cm** — Go up from 3:30 pm on the horizontal axis until you get to the green line. Then go across to the vertical axis and read off the depth. It's two divisions below 40 cm, which is 36 cm.

18 **C** — The sector for irises is larger than the sector for lilies, so more children chose irises than lilies, so A is false.
The sector for tulips is larger than the sector for lilies, so more children chose tulips than lilies, so B is false.
Roses make up $\frac{1}{4}$ (90°) of the pie chart. $\frac{1}{4}$ of 72 is 72 ÷ 4 = 18, so C is true. The sectors for daisies and bluebells are different sizes, so D is false.
60° is $\frac{1}{6}$ of 360°. $\frac{1}{6}$ of 72 is 72 ÷ 6 = 12 (not 9), so E is false.

19 **£2.40** — The total she spent over the six months was
6 × £4.50 = (6 × £4) + (6 × £0.50) = £24 + £3 = £27.
Her total spend in the other 5 months was
£4.80 + £5.40 + £3.90 + £6.20 + £4.30 = £24.60.
So in the missing month she spent £27 – £24.60 = £2.40.

20 **11 °C** — Add up the temperatures: 11 + 9 + 8 + 10 + 12 + 13 + 14 = 77. There are 7 days, so divide the total by 7: 77 ÷ 7 = 11 °C.

21 **Saturday: 4 mph, Sunday: 10 mph** — The total for the 7 days is 9 × 7 = 63. Subtracting the values for Monday-Friday leaves 63 – 9 – 11 – 7 – 14 – 8 = 63 – 49 = 14.
Find two numbers that add up to 14 and have a difference of 6:
4 + 10 = 14, 10 – 4 = 6. The wind speed was greater on Sunday, so it was 4 mph on Saturday and 10 mph on Sunday.

22 **D** — Statements A-C and E are all true, but don't matter for the pictogram. Statement D does matter — the symbols are different in each row, so you can't tell how many of each type of house there are.

23 **D** — TJ got 25 votes and Leo got 22 votes. 25 isn't double 22, so A is false. Leo got 22 votes and Mai got 21 votes. 21 isn't $\frac{2}{3}$ of 22, so B is false. Mai got 21 votes and Amy got 20 votes. 20 isn't half of 21, so C is false. TJ got 25 votes and Amy got 20 votes. 20 is $\frac{4}{5}$ of 25, so D is true. Leo got 22 votes and Amy got 20 votes. 22 isn't three times 20, so E is false.

Section Five — Shape and Space

Page 69 — Angles

1 **D** — Angle c is smaller than a right angle, so it is less than 90°. This means that it must be either 10° or 45°. You can tell that it is about half of the size of a right angle, so the correct answer is option D — 45°.

2 **135°** — The total size of the angles on the circular compass is 360°. There are 8 compass points, so the size of the angle between each point is 360 ÷ 8 = 45°. South is three points away from north-east so the size of the angle between them is 45 × 3 = 135°.

Page 73 — 2D Shapes

1 **C** — The shape has no right angles so it can't be a right-angled triangle. It has no equal sides so it can't be equilateral or isosceles. All the sides and angles in a scalene triangle are different, so the answer is C.

2 **A** — First, rule out the shapes that can't go in that row. A square, an equilateral triangle and a rhombus have all equal side lengths, so you can rule out B, D and E. Next, rule out the shapes that can't go in that column. A rectangle has all equal angles, so you can rule out C. The answer must be A — a trapezium.

3 **Isosceles triangle** — The shape has no obtuse angles, so all the angles inside the shape must be 90° or less — this means the shape can only be a square, a rectangle or a triangle. The next clue says that it has no right angles, so it can't be a square or a rectangle — it must be a triangle. The final clue says that two of its sides are equal in length. A right-angled triangle or an isosceles triangle can have two equal side lengths, but this shape doesn't have any right angles. The shape is an isosceles triangle.

4 **9 cm** — The diameter of the circle is 18 cm, so the radius is 18 ÷ 2 = 9 cm.

Page 77 — 2D Shapes — Area and Perimeter

1 **7.5 cm** — The perimeter of the shape is made up of 10 equal length sides. The length of each side is 75 ÷ 10 = 7.5 cm. So, side Z is 7.5 cm.

2 **C** — Split the shape into two rectangles as shown in the diagram. Work out the length of the missing sides — the horizontal side is 13 – 5 – 5 = 3 cm and the vertical side is 8 – 4 = 4 cm.

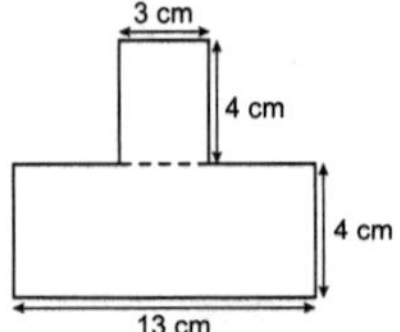

Then work out the area of each rectangle. The smaller rectangle is 3 × 4 = 12 cm². The larger rectangle is 13 × 4 = 52 cm². The total area of the shape is 52 + 12 = 64 cm².

Page 79 — Symmetry

1 **A** — The shape is a trapezium. The diagram shows the reflected shape.

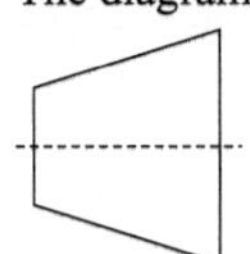

2 **5** — The star has 5 lines of symmetry, as shown on the diagram.

Page 83 — 3D Shapes

1 **B** — Option B is the only net that will not fold up to make a cube — two of its faces would overlap. The diagram below shows which faces would overlap if you folded it up.

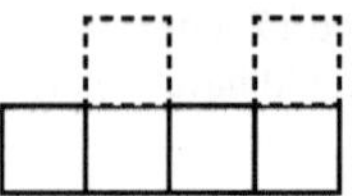

2 **64** — The number of vegetable stock cubes that will fit along the length of the box is 4 cm ÷ 1 cm = 4. The number that will fit along the width of the box is 8 cm ÷ 1 cm = 8. The number that will fit up the height of the box is 2 cm ÷ 1 cm = 2. The total number of cubes is 4 × 8 × 2 = 64 stock cubes.

3 **Cuboid** — The net has 4 rectangular faces in a line, then 2 squares at the top and bottom — it will fold up to make a cuboid.

Page 85 — Shape Problems

1 **C** — When you look at the logo from the back of the window it will be flipped over, so you need to look for the option that's a reflection of the original logo. Option C is a reflection of the original logo.

Page 89 — Coordinates

1 **D** — Go through the options one by one. Imagine plotting each point on the grid. A parallelogram is a shape with two pairs of equal length, parallel sides, a pair of equal obtuse angles and a pair of equal acute angles. Only the coordinates for option D make a parallelogram with the existing points on the grid.

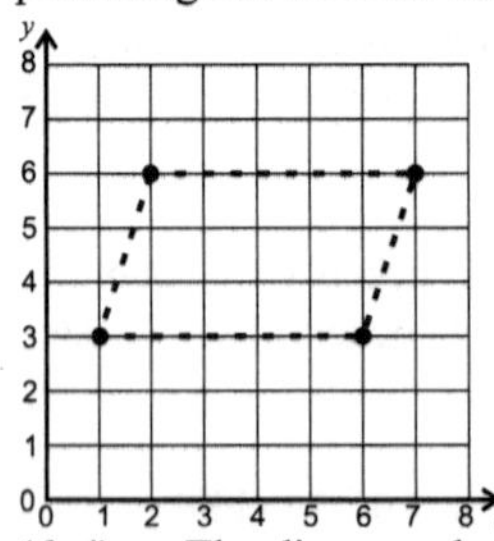

2 **(6, 4)** — The diagram shows the shape after it has been reflected in the mirror line. The coordinates of corner Y are now (6, 4).

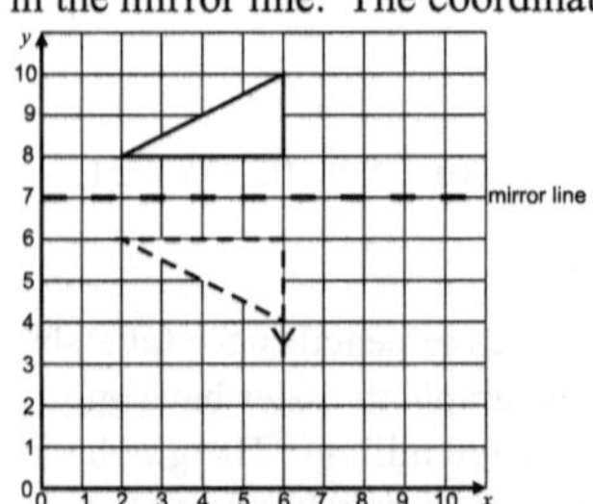

Pages 90-95 — Practice Questions

1 **B** — Angle w is smaller than a right angle but larger than half of a right angle ($90° \div 2 = 45°$), so it must be 60° — option B.

2 **131°** — Angles on a straight line add up to 180°, so S = 180° – 49° = 131°.

3 **302°** — Angles in a triangle add up to 180°, so the missing angle in this triangle is 180° – 38° – 84° = 58°. This angle is around a point with angle x, so these two angles must add up to 360°. So angle x is 360° – 58° = 302°.

4 **D** — Obtuse angles measure more than 90° but less than 180°, so three obtuse angles together must measure more than $90° \times 3 = 270°$. Angles around a point add up to 360°, so angle k must measure less than 360° – 270° = 90°. The only option less than 90° is D — 73°.

5 **44°** — First, look at the quadrilateral made up of the outside edges of the diagram. The angles in a quadrilateral add up to 360°, so the top angle must be 360° – 68° – 122° – 51° = 119°. This angle is made up of angle y and a 75° angle, so angle y is 119° – 75° = 44°.

6 **C** — The shape has six sides, so it is a hexagon.

7 **D** — She would need at least six sticks to make a rectangle, since the smallest rectangle would have two sides made up of one stick each and two sides made up of two sticks each — 1 + 1 + 2 + 2 = 6. The diagram below shows how she could make the other shapes.

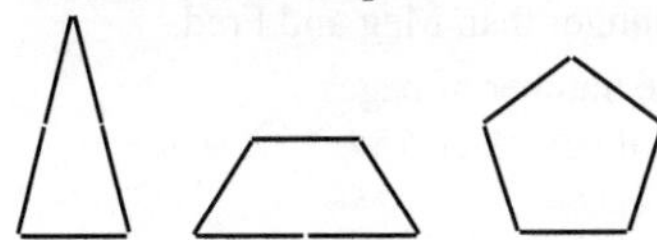

8 **B** — The outside edge of a circle is called the circumference.

9 **1** — A kite has 2 pairs of equal sides and 2 equal angles, so it has 1 pair of equal angles.

10 **120 mm** — The diameter is twice the radius, so the radius is $240 \div 2 = 120$ mm.

11 **76°** — The angles in a triangle add up to 180°, so the two missing angles must add up to 180° – 28° = 152°. The triangle is isosceles, so these two angles are equal. So each of them is $152° \div 2 = 76°$.

12 **120°** — Angle b is around a point with four angles in equilateral triangles. Each angle in an equilateral triangle is 60°, so these four angles add up to $60° \times 4 = 240°$. Angles around a point add up to 360°, so angle b is 360° – 240° = 120°.

13 **C** — A square has four equal sides and four equal angles, so it is a regular quadrilateral. All of the other options have at least one side or angle that is different in size, so they are irregular quadrilaterals.

14 **12 cm** — A regular heptagon has seven equal sides, so each side is $84 \div 7 = 12$ cm long.

15 **4** — First, find the perimeter of the pitch. 70 + 130 + 70 + 130 = 400 m, so he needs to paint 400 m of lines. So he needs $400 \div 100 = 4$ cans.

16 **21 cm** — A regular pentagon has five sides of equal length, so the length of each side is $35 \div 5 = 7$ cm. Each of the three sides of the triangle in the centre is also a side of a pentagon, so the perimeter of the triangle is $7 \times 3 = 21$ cm.

17 **80 m** — The original fence around field A was 60 + 50 + 60 + 50 = 220 m long. The fence around the combined fields is 60 + 50 + (60 – 40) + 40 + 40 + 40 + 50 = 300 m long. So the new fence is 300 – 220 = 80 m longer.

18 **D** — The area of a rectangle = length × width, so divide the area by the width to find the length. So the length is $56 \div 7 = 8$ cm — option D.

19 **5 m²** — The area of a triangle = $\frac{1}{2}$ × base × height. So the area of this triangle = $\frac{1}{2} \times 2 \times 5 = 1 \times 5 = 5$ m².

20 **47 m²** — Split the shape into two rectangles as shown in the diagram. The missing side in the smaller rectangle is 8 – 2 – 1 = 5 m.

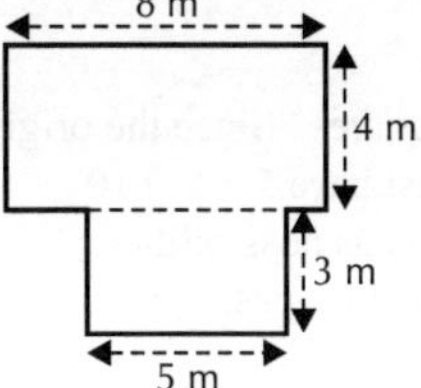

Work out the area of each rectangle. The area of the smaller rectangle is $5 \times 3 = 15$ m². The area of the larger rectangle is $8 \times 4 = 32$ m². So the total area of the shape is 15 + 32 = 47 m².

21 **A** — A regular pentagon has 5 lines of symmetry, which is more than the 3 lines of an equilateral triangle, the 4 lines of a square and the 2 lines of a rhombus. All of these lines are shown in the diagram below.

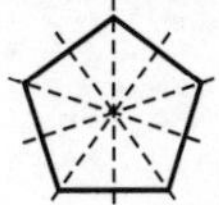
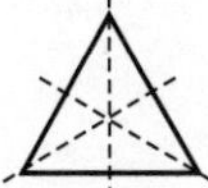
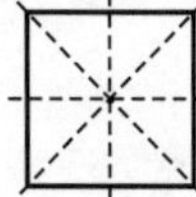
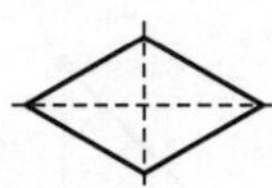

22 **2** — The shape has 2 lines of symmetry, shown on the diagram on the right.

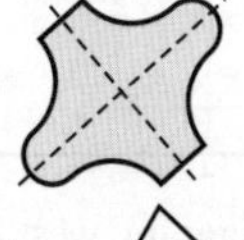

23 **D** — The reflected shape has seven sides, so it is a heptagon.

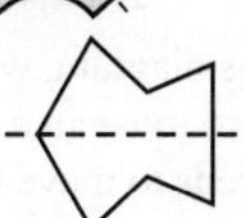

24 **E** — There are two end faces, so there are 7 – 2 = 5 side faces on the prism. The number of side faces is equal to the number of sides on the end face (e.g. a triangle has three sides, so a triangular prism has three side faces), so the end faces have 5 sides, meaning they are pentagons.

25 **4** — Vertices are corners. A triangle-based pyramid has 4 vertices.

26 **Square-based pyramid** — The net has one square and four triangles. The net will fold so that each triangle shares a side with the square and the four triangles meet at a point, so the shape will be a square-based pyramid.

27 **72** — The number of sugar cubes that will fit along the length of the container is $12 \div 2 = 6$ cubes. The number of cubes that will fit along the width of the container is $8 \div 2 = 4$ cubes. The number of cubes that will fit up the height of the container is $6 \div 2 = 3$ cubes. Multiply the number of cubes that will fit along the length, width and height to find the total number that will fit in the container. $6 \times 4 \times 3 = 24 \times 3 = 72$ cubes.

28 **D** — Option D is the only net that will not fold up to make a prism — the shaded faces in the diagram below would overlap.

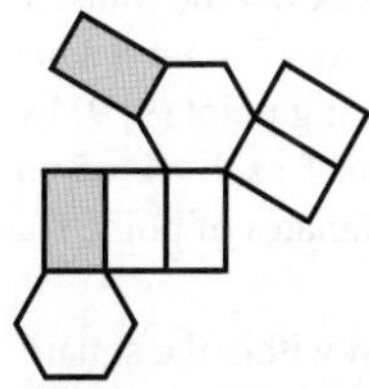

29 **2.5 m** — The planter is a cuboid, so its volume = length × width × height. So 5 = length × 2 × 1 = length × 2. So length = $5 \div 2 = 2.5$ m.

30 **160 cm³** — First, find the volume of the container. The container is a cuboid, so its volume = length × width × height = $8 \times 10 \times 7$ = $80 \times 7 = 560$ cm³. This is how much water the container could hold, so he needs to add 560 – 400 = 160 cm³ more to fill the container.

31 **26** — Count all of the faces that would be visible from any angle. There are 12 vertical faces on the bottom layer of the shape, 4 vertical faces on the top layer, 5 horizontal faces on the top and 5 horizontal faces on the bottom.
So she painted 12 + 4 + 5 + 5 = 26 faces.

32 **B** — Each of the original shapes has 5 squares. Since the original shapes do not overlap, the new shape must have 5 + 5 = 10 squares. This leaves only options B and D as possibilities.
Option D cannot be made from the original shapes.
Option B can be made as shown below.

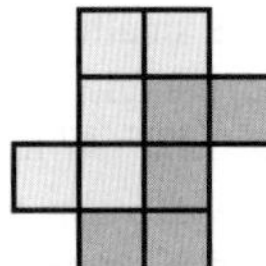

33 **E** — The diagram below shows Nneka's location after her first two moves.

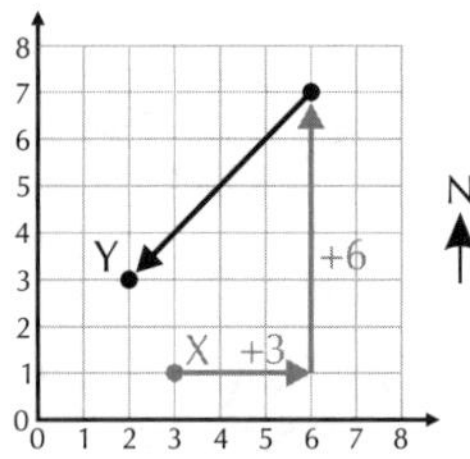

On this diagram, west is to the left and south is down. Since she needs to move in a direction halfway between the left and down, she needs to move to the south-west — option E.

34 **(3, 1)** — Corner H is directly below the corner at (3, 5), so it has the same *x*-coordinate of 3. The side length of the square is equal to the difference between the *x*-coordinates of the top corners, so each side is 7 – 3 = 4 units long. The side length is also equal to the difference between the *y*-coordinates of the top-left corner and corner H, so the *y*-coordinate of corner H is 5 – 4 = 1.
So the coordinates of corner H are (3, 1).

35 **(–2, 7)** — The reflection will not change the *y*-coordinate of point A, so that is still 7. Point A is 4 units to the right of the mirror line, so it will be 4 units to the left of the mirror line in the reflection. The mirror line is at *x* = 2, so the *x*-coordinate of the reflected point A is 2 – 4 = –2. So the coordinates of the reflected point A are (–2, 7).

36 **(–3, 2)** — Point B on the original shape is at (5, 4). Translating the shape 2 squares down decreases the *y*-coordinate by 2, leaving it at 4 – 2 = 2. Translating the shape 8 squares to the left decreases the *x*-coordinate by 8, leaving it at 5 – 8 = –3. So the coordinates of point B on the translated shape are (–3, 2).

37 **(5, 11)** — Every point is translated by the same amount, so take matching points from the two shapes and work out the translation. Point (7, 1) goes to (3, 3), so the translation was 7 – 3 = 4 squares to the left and 3 – 1 = 2 squares up. Translating point (9, 9) by the same amount leaves the *x*-coordinate of point T as 9 – 4 = 5 and the *y*-coordinate as 9 + 2 = 11. So the coordinates of point T are (5, 11).

38 **B** — The point for the statue must be located within the square on the grid. The *x*-coordinates of the corners of the square are 4 and 8, so the *x*-coordinate of the statue must be between 4 and 8. The *y*-coordinates of the corners of the square are 6 and 10, so the *y*-coordinate of the statue must be between 6 and 10. The only option that fits the criteria for the *x*- and *y*-coordinates is (5, 9).

Section Six — Units and Measures

Page 98 — Units

1 **D** — 0.3 g, 3 g and 30 g are all very light — less than the weight of an empty schoolbag, so the answer can't be any of these options. 30 kg is very heavy — about the weight of a child, so this can't be the answer either. The answer must be 3 kg — this is about the weight of 3 bags of sugar, which could easily be carried.

2 **71 servings** — There is originally 28.75 litres = 28.75 × 1000 = 28 750 ml of soup. 350 ml is spilt, so there is 28 750 – 350 = 28 400 ml left. Now you need to divide 28 400 ml by 400 ml to find the number of servings. To simplify the calculation, you could divide both numbers by 100: 28 400 ÷ 400 = 284 ÷ 4.
Now use a written method to do the division: $4\overline{)2\,{}^{2}8\,4}$ = 7 1

3 **A** — Each stride is 50 cm so 2 strides will cover 2 × 50 cm = 100 cm. 100 cm = 1 m, so Ashanti takes 2 strides to walk 1 m. 1000 m = 1 km, so in 10 km, there are 10 × 1000 = 10 000 m. To walk 10 000 m, Ashanti must take 10 000 × 2 = 20 000 strides.

Page 101 — Time

1 **Max** — The youngest child must have the latest date of birth. Children born in 2009 must be younger than those born in 2008, so it can't be Jim or Geeta. October is later in 2009 than March and May, so Max must be younger than Meg and Fred.

2 **February** — Keep adding the number of pages she completes each month until you reach 154.
Sep = 30
Sep + Oct = 30 + 31 = 61
Sep + Oct + Nov = 61 + 30 = 91
Sep + Oct + Nov + Dec = 91 + 31 = 122
Sep + Oct + Nov + Dec + Jan = 122 + 31 = 153
There are 153 days between September and the end of January, so she will finish her 154-page book in February.

3 **D** — 4:53 pm + 7 mins = 5 pm, then 5 pm + 2 hours = 7 pm, and 7 pm + 15 mins = 7:15 pm. The total is 7 mins + 2 hours + 15 mins = 2 hours 22 minutes. Watch out — this isn't the same as 2.22 hours. 2.22 hours is 2 hours and 22 hundredths of an hour.

Pages 102-103 — Practice Questions

1 **C** — 17 m, 1.7 km and 0.17 km are far too tall for a car (17 m is the shortest of these options, and this is about the height of a 5-storey building), and 17 cm is far too short (it's about the height of a paperback book). The most likely answer is 1.7 m.

2 **350 ml** — There are 5 divisions between 250 ml and 500 ml, so each division is worth 250 ml ÷ 5 = 50 ml.
The liquid is 3 divisions above 250 ml, which is 250 ml + (3 × 50 ml) = 250 ml + 150 ml = 400 ml.
To get to 750 ml, you need another 750 ml – 400 ml = 350 ml.

3 **D** — Convert all the measurements into the same units:
Sebastian: 340 mm = 340 ÷ 10 = 34 cm,
Khalid: 0.3 m = 0.3 × 100 = 30 cm, Lola: 34.5 cm,
Thea: 0.35 m = 0.35 × 100 = 35 cm. So Thea has knitted the most.

4 **13.5 km** — Convert all the distances into km:
600 m = 600 ÷ 1000 = 0.6 km, 4500 m = 4500 ÷ 1000 = 4.5 km.
Now add them up: 0.6 km + 8.4 km + 4.5 km = 13.5 km

5 **£67.50** — There are 2 lots of 500 m in every km, so Priti travels 2 × 13.5 = 27 lots of 500 m in total. So she gets sponsored 27 × £2.50 = (27 × £2) + (27 × £0.50) = £54 + £13.50 = £67.50.

6 **8** — In 2 bags of lentils there are 2 × 1.6 = 3.2 kg.
3.2 kg = 3.2 × 1000 = 3200 g of lentils. Divide this by the amount of lentils in one batch: 3200 ÷ 400 = 32 ÷ 4 = 8 batches.

7 **6** — 2.7 kg = 2.7 × 1000 = 2700 g. 2700 ÷ 450 = 270 ÷ 45 = 30 ÷ 5 = 6. (To make the division easier, we divided everything by 10, then by 9. You can do this in whatever way you prefer.)

8 **18** — She uses 2.4 litres = 2.4 × 1000 = 2400 ml of lemonade. Twice as much as 400 ml is 800 ml, so she uses 800 ml of apple juice. So she makes 2400 ml + 400 ml + 800 ml = 3600 ml of punch. This fills 3600 ÷ 200 = 36 ÷ 2 = 18 cups.

9 **D** — 4 minutes before 16:04 is 16:00, then another 12 – 4 = 8 minutes before that is 15:52, or 3:52 pm in the 12-hour clock.

10 **3 hours 35 minutes** — 9:45 am + 15 minutes = 10:00 am, 10:00 am + 3 hours = 1:00 pm, 1:00 pm + 20 minutes = 1:20 pm. So the tournament lasts for 15 minutes + 3 hours + 20 minutes = 3 hours 35 minutes.

11 **24th June** — Count back 14 days in July from Isla's birthday. Then count back another 20 – 14 = 6 days. There are 30 days in June, so 6 days before the end of June is 30 – 6 = 24th June.

12 **B** — There are 5 × 60 = 300 seconds in 5 minutes, so in 5 minutes and 24 seconds there are 300 + 24 = 324 seconds.

13 **44 mins** — The first train in the timetable leaves North River at 11:18 and arrives at East Water at 12:02. 11:18 + 2 minutes = 11:20, 11:20 + 40 minutes = 12:00, 12:00 + 2 minutes = 12:02. So the train journey takes 2 + 40 + 2 = 44 minutes.

14 **12:21** — The latest train to arrive in West Mile before 1:30 pm (13:30) gets in at 13:04. This train leaves South Path at 12:21.

15 **13:09 (or 1:09 pm)** — 35 minutes after 11:15 am is 11:50 am. 15 minutes after 11:50 am is 12:05 pm. The next train from North River after 12:05 pm leaves at 12:25 pm and arrives at East Water at 13:09 (or 1:09 pm).

16 **28 mins** — Mr Adams will arrive at East Water train station at 12:03 pm. The next train leaves at 12:31 pm, so he will have to wait for 31 – 3 = 28 minutes.

Section Seven — Mixed Problems

Page 107 — Mixed Problems

1 **£40** — Work out the volume of the swimming pool. 10 × 10 × 1.6 = 160 m³. If it costs 25p to fill 1 m³ then it will cost £1 to fill 4 m³. 160 ÷ 4 = 40, so it will cost £40 in total.

2 **B** — The pie chart is a circle so all of the angles add up to 360°. A section that is 90° would cover $\frac{1}{4}$ (or 25%) of the pie chart (360 ÷ 4 = 90°). The section for red flowers covers 45°, which is half of 90°. So as a percentage, 45° is 25% ÷ 2 = 12.5%. The correct answer is option B.

Pages 108-109 — Practice Questions

1 **£28** — Area of his garden: 13 × 8 = (10 × 8) + (3 × 8) = 80 + 24 = 104 m². 104 ÷ 30 = 3 remainder 14, so Horace will need 4 bags of fertiliser. So he will have to spend 4 × £7 = £28.

2 **B** — There are 60 seconds in a minute, so in $7\frac{1}{2}$ minutes, there are $7\frac{1}{2}$ × 60 = (7 × 60) + ($\frac{1}{2}$ × 60) = 420 + 30 = 450 seconds. So originally there were 450 × 10 = 4500 g of flour in the sack. Convert this into kilograms: 4500 ÷ 1000 = 4.5 kg.

3 **£210** — It costs 300 × 80p = 24 000p = £240 to make 300 cards. $\frac{1}{5}$ of 300 = 300 ÷ 5 = 60, so $\frac{3}{5}$ of 300 = 60 × 3 = 180. He sells 180 cards. 180 × £2.50 = (180 × £2) + (180 × £0.50) = £360 + £90 = £450, so he earns £450 – £240 = £210 in total.

4 **D** — A regular pentagon has 5 equal sides, so the perimeter of the pentagon is 5 × 16 = 80 cm. The regular octagon has 8 equal sides and its perimeter is also 80 cm, so each side is 80 ÷ 8 = 10 cm long.

5 **6 km** — Read off the graph to find the distance each day, then add them together to find the total distance: 9 + 4 + 8 + 3 + 6 = 30. There are 5 days, so divide by 5 to find the mean: 30 ÷ 5 = 6 km.

6 **30%** — She walks 30 km in total, and she walks 9 km on Monday. $\frac{9}{30}$ is the same as $\frac{3}{10}$, which is 30%.

7 **450 ml** — He makes 2.7 litres = 2.7 × 1000 = 2700 ml of cleaning solution. There are 1 + 8 = 9 parts in total, so one part is 2700 ÷ 9 = 300 ml. He uses 300 ml of bleach, so there is 750 – 300 = 450 ml left.

8 **E** — Write $\frac{3}{4}$ as a percentage: $\frac{1}{4}$ = 25%, so $\frac{3}{4}$ = 3 × 25% = 75%. Work out how many lots of 5% make up 75%: 75 ÷ 5 = 15, so it takes 15 days.

9 **Rectangle** — You know (x + 2, y) is 2 units to the right of (x, y), and that (x, y – 6) is 6 units down from (x, y). Do a rough sketch:

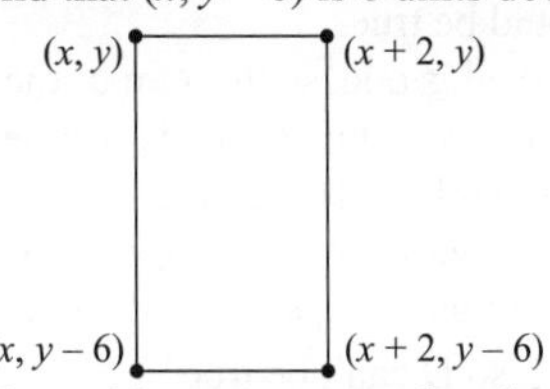

From this, you can see that the shape is a rectangle.

10 **B** — Work out how much she earns in total. For the first 10 km, she is sponsored £5 per km, so she gets £5 × 10 = £50. For the remaining 5 km, she is sponsored £8 per km, so she gets £8 × 5 = £40. So she is sponsored £50 + £40 = £90 in total. So the mean amount is £90 ÷ 15 = £6 per kilometre.

11 **72%** — Add up the cost of her items: £1.80 + £1.50 + £2.30 = £5.60. Then write the amount she spent as a fraction of £20: $\frac{5.6}{20}$ is the same as $\frac{56}{200}$ or $\frac{28}{100}$, and $\frac{28}{100}$ is 28%. She spent 28%, so she has 100% – 28% = 72% left.

12 **£5** — Work out how much they spent in total: £1.80 + £1.80 + £2.30 + £1.60 = £7.50. The ratio 2 : 1 has 2 + 1 = 3 parts in total, so one part is £7.50 ÷ 3 = £2.50. So Annabel pays £2.50 × 2 = £5.

13 **C** — List the prime numbers between 1 and 20: 2, 3, 5, 7, 11, 13, 17, 19. There are 8 prime numbers between 1 and 20, so $\frac{8}{20}$ are prime. This isn't one of the options, so you need to simplify it: $\frac{8}{20}$ is equivalent to $\frac{2}{5}$, so the answer is C.

14 **42°** — The sum of the angles in a quadrilateral is 360°: 65° + 85° + $2p$ + $3p$ = 360°, so $5p$ = 360° – 65° – 85° = 210°. $5p$ = 210°, so p = 210° ÷ 5 = 42°.

15 **D** — Count up to find how many days the flower has been growing for. There are 31 days in May, so it is 26 days to the end of May, then another 16 days of June, so it has been 26 + 16 = 42 days. The flower grows 4 mm each day, so it has grown 42 × 4 = (40 × 4) + (2 × 4) = 160 + 8 = 168 mm. 168 mm = 168 ÷ 10 = 16.8 cm. The flower was 5 cm tall when it was planted, so now the flower is 5 + 16.8 = 21.8 cm tall.

Mixed Practice Tests

Pages 110-111 — Test 1

1 **8** — A regular octagon has 8 equal sides and 8 lines of symmetry.

2 **E** — The shape is made from nine identical small triangles. Three of the triangles are shaded, so $\frac{3}{9}$ of the shape is shaded. This isn't one of the options, so simplify it: $\frac{3}{9}$ is the same as $\frac{1}{3}$, so the answer is E.

3 **D** — Add the 37 minutes in stages: 4:55 pm + 5 minutes = 5 pm. 37 – 5 = 32, so add another 32 minutes. 5 pm + 32 minutes = 5:32 pm, which is 17:32 in the 24-hour clock.

4 **426** — First, work out the rule for the sequence. 404 – 393 = 11 and 415 – 404 = 11, so the rule is 'add 11'. So the missing number is 415 + 11 = 426. You can check this by adding 11 again: 426 + 11 = 437, which is the next number in the sequence.

5 **A** — 30 cakes were sold in total and 10 were large cakes, so 30 – 10 = 20 cupcakes were sold. 12 vanilla cakes were sold in total and 3 of them were large cakes, so 12 – 3 = 9 vanilla cupcakes were sold. So 20 – 7 – 9 = 4 lemon cupcakes were sold.

6 **£90.97** — First add the money she gets for her birthday to the money she has in savings. Partition £34.50 into £34 + £0.50. £271.42 + £34 = £305.42, and then £305.42 + £0.50 = £305.92. Then subtract the cost of the bicycle. Partition £214.95 into £200 + £15 – 5p. £305.92 – £200 = £105.92, then £105.92 – £15 = £90.92. Then add the 5p back on: £90.92 + 5p = £90.97.

7 **B** —

A: The number of meals served is odd, and an odd number can't be divided into two equal whole numbers, so A can't be true.

B: If twice as many meals were served with salad, $^2/_3$ of the meals were served with salad and $^1/_3$ of them were served with chips. 39 is a multiple of 3, so B could be true.

C: The total number of meals served is odd, so the sum of the number of meals served with chips and with salad must be an odd number added to an even number. The difference between an odd number and an even number is always odd, so 4 more meals couldn't have been served with chips. C can't be true.

D: $^3/_4$ of 39 isn't a whole number, so D can't be true.

E: 12 is even, so this can't be true for the same reason as C.

8 **D** — P has been translated 2 units to the right and 1 unit down, so S has also been translated by the same amount. The original coordinates of S are (1, –1), so the new coordinates are (1 + 2, –1 – 1) = (3, –2).

9 **468** — 4 = 12 ÷ 3, so the answer to 1872 ÷ 4 will be three times bigger than 156 (the answer to 1872 ÷ 12): 1872 ÷ 4 = 3 × 156 = (3 × 150) + (3 × 6) = 450 + 18 = 468

10 **90°** — First work out the percentage of people who said milk or white: $^2/_5$ is the same as 40%, so 40% + 35% = 75% said milk or white. This means 100% – 75% = 25% of people said dark chocolate. Angles in a pie chart add up to 360°, so 25% of the pie chart will have an angle of 360° ÷ 4 = 90°.

Pages 112-113 — Test 2

1 **D** — The number will be smaller than 15 cm so the answer will have 1 ten and 4 ones. The digit in the tenths column has to be the smallest digit that rounds up, which is 5, so the answer is 14.5 cm.

2 **4.03 litres** — 4030 ml = 4030 ÷ 1000 = 4.03 litres.

3 **B** — There are 5 + 4 = 9 parts in total, so one part is 36 ÷ 9 = 4 sweets. So Julian gets 4 × 4 = 16 sweets.

4 **£192** — First find how many boxes of pencils you need: 2400 ÷ 100 = 24 boxes. Each box costs £8, so 2400 pencils will cost 24 × £8 = (20 × £8) + (4 × £8) = £160 + £32 = £192.

5 **E** — 8 × 60p = 480p. Convert £5 into pence: £5 = 5 × 100 = 500p. So he will get 500p – 480p = 20p change.

6 **105 cm²** — Split the shape into two rectangles and work out any missing lengths:

E.g.

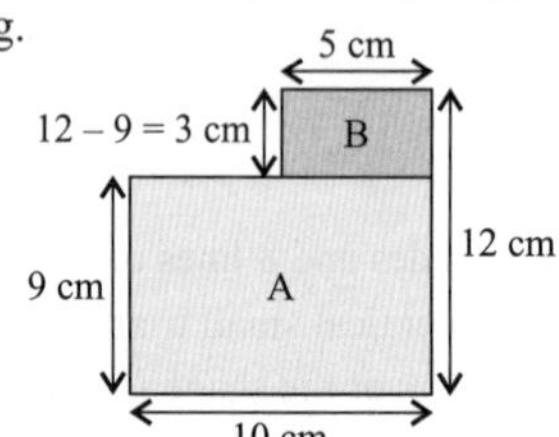

Then work out the two areas separately: The area of A is 9 × 10 = 90 cm² and the area of B is 5 × 3 = 15 cm², so the total area of the shape is 90 cm² + 15 cm² = 105 cm².

7 **1657** — M = 1000 and IX = 10 – 1 = 9, so MMIX = 1000 + 1000 + 9 = 2009. So the church was built 352 years before 2009. Partition 352 into 300 + 50 + 2 and then subtract from 2009: 2009 – 300 = 1709, then 1709 – 50 = 1659, and 1659 – 2 = 1657.

8 **C** — Add the lengths to find the total: 6 + 8 + 9.5 + 5 + 6.5 = 35 Then divide by the number of keys (5): 35 ÷ 5 = 7 cm

9 **9** — Work out how many packs of hair clips Lucy can make: 72 = 12 × 6, so 729 ÷ 12 = 60 remainder 9. So Lucy can fill 60 packs, and she will have 9 hair clips left over.

10 **E** — There are $1^1/_2$ circles in the USA row. Each circle represents 2 pupils, so $1^1/_2$ × 2 = 3 pupils went to the USA on holiday. Then add up the circles to work out how many pupils there are in total. There are 3 + 4 + 3 + 1 = 11 full circles, so this is 11 × 2 = 22 pupils. There are also 2 half circles, which is another 2 pupils. So there are 22 + 2 = 24 pupils, and $^3/_{24}$ pupils went to the USA. This isn't one of the options, so simplify it: $^3/_{24}$ is the same as $^1/_8$.

Pages 114-115 — Test 3

1 **E** — The only options that have four sides of equal length are a square and a rhombus. Both of these shapes also have two pairs of parallel sides. A rhombus has two pairs of equal angles but a square has 4 equal right angles, so the shape must be a rhombus.

2 **16 °C** — Count up 4 °C to go from –4 °C to 0 °C, then count up another 12 °C. So it is 4 + 12 = 16 °C warmer in Madrid.

3 **A** — 25% is the same as $^1/_4$, so 25% of 48 = 48 ÷ 4 = 12.

4 **10.43 kg** — Partition 2.15 into 2 + 0.1 + 0.05. 3.78 + 2 = 5.78, then 5.78 + 0.1 = 5.88, and 5.88 + 0.05 = 5.93.
Partition 4.5 into 4 + 0.5. 5.93 + 4 = 9.93, and 9.93 + 0.5 = 10.43.
So the total weight of the parcels is 10.43 kg.

5 **D** —

A: The horizontal axis goes up in even steps so this isn't true.

B: The graph is only supposed to show data from those years, so this isn't a reason why the graph is misleading.

C: The graph is about ice cream sales in general, so it doesn't matter what flavour the ice cream is.

D: This is misleading because it makes the differences between the years look bigger than they actually are. Daily ice cream sales have only increased by 20 in 5 years, but the graph makes it look like they have increased by a lot more than that.

E: The graph is about the average daily sales, so it doesn't matter exactly how many ice creams were sold each day.

6 **7700** — 32 and 68 are both multiplied by 77, so you can work out the answer quicker by adding them together first.
So 32 × 77 + 68 × 77 = (32 + 68) × 77 = 100 × 77 = 7700.

7 **B** — It costs £5 per hour, so for *H* hours, it would cost 5 × *H* or 5*H*. Then add this to the fixed £8 to get 8 + 5*H*.

8 **12:22 (pm)** — 2:45 pm is written as 14:45 in the 24-hour clock. The train that arrives at 14:56 is too late, so he needs to catch the train that arrives in Castleton at 13:13. This train leaves Angelby at 12:34. He needs to leave home at least 12 minutes before this, so the latest time he can leave home is 12:34 – 12 minutes = 12:22

9 **2 litres** — 800 ml is two parts of the ratio, so one part is 800 ml ÷ 2 = 400 ml. There are 3 + 2 = 5 parts in total, so she can make 5 × 400 = 2000 ml of salad dressing.
2000 ml = 2000 ÷ 1000 = 2 litres.

10 **D** — This is a rotation of Olive's shape, as shown below.

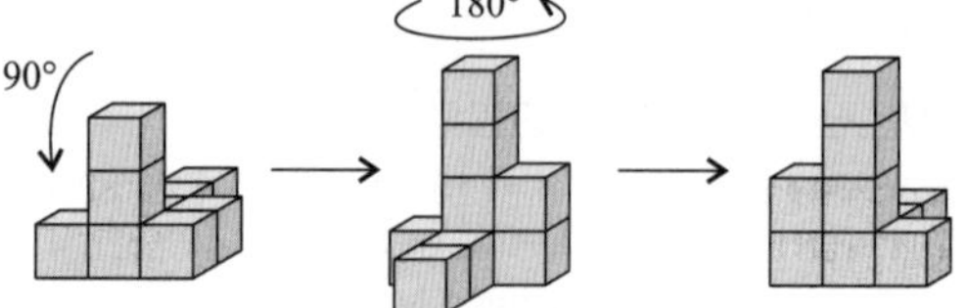

Pages 116-117 — Test 4

1 **D** — All of the numbers have a 1 in the thousands column, so look at the hundreds column. Luke's score has a 6 in the hundreds place and Patrick's score has a 7, and the rest have an 8, so neither Luke nor Patrick have the highest score. Then look at the tens column — Halima's score has a 2 in the tens column and Jemma's and Suzy's both have a 3, so Halima doesn't have the highest score. Finally look at the ones column — Jemma's score has a 1 in the ones column and Suzy's has a 9, so Suzy's score is the highest.

2 **12.37** — Partition 24.83 into 24 + 0.8 + 0.03.
37.2 – 24 = 13.2, then 13.2 – 0.8 = 12.4, and 12.4 – 0.03 = 12.37.

3 **6.36 km** — 1000 m = 1 km, so 660 m = 660 ÷ 1000 = 0.66 km.
So in total, Nick's journey is 5.7 + 0.66 = 6.36 km long.

4 **4** — Add the heights of the columns: 1 + 3 + 2 + 6 + 13 + 11 = 36.
40 pupils voted in total, so 40 – 36 = 4 pupils voted for Thursday.

5 **A** — Angles on a straight line add up to 180°, so the other angle inside the triangle is 180° – 108° = 72°. Angles in a triangle also add up to 180°, so *x* = 180° – 32° – 72° = 76°.

6 **58.4 cm** — Partition 7.3 into 7 + 0.3.
Then 8 × 7.3 = (8 × 7) + (8 × 0.3) = 56 + 2.4 = 58.4 cm.

7 **B** — The volume of a cuboid = length × width × height, so 7500 = 20 × 15 × height = 300 × height. So the height of the cuboid is 7500 ÷ 300 = 75 ÷ 3 = 25 cm.

8 **E** — The number must be both prime and a factor of 12. The factors of 12 are 1, 2, 3, 4, 6 and 12, so the factors that are also prime are 2 and 3. 3 isn't one of the options, so the answer is E.

9 **D** — Add the masses of the ingredients: 350 g + 180 g + 120 g = 650 g. So she can make 650 ÷ 30 = 65 ÷ 3 = 21 biscuits, with 20 g of dough left over. She gives 5 biscuits away, so she has 21 – 5 = 16 biscuits left.

10 **16 cm²** — The star is made from the sides of equilateral triangles, so all of the sides of the star are the same length. There are 8 sides, so each side is 32 ÷ 8 = 4 cm long. The sides of the square are also sides of the equilateral triangles, so each side of the square is 4 cm long as well. So the area of the square piece of card is 4 × 4 = 16 cm^2.

Pages 118-129 — Practice Paper 1

1 **E** — The first few multiples of 3 are: 3, 6, 9, 12, 15... The first few multiples of 4 are: 4, 8, 12, 16, 20... The only option that appears on both lists is 12.

2 **C** — There are 3 points on the grid where two lines intersect: on match day 3 (Rivertown and Park Rovers both scored 0 goals), on match day 5 (Wood United and Village FC both scored 3 goals), and on match day 9 (Park Rovers and Village FC both scored 2 goals).

3 **A** — Each passenger pays $^{1}/_{20}$ of the cost. Convert this fraction into a percentage: $^{1}/_{20} = ^{5}/_{100}$ = 5%

4 **B** — 12 shirts have collars, so 30 – 12 = 18 shirts do not. 18 out of 30 is $^{18}/_{30} = ^{3}/_{5}$

5 **E** — 11:52 + 5 hours = 16:52, 16:52 + 20 minutes = 17:12. So Peter's train journey lasted 5 hours and 20 minutes.

6 **A** — Centimetres (cm) and millimetres (mm) are too small (you might use them to measure the length of a pencil), and kilometres (km) are too big (you'd use them to measure the distance between two cities). Millilitres (ml) aren't a measure of length.

7 **D** — There are 10 divisions between 2.6 and 2.7, so each division represents 0.1 ÷ 10 = 0.01. The arrow points to the third division, so the number is 2.6 + (0.01 × 3) = 2.6 + 0.03 = 2.63.

8 **C** — 9.624 = 9.62 to the nearest hundredth. The rest round to 9.63.

9 **E** — Compare the numbers in the totals row: 49 pupils voted for a clip-on tie and only 23 pupils voted for a regular tie.

10 **C** — 72 hours ÷ 24 = 3 days. March has 31 days, so 3 days after 29th March is 1st April.

11 **C** — 9 tickets cost £63, so 1 ticket costs £63 ÷ 9 = £7. Then 4 tickets cost £7 × 4 = £28.

12 **B** — There are 3 whole circles in Animation and $2^{1}/_{2}$ circles in Romance. Each circle represents 4 films, so there are a total of $5^{1}/_{2}$ × 4 = (5 × 4) + ($^{1}/_{2}$ × 4) = 20 + 2 = 22 films.

13 **C** — A: $^{1}/_{2}$ of 30 = 30 ÷ 2 = 15 B: 25% of 40 = 40 ÷ 4 = 10
C: $^{4}/_{5}$ of 25 = 25 ÷ 5 × 4 = 20 D: 50% of 20 = 20 ÷ 2 = 10
E: $^{1}/_{4}$ of 60 = 60 ÷ 4 = 15

14 **D** — Alex paid p pounds and Jin paid p – 6 pounds. Add together the expressions: $p + p - 6 = 2p - 6$.

15 **D** — Shape D has 2 lines of symmetry. Shape E has no lines of symmetry, and the other shapes all have 1 line of symmetry, as shown by the dashed lines:

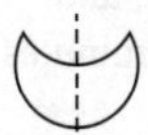  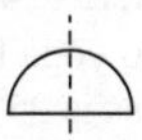  

16 **E** — 3 parts = 45 red roses, so 1 part = 45 ÷ 3 = 15 roses. So there are 15 × 7 = (10 × 7) + (5 × 7) = 70 + 35 = 105 white roses.

17 **D** — Angles on a straight line add up to 180°. So the unmarked angle is 180° – 90° – 40° = 50°. Angles in a triangle add up to 180°, so the shaded angle is 180° – 80° – 50° = 50°.

18 **D** — Find the option that costs £3.45 in total.
A: £1.80 + 95p = £2.75 B: £2.75 + £1.10 = £3.85
C: £3.20 + 95p = £4.15 D: £2.75 + 70p = £3.45
E: £3.20 + £1.10 = £4.30

19 **B** — You need to find 3 lots of £7.99. £7.99 is 1p less than £8, so £7.99 × 3 = £8 × 3 – 3p = £24 – 3p = £23.97.

20 **B** — Each line that Vicky draws has the same length, so every triangle will have two equal sides. The third side is shorter, so the triangles are all isosceles.

21 **D** — 60° + 90° = 150° represents 15 pupils, so 150° ÷ 15 = 10° represents 1 pupil. The 'Undecided' sector has an angle of 360° – 150° = 210°, so it represents 210° ÷ 10° = 21 pupils.

22 **A** — Width = (6 cm × 3) + (1 cm × 4) = 18 cm + 4 cm = 22 cm
Height = 8 cm + (1 cm × 2) = 8 cm + 2 cm = 10 cm
Area of card = width × height = 22 cm × 10 cm = 220 cm^2

23 **B** — Read the number of silver and yellow cars off the bar chart. Joanna saw 18 silver cars and 5 yellow cars in the car park, so she saw 18 – 5 = 13 more silver cars than yellow cars.

24 **E** — The second number is (3 × 2) – 2 = 6 – 2 = 4, so the third number is (3 × 4) – 2 = 12 – 2 = 10.

25 **B** — Substitute n = 3 into the formula to calculate T (in minutes): $T = 5n + 4$ = (5 × 3) + 4 = 15 + 4 = 19
Convert this time to seconds. 1 minute = 60 seconds, so 19 × 60 = (20 × 60) – 60 = 1200 – 60 = 1140 seconds.

26 **A** — East is right on the x-axis and south is down on the y-axis. So add 2 to the x-coordinate of Mike's house (3 + 2 = 5) and subtract 3 from the y-coordinate of Mike's house (5 – 3 = 2). So Lisa's house is at the coordinates (5, 2).

27 **B** — The area of the small square is 4 cm × 4 cm = 16 cm^2. The area of the large square is 8 cm × 8 cm = 64 cm^2. The percentage is $^{16}/_{64} = ^{1}/_{4}$ = 25%

28 **D** — There is 1.5 litres of lemonade in the jug. 1.5 litres = 1500 ml. Subtract 570 ml: 570 = 500 + 70, so 1500 – 500 = 1000, 1000 – 70 = 930. There is 930 ml of lemonade left in the jug.

29 **B** — Compare each digit in turn to order the numbers. E.g. 2.006 is less than 2.06. They have the same number of ones and tenths, but 2.006 has less hundredths than 2.06.

30 **C** — Total number of books = 6 + 7 + 14 + 3 + 10 = 40
Then divide by 5 to find the mean: 40 ÷ 5 = 8

31 **D** — Work out the total amount for each combination:
A: (80 g × 5) + (150 g × 4) = 400 g + 600 g = 1000 g
B: (80 g × 1) + (150 g × 7) = 80 g + 1050 g = 1130 g
C: (80 g × 3) + (150 g × 6) = 240 g + 900 g = 1140 g
D: (80 g × 5) + (150 g × 5) = 400 g + 750 g = 1150 g
E: (80 g × 10) + (150 g × 2) = 800 g + 300 g = 1100 g
To leave the smallest amount, he would need to sell the largest amount, which is 1150 g — option D.

32 **D** — 31.82 is 100 times smaller than 3182, so then 31.82 ÷ 43 is 100 times smaller than 3182 ÷ 43 = 74. 74 ÷ 100 = 0.74.

33 **D** — The reflected shape has 6 sides, so it's a hexagon.

mirror line

34 **B** — Notice that all options begin in the same way — with both two-digit numbers having been rounded to the nearest ten. Work out by how much you need to adjust to get the right answer: 39 rounds up to 40 and there are 5 lots, so 5 must be subtracted. 91 rounds down to 90 and there are 7 lots, so 7 must be added. So the calculation is 5 × 40 + 7 × 90 – 5 + 7 = 5 × 40 + 7 × 90 + 2.

35 **D** — There are 4 lots of 25 in 100, so there are 4 × 3 = 12 lots of 25 in 300. So he gave 12 manicures. Each manicure cost £32, so he earned a total of £32 × 12 = (£32 × 10) + (£32 × 2) = £320 + £64 = £384.

36 **D** — 125 = 5 × 5 × 5 = 5^3 is a cube number. It doesn't divide equally by 2, so it's also an odd number. (It's divisible by 5, so it's not prime.)

37 **A** — Looking down from directly above, he can see only the 6 faces shaded in the diagram. Options B, C and E have too many or too few faces. Option D has the correct number of faces, but in the wrong position.

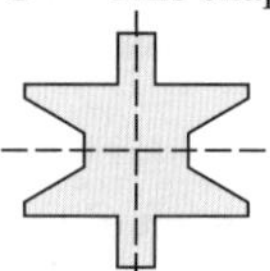

38 **B** — Subtract the base length from the side length to find the unknown lengths on the perimeter: 25 cm – 19 cm = 6 cm. Add up the lengths to find the total perimeter: 25 + 25 + 25 + 6 + 19 + 6 + 25 = 131 cm.

39 **E** — The prism has two triangular faces, so it's a triangular prism. It has three more faces that are rectangular. Each triangular face has 1 right angle and each rectangular face has 4 right angles, so there are (2 × 1) + (3 × 4) = 2 + 12 = 14 right angles.

40 **C** — She has spent £2.00 + (£2.25 × 2) = £6.50, so she has £25 – £6.50 = £18.50 left. 4 rides on the roller coaster cost £4.75 × 4 = £19 (too much), but 3 rides cost £14.25.

41 **D** — Follow the rules of BODMAS to work out the answer: $(9 - 4)^2 + 3 \times 7 = 5^2 + 3 \times 7 = 25 + 3 \times 7 = 25 + 21 = 46$

42 **E** — The scale shows the bowl and flour weigh 945 g together. Subtract 84: 84 = 80 + 4, 945 – 80 = 865, 865 – 4 = 861. Josh has 861 g of flour in the bowl. 1.5 kg = 1500 g, so subtract 861 g from 1500 g. 861 = 800 + 60 + 1, so 1500 – 800 = 700, 700 – 60 = 640, 640 – 1 = 639. So he needs 639 g.

43 **D** — The other piece is 100% – 65% = 35% of the original ribbon. 10% of 80 = 80 ÷ 10 = 8 cm and 5% of 80 = 8 ÷ 2 = 4 cm, so 35% of 80 = (3 × 8) + 4 = 24 + 4 = 28 cm. 28 cm = 28 ÷ 100 = 0.28 m.

44 **A** — The triangular prism would fit inside a cuboid with a height of 10 cm, a width of 20 cm and a depth of 15 cm. The volume of this cuboid is 10 cm × 20 cm × 15 cm = 3000 cm^3.

45 **D** — 3 : 4 has 3 + 4 = 7 parts and there are 7 numbers. So each number is 1 part. The set has 3 primes (2, 3 and 7) and 3 non-primes (8, 9, 4), so the missing number is not prime. 2 : 7 also has 2 + 5 = 7 parts. The set has 2 squares (9 and 4) and 4 non-squares (8, 2, 7 and 3), so the missing number isn't square. The only option that isn't prime or square is 12.

46 **D** — The point at (2, 5) moves to the point at (5, 6). So the shape has been translated 5 – 2 = 3 units right and 6 – 5 = 1 unit up. The point at (5, 6) moves to P: 5 + 3 = 8 and 6 + 1 = 7, so P has the coordinates (8, 7).

47 **D** — $4(x + 8)$ is 4 lots of $x + 8$. This is $(4 \times x) + (4 \times 8) = 4x + 32$.

48 **C** — The gap between the bars changes from 10 years to 40 years, so it looks like there has been a big jump in sales. The other options aren't correct: The graph is about the UK, so sales in other countries don't matter. The sales before 1960 have little effect on the sales in 2020. Writing the numbers in thousands would not change the difference in the heights of the bars. A bar chart is a suitable choice to display this data.

49 **B** — There are 3 × 8 = 24 slices of pizza in total. 3 people (Jodie and two friends) have each taken 3 slices — so 3 × 3 = 9 slices are gone and 24 – 9 = 15 slices remain. 15 out of 24 = $^{15}/_{24} = {}^{5}/_{8}$.

50 **C** — The nets for options A, B, D and E all result in cubes with the two shaded faces sharing an edge, and not opposite.

Pages 130-141 — Practice Paper 2

1 **C** — 1 litre = 1000 ml, so 2.75 litres = 2.75 × 1000 = 2750 ml.

2 **D** — Add up the Year 5 and Year 6 values for each row:
Choir: 7 + 24 = 31 Football: 16 + 18 = 34
Chess: 21 + 13 = 34 Orchestra: 18 + 17 = 35
So the club attended by the most pupils is orchestra.

3 **B** — The thousands place is the fourth column from the right in a whole number. The digit in this column is 0.

4 **D** — Four of the bars go above 5 on the vertical axis: March, June, September and November.

5 **A** — Convert the amount into millilitres: 1.756 litres = 1756 ml. The 5 (in the tens column) is being rounded. The 6 (in the ones column) is more than 5, so 1756 ml rounds up to 1760 ml. Then convert back to litres: 1760 ml = 1.76 litres.

6 **C** — This shape has two lines of symmetry, shown below:

7 **D** —
A: 8 and 27 aren't square numbers, so this isn't true.
B: 27 can't be divided exactly by 2, so this isn't true.
C: 27 does not have 4 as a factor, so this isn't true. (The factors of 27 are 1, 3, 9 and 27.)
D: $8 = 2 \times 2 \times 2 = 2^3$, $27 = 3 \times 3 \times 3 = 3^3$ and $64 = 4 \times 4 \times 4 = 4^3$, so this is true.
E: 8 and 64 are not multiples of 3, so this isn't true.

8 **E** — There are seven days in a week, so seven days after Megan's birthday is also a Saturday. There are 31 days in July, so 25th July and 1st August are both Saturdays. Then 4th August is a Tuesday.

9 **A** — Point A has the same x-coordinate as (5, 1) and the same y-coordinate as (2, 4), so it has the coordinates (5, 4).

10 **A** — To divide by 1000, move the digits three places to the right. 58 m ÷ 1000 = 0.058 m. This isn't one of the options, so convert into cm: 1 m = 100 cm, so 0.058 m = 0.058 × 100 = 5.8 cm.

11 **B** — Angles on a straight line add up to 180°. The middle angle is a right angle, so $2k + 90° + k = 180°$. $3k = 90°$, so $k = 30°$.

12 **B** — The first few multiples of 9 are 9, 18, 27, 36, 45, 54... The first few multiples of 12 are 12, 24, 36, 48, 60... The smallest number to appear in both lists is 36.

13 **C** — Isosceles triangles aren't quadrilaterals, so the answer can't be B. A square has 4 lines of symmetry, a rhombus has 2 lines of symmetry and a parallelogram has 0 lines of symmetry. A kite has 1 line of symmetry, so it is the only option that can go in the shaded area.

14 **B** — 35 × 40 = (30 × 40) + (5 × 40) = 1200 + 200 = 1400. Convert 1400 g into kg: 1400 g = 1400 ÷ 1000 = 1.4 kg.

15 **D** — The clock shows 2:40 pm, so add on 2 hours and 25 minutes: 2:40 pm + 2 hours = 4:40 pm, 4:40 pm + 25 minutes = 5:05 pm. 5 + 12 = 17, so 5:05 pm = 17:05 in the 24-hour clock.

16 **E** — Count the hexagons in each shape. Shape 1 has 7 hexagons, Shape 2 has 12 hexagons and Shape 3 has 17 hexagons, so the rule is 'add 5 hexagons'. Shape 4 will have 17 + 5 = 22 hexagons, and Shape 5 will have 22 + 5 = 27 hexagons.

17 **A** — Diameter = radius × 2, so the diameter of the mirror is 12 × 2 = 24 cm.

18 **B** — $^{7}/_{10}$ = 70%, so he has 100% – 70% = 30% left.

19 **C** — On net C, the triangle faces will overlap and there will be no triangular face on the other end of the prism.

20 **A** — 4 in every 7 animals are goats, so $^{4}/_{7}$ of the animals are goats. $^{4}/_{7}$ of the total number of animals is 32, so $^{1}/_{7}$ = 32 ÷ 4 = 8. So there are 8 × 7 = 56 animals in total.

21 **D** — Partition 36.8 into 36 + 0.8. 23.5 + 36 = 59.5, and 59.5 + 0.8 = 60.3. Partition 16.4 into 16 + 0.4. 60.3 + 16 = 76.3, and 76.3 + 0.4 = 76.7. So he cycled 76.7 km.

22 **E** — Karate starts at 11:35 and ends at 12:55. 11:35 + 1 hour = 12:35, and 12:35 + 20 minutes = 12:55, so karate lasts 1 hour 20 minutes = 80 minutes. Yoga starts at 14:15 and ends at 15:10. 14:15 + 45 minutes = 15:00, and 15:00 + 10 minutes = 15:10, so yoga lasts 45 + 10 = 55 minutes. 80 – 55 = 25, so the karate class is 25 minutes longer.

23 **E** — The square has four 90° angles, so the other angle in the triangle is 90° – 55° = 35°. Angles in a triangle add up to 180°, so 35° + 70° + x = 180°. 105° + x = 180°, so x = 75°.

Index

24 **D** — $\frac{2}{7} \div 4 = \frac{2}{28}$. This isn't one of the options, so simplify the fraction. $\frac{2}{28}$ is the same as $\frac{1}{14}$, so $\frac{1}{14}$ of the bag is in each bowl.

25 **A** — He buys 4 packs of 8 buttons and 2 packs of 24 buttons, so he buys $(4 \times 8) + (2 \times 24) = 32 + 48 = 80$ buttons.

26 **C** — The hottest day was Thursday and the temperature was 22 °C. Look for the day that was 22 °C – 5 °C = 17 °C. Read across from 17 °C on the y-axis until you reach the line, then read down to the x-axis. The first time you reach the line is between two days, so keep going across until you reach the line again — it is 17 °C on Friday.

27 **D** — Eliminate numbers that clearly aren't prime — 93 and 99 are both multiples of 3, and 95 is a multiple of 5, so they can't be prime. Then work through some multiples. $7 \times 13 = 91$, so this isn't prime. 97 only has 1 and itself as factors, so the answer is D.

28 **D** — $99 = 100 - 1$, so 218×99 is the same as $(218 \times 100) - (218 \times 1)$. $218 \times 100 = 21\ 800$, so the missing number is $218 \times 1 = 218$.

29 **E** — Partition 3660 into 3600 + 60.
$3660 \div 12 = (3600 \div 12) + (60 \div 12) = 300 + 5 = 305$ g.
You could use any method to calculate the division here.

30 **B** — Check that the numbers in each box meet both criteria.
81 is odd, but $81 = 9 \times 9 = 9^2$, so it is a square number.

31 **B** — Jamal's brother gets $\frac{2}{5}$ of $100 = 100 \div 5 \times 2 = 40$ cards, and his friend gets 32% of 100 = 32 cards. Jamal gives away $40 + 32 = 72$ cards, and keeps $100 - 72 = 28$ cards.

32 **E** — The design has 16 sides. Each side is the side of a regular hexagon, so each side is 32 cm ÷ 16 = 2 cm long. The shaded region has four sides, and each one is also the side of a hexagon, so they are 2 cm long as well. So the perimeter of the shaded region is 4 × 2 cm = 8 cm.

33 **A** — Use BODMAS to do the calculation in the right order.
$160 \div 4^2 + 4 = 160 \div 16 + 4 = 10 + 4 = 14$

34 **C** — The expressions are in grams, so convert 1 kg into 1000 g. He uses $3 \times x = 3x$ grams of compost, so he has $1000 - 3x$ left.

35 **D** — Find the total of the times: $26 + 24 + 22 + 32 = 104$
Then divide the total by 4 to find the mean: $104 \div 4 = 26$ minutes.

36 **C** —
A: $1^3 - 4 = 1 - 4 = -3$, which isn't prime.
B: $2^3 - 4 = 8 - 4 = 4$, which isn't prime.
C: $3^3 - 4 = 27 - 4 = 23$, which is prime.
D: $4^3 - 4 = 64 - 4 = 60$, which isn't prime.
E: $5^3 - 4 = 125 - 4 = 121$, which isn't prime.
So the only possible option is C.

37 **A** — August is between April and September, so the tickets will cost £12.20 for each adult and £8.50 for each child.
3 × £12.20 = (3 × £12) + (3 × £0.20) = £36 + £0.60 = £36.60
2 × £8.50 = (2 × £8) + (2 × £0.50) = £16 + £1 = £17.
So the tickets will cost £36.60 + £17 = £53.60.

38 **D** — Each piece of cardboard has an area of $12 \times 12 = 144$ cm^2.
Multiply by 5 to find the total area of cardboard: $144 \times 5 = (100 \times 5) + (40 \times 5) + (4 \times 5) = 500 + 200 + 20 = 720$ cm^2

39 **D** — The volume of one cube is $2 \times 2 \times 2 = 8$ cm^3.
The shape is made from 10 identical cubes, so the volume of the shape is 10×8 cm^3 = 80 cm^3.

40 **A** — He spends (2 × £20) – £2.50 = £37.50. There are six people in the group, so the cost for one person is £37.50 ÷ 6.
Partition £37.50 into £30 + £7.50.
£37.50 ÷ 6 = (£30 ÷ 6) + (£7.50 ÷ 6) = £5 + £1.25 = £6.25.

41 **E** — Count up how many drama club members there are in total. There are $2 + 4 + 3 + 2 = 11$ whole squares, which stands for $11 \times 4 = 44$ members. There are 2 half squares, which is another 4 members, and 2 quarter squares, which is another 2 members. So there are $44 + 4 + 2 = 50$ members in total.
In the last two rows, there are 2 whole squares, 1 half square and 1 quarter square, so there are $8 + 2 + 1 = 11$ members that are at least 150 cm tall. So the answer is $\frac{11}{50} = \frac{22}{100} = 22\%$.

42 **B** — The volume of the fish tank is $30 \times 40 \times 50 = 60\ 000$ cm^3.
So it will take $60\ 000 \div 3000 = 60 \div 3 = 20$ minutes.
09:45 + 20 mins = 10:05.

43 **D** — The mean is 18, so the sum of the 5 numbers is $5 \times 18 = 90$.
Add up the numbers you know: $16 + 23 + 15 + 14 = 68$
So the fifth number is $90 - 68 = 22$.

44 **D** — 10% of 50 = 50 ÷ 10 = 5, so 40% of 50 = 20 people said apples. Now look at each option. A, B and E aren't relevant — it doesn't matter what fruit the other people said, how old the people are, or where the survey was done. C isn't true — 20 people chose apples but 25 people chose pears. The answer is D — the headline says apples were the most popular, but five more people said pears than apples.

45 **A** — First work out how many of each type of coin she has:
There are $2 + 3 = 5$ parts in total, so one part is $60 \div 5 = 12$.
So she has $2 \times 12 = 24$ 20p coins and $3 \times 12 = 36$ 50p coins.
(24 × 20p) + (36 × 50p) = 480p + 1800p = 2280p = £22.80

46 **E** — 45° is $\frac{1}{8}$ of the pie chart, so $135° = 3 \times 45°$ is $\frac{3}{8}$ of the pie chart. The 18 pupils who travel by car are $\frac{3}{8}$ of the number of pupils asked. $\frac{1}{8}$ of the pupils asked is $18 \div 3 = 6$, so he asked $6 \times 8 = 48$ pupils.

47 **C** — The numbers in the sequence $5n + 1$ are one more than a multiple of 5.
The first few numbers in the sequence are 6, 11, 16, 21, 26, 31...
The first few square numbers are 1, 4, 9, 16, 25, 36, 49...
The smallest number to appear in both lists is 16.

48 **B** — Work out how many purple balloons there are to start with:
$\frac{1}{4}$ = 25%, so 25% + 20% = 45% of the balloons are not purple, so 100% – 45% = 55% of the balloons are purple.
50% of 80 = 80 ÷ 2 = 40 and 5% of 80 = 40 ÷ 10 = 4, so 55% of 80 = 40 + 4 = 44 balloons are purple.
7 of them burst, so there are $44 - 7 = 37$ purple balloons left.

49 **A** — The coordinates of the corners after translation are (–4, 1), (–3, 3), (–1, 3) and (0, 1).

50 **D** — E.g. A, B, C and E can be made like this:

Shape D can't be made without reflecting one of the shapes.